THE MINNESOTA

LIBRARY

ON AMERICAN WRITERS

Leonard Unger
and George T. Wright,
editors

THE SEVEN *essays which appear in this book were first published separately in the series of University of Minnesota Pamphlets on American Writers and, together with the other pamphlets in the series, are intended as introductions to authors who have helped to shape American culture over the years of our colonial and national existence. The editors of the pamphlet series have been Richard Foster, William Van O'Connor, Allen Tate, Leonard Unger, Robert Penn Warren, and George T. Wright. Many pamphlets, in addition to the seven represented here, are available from the University of Minnesota Press.*

SEVEN NOVELISTS IN THE AMERICAN NATURALIST TRADITION

An Introduction

edited by Charles Child Walcutt

UNIVERSITY OF MINNESOTA PRESS
MINNEAPOLIS

Library of Congress Catalog Card Number: 74-14209

ISBN 0-8166-0730-3

CONTENTS

SEVEN NOVELISTS IN THE
AMERICAN NATURALIST TRADITION

INTRODUCTION

The naturalistic novel is a phenomenon — that is, an appearance — whose image is dependent upon the historical perspectives in which it is seen. It has appeared to successive decades of critics since 1900 in a series of shapes that have taken their form from the foreground and the background of ideas among or against which it has been seen. Everything has depended upon the particular setting. It may also be thought of as a great new tree suddenly bursting from the ground and occupying totally the vision of readers and critics. As the years pass, one tree after another springs up, and the naturalistic tree recedes bit by bit into the distance, until it is seen at the end of a long diminishing line of trees. That is how we see it today — and that is why we may find it surprising to hear that it once seemed so overpoweringly new. Today it is merely the first tree in a long line, obscured by the qualities of all the trees that grow larger and larger (in appearance, always) as the observer moves farther down the line, away from the original tree.

Depending on foreground, background, and this diminishing historical perspective, the naturalistic novel has been called scientific, experimental, objective, pessimistic, optimistic, despairing, revolutionary, sensational, mindless, and philosophi-

3

cal. As the essays in this volume show, it has taken such different forms in the writings of various authors who have borne the label of naturalist that we are now able to isolate a number of "naturalistic" qualities and show how they color the works of such different authors in very different ways.

If naturalism is an element that mixes into the flowing, changing stream of the novel, we may perhaps see it more clearly if we explore that stream up to its source. I propose that a new but fruitful way of locating naturalism in the long flow of the novel is to consider it in terms of the *attenuation of story*, which is indeed a movement toward its dissolution into the often chaotic forms of the contemporary novel. To design a purely theoretical history of the novel, we have to go back even behind its beginnings to what we can observe and deduce about the earliest story. Story was at first the telling of an event, specifically a heroic exploit or adventure. Such an exploit was more important as an action than the hero who enacted it. At first I assume there was no hero but only a figure who existed to enact the exploit. The exploit or adventure was wondrous, strange, exciting; the man involved was any man of the people (the Anglo-Saxon "Wanderer"). A second stage of story brought more attention to the actor, the prototypal hero, whose presence became an aspect of the event (Beowulf). In a third stage the hero became a Hero, and his conduct drew attention. It drew attention and it was evaluated, regarded as an example of courage, fidelity, endurance, or guile — but *still* the values were seen in the deed rather than in the character or motives of the hero (still true of Beowulf). The event was still central. The next stage, which opened the Pandora's box of modern literature, came when the hero's motives, plans, intentions were conceived as separate from the deed and not merely as responses to the critical situations in which the hero found himself. Then he was seen as an individual apart from his acts and judged, like the modern hero, for his intentions as well as for the decisions that he made at the climax of the story. But at first there would have been no thought of a decision; the deed would have happened, and the hero would merely have been there in it.

The separation of the motive from the deed marks the first suggestion of a hero who exists in spirit or character as well as in his acts (Achilles sulking in his tent, Odysseus longing for home). There is also the complicating factor that the author, in modern times, enters the story and frequently gets between the hero/action and the reader: irony, speculation, autobiography, and verbal performance (to say nothing of religious, political, and philosophical ideas) become significant aspects of the novel. It has traveled a long way from the simple condition where a listener heard an account of a deed. Now it is triangular at least: the author, the reader, and the story assume various relations to each other. And this is only the start, for the author may come to be more interesting than his characters, and the author's mental or spiritual growth may become more interesting than what is presumably enacted by the hero of his elusive action. The author may also discuss or speculate many more meanings than can be enacted in his story, so that the reader wanders among hints, clues, and symbols looking for meanings that are peripheral and hermetic.

But above all these growing complexities — of which I have noted only a few — there is one that marks a turning, a second major turning perhaps as important as the one that I have identified as the separation of the motive from the deed. It comes where the conditions, the circumstances, the forces that limit the hero's freedom of choice grow in strength and complexity to the point where they take control. It is perfectly apparent to anyone who thinks about it at all that there is no such thing as a completely free choice. The earliest hero of story faced what was probably a physical threat that he had to decide how to meet. When the story becomes more complex it is because the problem and the circumstances become more complex, so that the hero has to consider a great many more elements as he decides what path he will choose. It is of course these complicated problems that make fiction interesting. As we move down into the Victorian period of the English novel, we find the movement of realism to be more than anything else an exploration of the dense, complex fabric of society which contains and limits the individual's "freedom" of choice. This complex fabric includes threads of heredity, education, social values, manners, traditions, political, national, and philosophical movements, and so on. The great realistic novelist gives us the fullest account of these limiting elements in his characters' lives, yet he still organizes his action to concentrate our attention on the reaction of his character to whatever choice is open to him. This is the climax of the novel. Here the hero discovers and reveals himself, and the denouement follows with the unwinding of the original complication. However limited, the free human choice still binds the novel together and constitutes the source of its interest — the choice and of course all the consequences that it produces.

The major turning occurs when the individual becomes merely another thread in the fabric, when his freedom disappears (theoretically) in the concept that all human events may be understood as products of the hereditary, social, chemical, economic, and historical forces that compel them. But this simple formulation, which represents more or less accurately the views of the early interpreters of naturalism, is very far wide of the facts. We did not begin the naturalistic era by affirming that man was helpless against external forces. Rather, we turned to those forces and made them the heroes of our novels, but always — and most paradoxically — impelled not by any despairing pessimism but by an almost religious belief that man would be truly free, for the first time, under the auspices of this philosophy of scientific determinism!

The critical and evolutionary philosophers of the nineteenth century saw man as struggling under a burden of received dogma — religious, moral, political — that crushed the spirit of freedom. Auguste Comte announced, in his *Cours de philosophie positive* (1830), that human thought moved from the mythic to the explanatory to the *descriptive*. The final stage would accumulate information that would bring to perfection the science of society that would at last dispel the clouds of superstition and ignorance through which man had been blundering for aeons. Charles Darwin not only showed that man had evolved like other species from earlier forms but also inspired Herbert Spencer to write his *Synthetic Philosophy* which made evolution a cosmic process and almost guaranteed that man and society must evolve toward the highest complexity *and* stability. The power of these ideas appears in the work of Émile Zola, who undertook in *le roman expérimental* to demonstrate the working out of social process as the product of hereditary and environmental forces. He translated the theory of a contemporary French doctor, Claude Bernard, in his *Introduction à l'étude de la médicine expérimentale* (1865), into a statement of how an experimental novel could be written. The author would first establish his subject and milieu; then he would go forth with his notebook and gather masses of "documentation"; and finally he would establish the hereditary traits of his characters. Then like a scientist in his laboratory he would put his characters in the setting and *record* what they did and how their lives worked out. The result would be scientific findings that would bring man closer to controlling his own destiny because he understood the forces that made it happen.

This extraordinary undertaking occupied Zola through the twenty-volume Rougon-Macquart series as well as through a literary controversy that produced thousands of pages of attack and defense, of charge and countercharge. For the amazing fact is that Zola's announced program of writing a scientific novel was taken very seriously by both his readers and his critics. It must be obvious to the modern student that the whole proposition is preposterous. There are no test tubes, no laboratory where the people (ingredients) act under controlled conditions and are scientifically observed by the author, who merely records what he sees. Every fact in a novel is devised and organized by the author. Every single word in it is written down by him, out of his own invention, regardless of what "data" he may use. Hereditary forces, moreover, upon which Zola put the greatest emphasis, cannot be observed in operation; they can only be inferred as explanations of what the character has done *after* he has done it. Insofar as the characters' actions suggest drives or motives, the latter can be assigned hereditary causes; but this is the purest assumption. It is by no stretch of the imagination demonstrated scientifically — least of all in a novel.

My intention is not to ridicule Zola's "experimental" program but to suggest the tremendous emotional force of "scientific" ideas at that time. People were intoxicated by the idea of a new era in human history, an era that would bring knowledge, control, and even the creative manipulation of man's condition. So if the forces became the heroes of the naturalistic novel, they were not repressive but liberating forces. They carried a promise that something equivalent to a devout Christian's heaven would be established on earth as a result of the evolutionary application of scientific method. Complexity plus stability equaled Utopia. The equation fired the imaginations of laymen, scientists, and philosophers. And at the same time the ago-old tyrannical mystery of supernatural dogma was threatened. The excitement was so great that when Herbert Spencer came to the United States to lecture, just after 1900, his remarks were reported in full on the front pages of the newspapers.

If all process is material and chemical, capable of being scientifically charted and described, then it follows logically that man's free will and moral responsibility, under the old dispensation, no longer exist. But the impact of this scientific revolution was not logical at this point. It was intoxicated with golden hopes for mankind — and what has ever been closer to the heart of man than more and more leisure, hope, and opportunity, in short, more freedom? So the second great turning point of the novel, which I have described as the step-over-the-line from the realistic attention to the hero's freedom within a great web of social and personal limitations, to the enthroning of the forces as the heroes of the story — this was not a step toward "pessimistic determinism" but a plunge into more glorious vistas of freedom than the realistic novelist had dared envisage. Explorations of diseases, manias, hereditary defects; of wild struggles on the frontier against polar bears or cannibals; of economic oppression or ghastly drudgery; of social corruption and the law's misuse — all these carried an enthusiasm for a new era of human deliverance. They were man-centered and man-hopeful.

Whatever the power of the forces in a novel and the zeal with which the writer celebrated them, he could not rid himself of a primary interest in the personal freedom of the character who moved "helplessly" among these forces; nor of course could he slough off the whole tradition of story that had brought to him thousands of literary pieces in which the action turned upon a moral or ethical problem and was moved, essentially, by the *choices* of the hero at the climax.

New forms, in which the forces were the controlling actors, proliferated; but they could not exclude those bright vistas of human freedom that were the inspiration of the whole movement. Every naturalistic novel therefore seems to contain and even be dominated by ideas that are completely contrary to its apparent philosophical base. It is this fact that has made the criticism of naturalism so controversial. I may illustrate with just one powerful example. Dreiser's *An American Tragedy* presents a hero who is completely dominated by social and economic forces that finally destroy him. The novel has been labeled "pessimistic determinism" and therefore a perfect example of naturalism (see Oscar Cargill, *Intellectual America*, 1941). But another critic has insisted that naturalism is "optimistic progressivism" and that *An American Tragedy* therefore cannot be considered naturalistic at all (George W. Meyer, "The Original Social Purpose of the Naturalistic Novel," *Sewanee Review*, October 1942).

The critical impasse over this novel opens to a richer definition of naturalism if we consider the fact that the overwhelming power of the environment can be demonstrated only if it destroys the individual: one simply cannot demonstrate the forces that carry a man from rags to riches. The upward movement celebrates will and freedom; the downward movement demonstrates the power of the forces. Inside the action, *An*

American Tragedy is completely deterministic; but the novel lives in an atmosphere of indignation and hope. It has demonstrated in depth the operation of social values and laws that have destroyed the hero. It has shown that the hero was helpless against them. It has therefore shown just what destroyed him and why it destroyed him — and this knowledge is presented as the tool that man can use to correct the *evils* of his social condition. An action depicting the forces that destroy a helpless hero involves the audience, outside that action, in responsibility, guilt, and knowledge of what has to be done to correct the situation. Aristotle said that tragedy evoked the emotions of pity and fear — pity for the protagonist and fear of the mysterious and terrifying forces in the universe that might, at any moment, burst over the noblest of heroes. Naturalistic tragedy evokes the emotions of pity and guilt — pity for the same reasons but guilt because the destroying forces are no longer mysterious but clearly *social*, for which the spectator shares the responsibility and therefore experiences guilt.

It is worth noting, however (and here we can tie the naturalistic tragedy back into the tradition), that the reader still identifies with Clyde Griffiths, helpless as he seems to be, and shares his plight *as if* he were free to cope with it. So powerful is the human attraction. Ignorant, misguided, amoral, and not very intelligent, Clyde is still a person for whom the reader suffers moral anguish. His own humanity is deeply involved, no matter how rational he may be. And it is not reason that controls such experience; it is the ardor of science against the passion of humanity, and the latter prevails. Thus all naturalistic novels are stretched in a perilous tension between man's freedom and his fated impotence.

To account for this tension somewhat more fully, and perhaps to show why naturalism has been a particularly American phenomenon, we must look back to its roots in American transcendentalism. There we find why the American Dream values science and technology above culture, and pragmatic action above analysis and reflection — and why these tendencies carried us so enthusiastically into the naturalistic movement.

Traditional Christian dualism divides reality between the divine and the mundane. It sees two realms, with the world of time and nature different and separated from the timeless holy perfection of God's dominion. Nature being the Devil's playground since the Fall, man's will and intellect have been corrupted by the Original Sin so that they are no longer trustworthy. In time, in nature, man is incapable of regaining that timeless Realm by his own efforts. He must submit to authority; he must pray for grace; he must subdue his natural impulses to err. Defying and subverting this conservative tradition, Ralph Waldo Emerson reformulated European transcendentalism into a distinctly American Dream. He declared that nature was the symbol of Spirit. There was a perfect correspondence between divine Ideas and the objects in nature that embodied them. Nature was God incarnate. In fact, God was nowhere *but* where his ideas, his essences appeared in the natural forms that gave them being. And since man's mind/spirit was a version of absolute Spirit, it followed that the natural world, with all its laws, was no less than a perfect model, image, and embodiment of man's mind and will — which constituted man's spirit.

When Emerson declared in "Fate" that "thought dissolves the material universe by carrying the mind up into a sphere where all is plastic . . . every jet of chaos which threatens to exterminate us is convertible by intellect into wholesome force. Fate is unpenetrated causes," he was affirming that the physical universe is a projection of man's will. It is there to serve him just insofar as he penetrates its causes, that is, seizes its laws, sees them as forms of his own will, and uses them. Man could penetrate these causes by two routes. One was through what the transcendentalists variously termed reason, intuition, or imagination; they were the highest powers of the mind by which man could apprehend truth directly, could know it by being it, by experiencing it. The other was science, which could discover the same truths by observation and analysis.

The heart of the American Dream, then, was to see reality and perfection in the present instant, here and now. As Henry David Thoreau said in *Walden*, in the same vein, "I have been anxious to improve the nick of time, and notch it on my stick too; to stand on the meeting of two eternities, the past and future, which is precisely the present moment; to toe that line." If whatever divinity there was revealed itself only through nature and at the present instant, truth was present and equally accessible to every man — to the mystic through intuition, to the common man through the gatherings of science. With this Dream, it was inevitable that science should have been welcomed as man's new savior. Science would dispel old superstitions; displace corrupt authority; be the acrid dissolvent of outworn repressive morality; bring man to mental and physical health; and transform the wilderness into a garden. Thus in the American Dream science carries the fervor of transcendentalism directly into literary naturalism: It will identify the "unpenetrated causes" of physiology, psychology, economics, and heredity — and subdue them to man's will. It will make the philosophy a weapon against the status quo of manners, values, and regulations that limit freedom, by showing that such limiting elements are man-made and so subject to change by man. It will make its hero a tragic victim not of fate but of human folly in the form of institutional rigidity. It will transform the Struggle for Existence into an aspect of cosmic amelioration.

We can find in this constellation of beliefs the reason why America has valued science and technology above manners and culture. The same impulses have led us to value action above reflection. William James, the father of American pragmatism, had one foot firmly planted on Emerson's thought. The naturalistic novel, in a variety of forms that render it almost unclassifiable, is everywhere informed by this scientific fervor, which is its incontestable hallmark. Confidence in progress and distrust of traditional values accompany it. After 1900, when confidence in science began to wane, the other elements continue but the fervor fades — and we no longer have a naturalistic movement.

The authors of the present volume admirably describe the implications of naturalism, as they also represent the variety of critical approaches that it supports. *The Red Badge of Courage*, which for many years was a crux in the debate over naturalism, can now be seen as an illustration of various critical insights into it. We used to line up and take sides over the question whether Henry Fleming matured or whether he acted like an animal and rationalized his actions to protect his ego. Under the essential principle of controversy (that it drives opposing sides further apart) defenders of the maturation position went still further to contend that the book was essentially religious and that Henry underwent an ordeal that led toward Redemption, symbolized by that sun that was pasted in the sky like a wafer. A wafer, it was firmly stated, could be only a communion wafer.

The defenders of the naturalistic extreme insisted more and more strongly that Henry was reacting like an animal and (here is where the naturalism took full charge) his thinking was like human thinking generally in being controlled by the demands of whatever situation the individual found himself in.

More recently, and more temperately, a new formulation has appeared. It describes Henry as walking on a moving sidewalk in a subway or airport, walking against the direction of the belt. The belt is naturalism, but Henry moves a little faster in the opposite direction, and that represents his free will. This image has the attraction of being available for the other view: that the belt moves just a bit faster than Henry moves against it; so that he has the illusion of freely moving according to his own will but in fact he is moving with the belt all the time. If the difference between realism and naturalism is, as I have said elsewhere, in the richness and complexity of the forces and conditions rep-resented as limiting/controlling man's freedom, then we might take a closer look at Henry and try to see whether the huge machine of war and the smaller but closer influence of the harried soldiers control Henry or merely constitute a rich texture of experience within which he exercises his tiny remnant of freedom. If the latter is true, one might proceed to argue that this is the universal condition of man but that in a war situation it is intensified and urgent, so that its meaning is more easily seen.

The latest criticism seems fairly well to have brought this issue down to a still nicer one: is Crane consistent, and does he know all the way through just how he wants us to look at Henry? The consensus seems to be that he did not. He began with an ironic view — an ironic view so strong that it veered toward parody of heroism and war — but toward the end moved slowly toward a recognition that anyone who had been through what Henry had known must have learned something, no matter how vainglorious about it he might have become in later years. There is, to be sure, still irony in the grand language Henry uses about himself as he emerges from his ordeal. Yet Crane felt that he had gone much too far with this irony, because we know that he cut a good deal of it out as he prepared the manuscript for the printer. Did he think he had cut it all out? Are we overreacting to the remnants of irony that remain?

Certainly the parodic elements are stronger in the first half of the novel. And the optimism, the idealism, the rebellion against traditional repressive authority, and the contempt for the public values that have cowed simple people for too many centuries burn in Crane's mocking tone. This brings the indignant humanity of the reader into the experience and makes it more aesthetically complex and more removed from any resemblance to scientific objectivity. War is a frightful obscenity. It is humanity's outrage upon itself. It is man's ultimate depravity. It reduces even the bravest to animal ferocity and, later, to simplistic bravado and rationalization. In this context men may nevertheless display superb fearlessness, through which they will grow; and it is most interesting to note that Mr. Cazemajou finds Crane's concern with war mounting to the point where "To him war, in its various manifestations, was the alpha and omega of human life, essentially a testing ground." The trend toward respect for Henry Fleming, which critics have seen within the novel, certainly operated in Crane during the few years of life that remained to him.

Frank Norris, beyond any question, thought a good deal about naturalism, reacted strongly to the literary model of Zola, and, beginning under the conscious tutelage of Professor Gates at Harvard, undertook to write what he considered naturalistic novels. He was consciously riding the new wave. He published a volume of essays entitled *The Responsibilities of the Novelist* in which he attempted to distinguish among naturalism, realism, and romanticism, declaring that Zola was tremendously romantic and thus avowedly linking naturalism with romanticism as I have done earlier in this Introduction. The reader may therefore consider it something of an oddity that Norris, of all the exhibits in this volume, seems to have the least of that earnest faith in science, that zeal for progress and reform, that I have claimed to be the unifying element among the varieties of naturalistic tendencies. The contradiction or paradox may be resolved if we consider the extent to which tradition — and in this case specifically the genteel tradition — prevailed over the "new" elements in Norris's writings. Norris is highly verbal. He plays with language as he plays with situations. He is alert to the possibilities of clever sentiment and literary facetiousness. He seems always to have his tongue somewhat in his cheek, and his simple heroes are likely to be presented as freakish wonders or, wide-eyed, as romantic extravagances that are not to be taken with ultimate seriousness. These qualifications are not meant to undercut his literary achievement, which is considerable, but to suggest that a lively awareness of the qualities of the genteel tradition may heighten the reader's appreciation of the curious mixture of elements that constitutes Norris's idiosyncrasy.

Mr. Frohock's treatment of Dreiser illustrates very well my assertion that naturalism is at most an element in the novel. Acknowledging that Dreiser "in his novels made a shambles of the public moral assumptions of his time," and doing full justice to an intellectual naturalism that assumed that "laws" controlled all process, he nevertheless describes Dreiser as a romantic realist who moved between poles of genuine compassion for misery and naive admiration of material success. His novels *demonstrate* nothing; rather they explore the bewildering varieties of lives that grope painfully among complexities they cannot fathom. He is not detached, not scientific; he was most influenced by Balzac, the abundant realism of whose works he strove toward with a craft that was considerably inferior to that of his master. Yet the impact of Dreiser's writings upon the post-Victorian moral complacency of America cannot be exaggerated. His depiction of a world with different standards, different aims, and different values from those of the traditional Puritan ethic constitutes a "naturalistic" statement of immense power and influence.

If Dreiser is a romantic realist, we might in a comparable vein call Jack London a sentimental Spencerian. He wrote of life as a two-fisted struggle with survival at stake, although it was always the virtuous heart that prevailed. His concepts are earnestly Darwinian or, somewhat later, Marxist, but his actions are traditionally plotted insofar as they test the traditional virtues of integrity, courage, and respect for womanhood. They are, that is, except when they are so freighted with pseudoscientific evolutionary ideas that they become mixtures of the traditional and the sensational. We shall see London fighting his personal battles; creating a golden image of himself that passes from book to book, aging with his years; exorcising his personal demons of poverty, drink, and impossible aspiration; flaunting Darwin, Spencer, Nietzsche, and Marx; and withal translating the personal battles of his childhood and youth into fables of a modern St. George slaying the dragons of privilege to make ready for the coming of socialism.

Sherwood Anderson was more detached from science even than Norris, but he considered the lives of his characters much more seriously. He has become, surely, a name one thinks of among the first when the question of modern alienation is raised. Anderson's prime concern was the buried life, the life that was warped, cheated, confined largely because it did not enjoy the social or cultural nourishment that would have enabled it to grow to a proper humane maturity. Coming on the literary scene a generation after Crane and Norris, he did not have to set about attacking the Victorian hypocrisies as they and Dreiser did; he found on every side lives that embodied nothing so much as cultural starvation, lives that so obviously suffered from the constrictions of repressive bigotry and narrow moral timidity that he eschewed attacking outworn official morality and devoted himself to finding the blighted roots, the low stumps of the spirit, from which the blooming sprays had been stripped. When we get to Anderson, the flaming revolt of naturalism has been curbed; science, as so many have observed, has been shown to be generating ten questions for every answer, ten threats to man's security for every wound it has healed. Anderson breathes tenderly on the dim spark of life. His later work, from which his reputation suffered badly, as Mr. Weber shows, became increasingly concerned with social injustice — and here his genius was not served as well as his earlier subjects had served it.

John Steinbeck represents a later generation of naturalistic thought, and what is of special interest is that he goes back to the Emersonian bridge between nature and Spirit and reaffirms its importance to the insights of contemporary science. His most conscientious statement of these concepts comes in a later work, *Sea of Cortez*, 1951. It is the log of a journey into Mexican seas (the Gulf of Lower California), with his great friend Edward F. Ricketts, looking for the same sort of mystical insights that transpire from a Thoreau's enraptured contemplation of nature and that had been expressed a dozen years earlier by Tom Joad in *The Grapes of Wrath*, 1939, when he affirmed that his spirit would be one with that of every poor working stiff who had become an outcast of the Great Depression.

But neither Steinbeck's merits nor his defects, which appear in the truly formidable range of his techniques and his qualities, can be tied very closely to his pervasive naturalistic thought. He ranges from the exuberant legend of *Tortilla Flat*, the perfectly controlled craftsmanship of *In Dubious Battle*, the stirring compassion of *The Grapes of Wrath*, and the glorious humor of *Cannery Row* — down to the meretricious philosophizing of *East of Eden* and the utter banality of *The Winter of Our Discontent*. An amusing thread that weaves its way through all the varying textures of his experimentation is the little symbolic legends of animals that he uses to give body or illustration to his themes. Men are like dogs in *In Dubious Battle*. A turtle struggling to cross a highway symbolizes the people in *The Grapes of Wrath*. A prairie dog with a perfect site for his burrow — but no mate — enriches the dilemma of freedom versus responsibility in *Cannery Row* . . . At his best, Steinbeck has one of the most enchanting styles in American literature. It is impossible to lay his best books aside.

Pouring out his fusillades of invective, attack, and defense on naturalism, Émile Zola ranged widely. He insisted, at one end of his scale, that the naturalistic writer gathered documentation like the most rigorous scientist, put his characters faithfully in the established setting, and then with total scientific objectivity recorded their actions. At the other end, he maintained that naturalism was reality viewed "*à travers un temperament*." Edgar Branch shows that James T. Farrell must be seen under the sign of the latter formulation. Science, with all its antitraditional implications, has been his passion; Balzac's penetrating dissection of the minutiae of ordinary/extraordinary life was his predecessor if not his model; left-wing politics were his obsession; yet his writings are informed by a vividly and intensely personal vision. Farrell is working out his brilliant and agonized recollections in every line that he writes. His vision is idealistic and moral. Richly as he captures the lives of a particular segment of society, what burns the hottest in his work is the moral intensity of his comment. He writes in an agony of love and hate that resembles, on its different scale, the love-hate relation of William Faulkner with the South. Studs Lonigan (3 volumes), Danny O'Neill (5 volumes), and Bernard Carr (3 volumes) are the same person, but each lives a life on a fuller and higher level than the previous one because he is seen, this same man, later in time and consequently in a mellower perspective. Farrell lived through the agon of Studs, but he also survived like Danny and succeeded like Bernard. When he wrote *The Face of Time*, in 1953, going back to the earliest memories of his protagonist, he could have been writing about the early childhood of any one of the three.

If the reader has noticed somewhat abrupt differences of stress and tone in the preceding paragraphs, as they move from one of our authors to the next, he will have been responding properly to my intention, for I have sought to demonstrate in part what I have stated earlier — that the "naturalism" of the main writers who have commonly been subsumed under the label not only differs markedly from one writer to the next but also never accounts for what is the special quality and hallmark of any of them. Crane is a vehement, parodic impressionist. Norris has a foot-and-a-half in the genteel tradition but is at the same time consciously exploiting the forms and the subjects that he found in Zola's work. Mr. Frohock admirably characterizes Dreiser as a romantic realist; his yearnings waver between compassion for the underprivileged and an outcast's wistful greed for material splendor. Jack London's work bristles equally with ideas and brutal action; he too cannot free himself from the genteel tradition although his continuing impact on the world must be due to the energy of his *ideas*. Anderson, with the most exquisite style, tenderly penetrates the buried life — until later when his social zeal dilutes his effectiveness. Steinbeck has been an engaging experimentalist, trying a new form with almost every book and succeeding in being the most charmingly readable of these authors. Farrell has bored deep deep into a segment of American life that he loves as much as he hates; he has recorded the life of a place and an era with extraordinary particularity. Personal involvement and public protest fill his pages with painful intensity. Yet all these writers have a new concept of physical-social-political-moral process; all protest in one way or another against convention and hypocrisy; all are seeking new forms for dealing with a world that has forever departed from the certain certainties of orthodox tradition. They carry us into the affirmation and the despair of the twentieth century.

JEAN CAZEMAJOU

STEPHEN CRANE

Some writers work their way up to popularity in a long and difficult climb. Others — and Stephen Crane was one of them — reach success almost overnight. Propelled into the limelight early in his brief career by the triumphal acclaim of his *Red Badge of Courage*, he lived only long enough to enjoy a few years of controversial fame.

Experimenting in various media — journalism, fiction, poetry, playwriting — Crane was for his contemporaries above all a picturesque figure of the world of the press. His professional commitments kept him in close touch with the life of his country, and he explored slums and battlefields with unabating eagerness, seeing war in two brief conflicts in 1897 and 1898. The conjunction of highstrung temperament and obstinate neglect of his health brought Crane's life to an early close when he was not yet twenty-nine.

During the two decades following his death, in 1900, he was to be almost forgotten. Then in 1923 Thomas Beer published an impressionistic biography which served to focus attention on Crane once more, and *The Work of Stephen Crane* (1925–27), edited by Wilson Follett, made most of his writings available to a scholarly audience. This limited edition contained laudatory

prefaces by creative writers such as Amy Lowell, Sherwood Anderson, H. L. Mencken, and Willa Cather, a few assessments by
professional critics, and reminiscences by fellow journalists.
Crane's reputation was also enhanced by the faithful support of
some of his friends, especially Edward Garnett, Joseph Conrad,
H. G. Wells, and Ford Madox Hueffer, later known as Ford
Madox Ford. The thirties saw in him a champion of the cause
of the common man, and the forties continued to fit him into a
realistic tradition; in the next two decades he appeared to critics
primarily as a symbolist, but a wide range of interpretations
confronted the student with a mass of conflicting scholarship. In
1950 John Berryman's *Stephen Crane* established him as an
American classic. The Modern Library edition of *The Red Badge
of Courage* came out the following year with a preface written by
R. W. Stallman, whose extensive work on Crane, climaxed by his
monumental biography in 1968, has aroused much enthusiasm
and controversy. D. G. Hoffman's *The Poetry of Stephen Crane*, a
very lively and perceptive study, appeared in 1957. Since 1951
there has also been a steady outpouring of articles, dissertations,
monographs, and reprints. When, in the summer of 1966, a
Stephen Crane Newsletter was founded and began to be issued
regularly by Ohio State University, Stephen Crane had come
into his own.

With deep roots in the soil of New Jersey he appeared ex-
tremely proud of his American heritage. One of his ancestors
bearing the same name had, according to Crane, "arrived in
Massachusetts from England in 1635." The man who wrote *The
Red Badge of Courage* was, on his father's side, descended from a
long line of sheriffs, judges, and farmers, and another Stephen
Crane had been one of the leading patriots of New Jersey during
the Revolution; in his mother's family, as he humorously put it,
"everybody, as soon as he could walk, became a Methodist cler-
gyman — of the old, ambling-nag, saddle-bag, exhorting kind."
Born in a Methodist parsonage in Newark, New Jersey, on
November 1, 1871, Stephen was the fourteenth child of Jonathan

Townley Crane, D.D. He grew up in various parsonages in New Jersey and New York State, his father being, according to the custom of his church, shifted from one charge to another every two or three years. The death of Dr. Crane in Port Jervis, New York, in 1880 brought this itinerancy to a close. Still a child when his father died, Stephen always cherished his memory.

After the death of her husband Mrs. Crane returned to Newark for a while, but soon made a permanent home in Asbury Park, New Jersey, which was a new stronghold of American Methodism. There she settled in 1883 and, that same year, was elected president of the Woman's Christian Temperance Union of Asbury Park and Ocean Grove. Frequently lecturing in neighboring towns, she occasionally traveled to distant cities as a delegate of that organization. A well-educated woman, she also dabbled in journalism to eke out her meager resources and reported on the summer religious meetings on the New Jersey shore, contributing mostly to the *New York Tribune* and the *Philadelphia Press*. She suffered from mental illness for some months in 1886 and was to die in 1891. Her religious zeal did not inspire a similar response in Stephen and he left the fold of the church; but he remained dominated by fundamental religious precepts and patterns — charity, fraternity, redemption, and rescue — which he usually kept at an earthly level.

At the age of fourteen he left Asbury Park to go to the Pennington Seminary, a Methodist academy in New Jersey, and thus attended a school over which his father had ruled for ten years (1849–58). He did not complete the four-year course there but transferred in the middle of the third year to Claverack College and Hudson River Institute, a semimilitary Methodist school near Hudson, New York. He stayed there from January 1888 to June 1890. His university education lasted only one year: it began at Lafayette College, a Presbyterian institution at Easton, Pennsylvania, where he spent the autumn term of 1890, and ended at Syracuse University the following June. All these schools stressed religious and classical studies and at no time did the young man feel any sympathy for these two branches of knowledge. He was already a rebel resolutely hostile to formal education and preferred to study "humanity."

Crane suffered both from his mother's moral severity and from her physical neglect of him, but in Asbury Park he enjoyed a happy freedom near the "soft booming sound of surf." The deaths of his father, his sister Agnes, his brother Luther, and finally his mother must have made his childhood and adolescence a period of many severe trials. Three of his older brothers played the part of father-substitutes, offering either material assistance or a questionable but attractive model. William, who became a lawyer in Port Jervis in 1881, and Edmund, a man of limited education but of generous heart who, in 1894, settled at Hartwood, near Port Jervis, often helped the young man in his financial difficulties at the beginning of his literary career. Jonathan Townley Jr.'s bohemian tastes exerted a powerful influence on his younger brother; almost twenty years older than Stephen, he was in the late 1880s the coast correspondent of the *New York Sun*, the *New York Tribune*, and the Associated Press in Asbury Park and so a well-known regional journalist. Stephen, as early as 1888, began helping him in his reportorial work on the New Jersey shore. His oldest sister, Nellie, who then kept an art school in Asbury Park, may have introduced Stephen to the world of color and prepared him for an aesthetic exploration of his environment.

Stephen Crane's sensitivity was thus early aroused and developed through a gradual training of his faculty of observation: Methodism forced him to probe his own soul, journalism taught him how to note facts with accuracy, and art provided his craving for reality with chromatic patterns.

After publishing a few pieces in *Cosmopolitan* and the *New York Tribune*, a paper for which he wrote his "Sullivan County Sketches," boyish tales of the woods, in the early part of 1892, he was fired by the *Tribune* for an ironic article about a parade of workers in Asbury Park, and became a free-lance journalist in New York. (This brief report had expressed, in the tone of a sententious aesthete, his mild amusement at the sight of "an uncut and uncarved procession" of men with "principles" marching past a "decorous" throng of "summer gowns" and predatory Asbury Parkers.) Then began his apprenticeship in bohemianism in the metropolis, where he lived with struggling young artists. Occasional visits to his brothers Edmund and William helped him keep from starving; they provided him with handy refuges where he could escape from the hardships and turmoil of New York. His pride, however, prevented him from making frequent use of them. In 1893 he published his first book, *Maggie: A Girl of the Streets*, under a pseudonym and at his own expense. The audacity of the subject did not deter Hamlin Garland and W. D. Howells from praising that novel, but they were almost the only critics to notice it. They both encouraged him to write proletarian sketches, some of which appeared in the Boston *Arena* and others in the *New York Press*, enabling him to attain some financial security. His picture of the big city was centered around the life of the underprivileged in their ordinary setting, the southern tip of Manhattan.

Gradually acquiring self-reliance, experience, and ambition, he immersed himself in the most significant venture of his literary life, the writing of *The Red Badge of Courage*, an imaginative reconstruction of a Civil War battle; it was first printed in an abbreviated form as a newspaper serial distributed by the Bacheller Syndicate in December 1894. The success of the story led to an assignment as roving reporter in the West and Mexico at the beginning of 1895. When he came back in May, his first volume of verse, *The Black Riders*, had just appeared in print and proved that the young man was impelled by the spirit of religious and social rebellion. Appleton published *The Red Badge* as a book in New York in October 1895, and the London firm of Heinemann included it in its Pioneer Series at the end of November. Warmly received by English reviewers, it soon became a popular novel in the United States as well and its tenth American edition was issued in June 1896.

In that year Crane's celebrity reached a peak. All at once praised, parodied, and harshly criticized, he found it difficult to cope with success. Going from one apartment to another in New York and probably from one girl to another, he ended up challenging the impregnable metropolitan police force on behalf of a prostitute who claimed she was being unjustly harassed. Then, rushing into escape, he accepted a commission to report the insurrection in Cuba against Spanish rule, but his ship sank off the coast of Florida on January 2, 1897, and he returned to Jacksonville, where before sailing he had met Cora Howorth (known there as Cora Taylor), the proprietress of the Hotel de Dream, a somewhat refined house of ill-fame. She had already been married twice and, at the time of her first meeting with Crane, was thirty-one years old. They were to live together for the rest of his life. His previous adventures with women had been inconclusive episodes. At the age of twenty he had fallen in love, at Avon-by-the-Sea, a resort near Asbury Park, with a certain Helen Trent, who was already engaged. In 1892 a love affair with a young married woman, Lily Brandon Munroe, enlivened his summer in Asbury Park and inspired some of his more moving love letters. Nellie Crouse, a provincial maiden whom he met at a social tea in New York, flirted with him by mail but finally rejected him. In 1896 he started sending money to Amy Leslie, a former actress now past her prime who had become a drama critic for the *Chicago Daily News*. He kept doing so until January 1898, when she succeeded in having a warrant of attachment issued against him to recover $550 of the $800 she had allegedly given him in 1896 to deposit for her. The details of their relationship remain somewhat obscure but, in November 1896, when he set out for Florida, he was probably fleeing from her as well as the New York police.

The year 1896 was not marked by any really new work from his pen, except his "Tenderloin" sketches for the *New York Journal*: Crane was too busy with his public and private life. *Maggie*, made respectable by the success of *The Red Badge* and slightly revised, came out under his real name, accompanied by another tale of the slums, *George's Mother*, which had been completed in November 1894. A volume of war stories, *The Little*

Regiment, appeared in New York late in 1896 and in London in February 1897.

Crane's longing for adventure had apparently been only whetted by the shipwreck off Florida, in which he nearly lost his life; periodically the urge to see violent action was aroused in him. The Greco-Turkish War, which he covered in a disappointing manner for the *New York Journal* and the *Westminster Gazette*, took him to Europe in the summer of 1897; his bad health interfered with his reportorial duties in Greece, but he saw enough fighting to conclude on his return to London that "*The Red Badge* [was] all right."

Obviously conscious of the impossibility of introducing his "wife" — there is no record of a marriage ceremony — to his family, and still afraid of retaliatory action by the New York police, he decided to stay on in England after the Greek war was over. His shipwreck had inspired him to write a brilliant short story, "The Open Boat," which *Scribner's* printed in June 1897. About the same time he published *The Third Violet*, a novel based on his experiences in the highly contrasted worlds of Hartwood, New York, and New York City. Crane's stay in England did not provide the writer with a fresh batch of literary topics but it did enable him to see his own life in a new perspective. Many of his western adventures and several accounts of urban poverty went into a volume published in 1898 under the title *The Open Boat and Other Stories*. This volume, which contains seventeen tales, gives a sample of Crane's best talent. His meeting with Joseph Conrad brought him into contact with a writer whose aesthetics was very close to his own. In his "villa," situated on the borderline between Oxted and Limpsfield, Surrey, where he settled in the fall of 1897, Crane was not far from Ford Madox Hueffer and Harold Frederic. A few English Fabians, the Sydney Oliviers and the Edward Garnetts notably, lived in the vicinity.

In 1898 he was hired by Pulitzer to write for the *New York World* and, seeing war for the second time, reported the Spanish-American conflict, which left deep scars on his body and mind; the symptoms of the tuberculosis that was to prove fatal had already set in. In the fall he lingered in Havana where he served as special correspondent for the *New York Journal* and wrote the first draft of a novel, *Active Service*, based on his Greek assignment.

Early in 1899 he was back in England and, because of harassing creditors in Oxted, decided to move from Surrey to Sussex, his new English residence being the medieval manor of Brede Place situated near Rye on the charming Sussex coast. There his literary production reached a peak, but his efforts to avoid bankruptcy proved vain in the face of a rising tide of debts and recurring signs of failing health. He kept writing doggedly, now coaxing, now threatening his literary agent, James B. Pinker, from whom he tried to obtain more and more advances, and even the best work of this period shows the effects of haste and worry. Drawing upon his recent experiences, he completed a series of eleven fictional and autobiographical accounts of the Cuban war, which were posthumously collected in *Wounds in the Rain* (1900). He also wrote thirteen children's stories which first appeared in *Harper's Magazine* and were assembled in book form after his death under the title *Whilomville Stories* (1900). In the course of 1899 three other books saw print: a volume of verse, *War Is Kind*, containing a variety of poems whose composition embraced a period of seven years; *Active Service*, a novel which he himself regarded as second-rate; and the American edition of *The Monster and Other Stories*. Reminiscing about his family's role during the Revolutionary War, he composed three "Wyoming Valley Tales" and, creating an imaginary country, chose it as the setting for a series of archetypal battles, the "Spitzbergen Tales," which began to appear in English and American magazines in 1900.

Taking a mild interest in Cora's passion for entertaining, he watched streams of guests come to visit him in his dilapidated mansion, among whom were some distinguished writers (Conrad, Wells, Henry James) and many parasites. He decided or was persuaded by Cora to arrange a Christmas party for his literary friends, producing an original play for the occasion. The play

was very aptly called *The Ghost* and, in spite of a widely adver-
tised collaboration with famous English and American authors,
most of it was written by Crane himself. During the festivities he
almost died of a lung hemorrhage. He was to drag on for a few
more months, his body and his brain gradually weakening, but
he went on writing to his deathbed. With the help of Kate Lyon,
Harold Frederic's mistress, he turned out a series of articles on
nine great battles of the world for *Lippincott's Magazine*, outlined
the plot and wrote the first twenty-five chapters of *The O'Ruddy*, a
picaresque novel of the eighteenth century with an Irish hero
and an English setting. But it was left uncompleted when Crane
died on June 5, 1900, in Badenweiler, Germany, where Cora had
seen fit to take him in the idle hope of a miraculous recovery
from tuberculosis. Crane's friend Robert Barr agreed to write
the final chapters of the novel which, after picaresque ups and
downs, was eventually published in New York in October 1903.

The inescapable trait of Crane as a writer is his desire to express his own mind candidly, regardless of accepted opinion,
conventions, and satirical attacks. The world first appeared to
him with the colors, shapes, and sounds of the Psalms and of
Wesleyan hymns, and he unconsciously made frequent use of
the rhythms and imagery of Biblical stories. His parents' participation in charitable work encouraged his interest in slum life,
and he soon discovered, through his own deep concern with the
mainsprings of fear, a strange curiosity about war.

In Crane's generation "low life" was a subject of reportage,
fiction, and melodrama. When he moved into this area of literature he did so with the seriousness, the intentness, and the
acuteness of a minister's son who had received his training as a
journalist. Even if he did not know New York well at the time he
wrote *Maggie*, he must have caught by then a few glimpses of the
poorer districts of the American metropolis, which was so close
to Asbury Park where he lived between his stays at boarding
school or college.

The approach to slum life of Crane's first novel was new in

that it did not preach and did not encourage "slumming"; it simply aimed, he said, to "show people to people as they seem[ed] to [him]." Maggie is the daughter of the Johnsons, a family of poor tenement dwellers living on the lower East Side of Manhattan. A large part of the story is devoted to drinking bouts, and Maggie's home is the scene of a daily fight for survival. We thus attend the growth and brutal extinction of the heroine who has "blossomed in a mud-puddle" to become a "pretty girl" strangely undefiled by her surroundings. She tries to escape the degrading atmosphere of her home by working in a collar-and-cuff factory, but soon discovers the dull routine and corruption of the sweatshop. Then Pete, a commonplace bartender, comes into her life, and to Maggie he seems to be "a supreme warrior," "a knight." He takes her to dime museums, beer gardens, and theaters, and thus satisfies her vague and romantic longings for culture and refinement. Seduced and abandoned by her lover, rejected by her drinking mother and callous brother on "moralistic" grounds, Maggie finally turns to prostitution. Shortly afterwards, "upon a wet evening," she abruptly ends her life in the East River while in the distance "street-car bells [jingle] with a sound of merriment."

The problem this story hinges on is not primarily a social one, and Crane is not merely content with studying the causes and consequences of prostitution. Mainly concerned with the "soul" of the young prostitute, he tries to challenge the beliefs of Sunday school religion. Can an "occasional street girl" be expected to end up in heaven, irrespective of the indignant frowns of "many excellent people"? The answer is never made explicit in a narrative brimming over with irony, but it could not be other than positive. Maggie falls because "environment is a tremendous thing in the world," because she herself is romantic and weak, and also because nobody is interested in her fate. She, however, redeems herself by committing suicide, her only possible escape from a life of moral degradation. By so doing she undergoes an ironic purification in the foul waters of the East River while her brother Jimmie, who had "clad his soul in armour," and her mother, who belatedly "ferg[ave]" her, are allowed to continue their degenerate lives of vice and hypocrisy in the human jungle to which they are perfectly adapted.

As a first novel *Maggie* revealed on the part of the author a deep seriousness and the powerful urge to gain an audience. It posited the imperative need for a new ethical code and, through a consistent use of irony, debunked the false values worshiped by society and exposed the part played by collective passivity in the destruction of innocence. "Indifference is a militant thing," Crane commented in a story of 1897; this idea is implied throughout *Maggie*. Much of this early Crane is reminiscent of the young Zola's passion for social rescue which found its most moving expression in *La confession de Claude* (1865). The critics who wonder whether *Maggie* should be called a tragedy or a melodrama raise a fruitless issue, because the book is undeniably filled with pity and fear, and Howells was right when he discovered in it "that quality of fatal necessity which dominates Greek tragedy."

George's Mother is a companion piece to the drama of the New York prostitute, and it takes up again the problem of the corruption of innocence, this time in the person of a young working-man, George, who has recently settled in New York and lives in a tenement with his widowed mother, a very religious woman. The path leading to George's physical and moral destruction opens early in the story when he meets a former acquaintance, a certain Jones who introduces him into a circle of alcoholics. He thus misses work one day and invents a lie as an excuse for his absence. His mother, who tries to keep him from drifting, induces him to go with her to a prayer meeting which only "prov[es] to him again that he [is] damned." Plunging more resolutely into drink and dissipation, the young man inflicts great moral torture upon his mother who finally dies, worn down by disappointed expectations. The last scene shows her in the grips of her death agony, while her son, hastily called to her bedside, suddenly feels "hideous crabs crawling upon his brain." This book shows more interest in abstract ideas than in real people; it demonstrates the baneful effects of Sunday school religion upon George, who seeks refuge from it in drink, and the failure of this primitive faith to succor the mother in her sorest need. It also points to the impossibility of communication between human beings. The power corruptive influences and environment exert on immature minds is here again illustrated. This rather flimsy novel raises a number of issues but solves none and throughout are heard distinct echoes of Crane's conflict with his own mother.

The confined world of *George's Mother* could easily be contrasted with the maelstrom of life in Crane's New York City sketches, which he ranked among his "best work." He started his field study in the poorer districts of southern Manhattan, observing the motley streams of passers-by on Broadway, breadlines, crowds gathering outside cheap lodging houses, jingling streetcars, fires, Italian fruit-vendors, tramps, policemen, and here and there his camera eye stopped on a detail, a "tiny old lady" lost in "the tempest of Sixth Avenue," or two children fighting for a toy. His sympathy drew him instinctively to the cause of the common man, but he was more inclined to study the actual working of minds than the possible consequences of economic systems. In his study of the "Tenderloin," undertaken for the *New York Journal* in 1896, he calls up a picture of restaurants, dance halls, and opium dens where, beneath the superficial gaiety, slumbers the fire of an ever-present violence.

His technique in these city sketches follows three main patterns: that of the journey of initiation, exemplified by "An Experiment in Misery" and "An Ominous Baby"; that of canvas painting, in "The Men in the Storm," "An Eloquence of Grief," and "The Auction"; and that of the parody, in some of his "Tenderloin" stories. The reporter-errant selects a certain situation which becomes a pretext for a psychological study of urban conflicts. To him "the sense of city [was] battle."

How did Crane's war novel, *The Red Badge of Courage*, come into being against this background of urban literature? The book is not an ordinary Civil War novel. Although the theme is the baptism of fire of a Union private, Henry Fleming, during the battle of Chancellorsville, the tone is psychological rather than military. Its main characters are most of the time designated as figures in an allegory, "the tall soldier," "the loud soldier," "the tattered man," "the man of the cheery voice"; and the protagonist, usually referred to as "the youth" in the early chapters, only acquires his full identity in Chapter XI.

The author's observation of "the nervous system under fire" is conducted on the level of Henry's restless mind; before the battle we witness the premonitory misgivings of this farm boy in uniform; then comes his moment of reassurance after a first onslaught of the enemy has been repulsed. A second attack launched against his side causes his sudden panic and flight. Driven by shame to wander on the fringe of the battlefield, he seems to be helplessly floating in a nightmarish atmosphere; this, for our cowardly private, is the beginning of a journey of expiation. He meets a "tattered soldier" whose wounds and embarrassing questions increase his sense of guilt. The two men are caught up in the procession of wounded soldiers who make their way to the rear. Among them they see Henry's friend, Jim Conklin, the mortally wounded "tall soldier" who, after horrible sufferings climaxed by a gruesome "danse macabre," dies under their petrified gaze. After this shattering experience Henry abandons the "tattered man" whose very presence seems to him an accusation. Retreating Union soldiers fly past him and one of them, whom the youth tries to question, knocks him down with the butt of his rifle, ironically giving him the "red badge of courage" he had been longing for. After regaining consciousness Henry meets a man with "a cheery voice" who takes him back to his regiment and, from then on, the protagonist's attitude is altogether changed. He feels full of aggressive but specious self-confidence and, because he does not reveal the real cause of his wound, derives much unmerited respect from his fellow soldiers for his ostensibly courageous conduct. The last chapters show him turning into a daredevil, fighting at the head of his unit during a victorious charge, but at the end of the story

— which is no pamphlet for recruiting officers — Henry's regiment finds itself recrossing the river it had crossed a few days before and thus going back to its previous position on the other bank of the Rappahannock as if nothing had happened. Henry's first impression had been right after all: "It was all a trap."

A constant ironic counterpoint aims to debunk the traditional concept of glorious war. The whole thing seems absurd: generals shout, stammer, and behave childishly on the battlefield; Henry's wound confers upon him a spurious glory; Wilson, the "loud soldier," has become as meek as a lamb in the last chapters, and the whole tumult has resulted in no gain of ground for the Union forces and no loss for the Confederates. What remains in the mind of the reader is a series of confused movements with, from time to time, "men drop[ping] here and there like bundles" and, in the protagonist's "procession of memory," sad nerve-racking images suddenly blurred with a sense of relief when the "sultry nightmare [is] in the past."

Like all the great classics of literature *The Red Badge of Courage* speaks of different things to different minds. However, only an oversimplified interpretation could see in Henry's final charge the proof that he has become, as he himself thinks, "a man." The pattern of this book is that of a spiritual journey, but the final goal remains in doubt when we reach the conclusion: "Over the river a golden ray of sun came through the hosts of leaden rain clouds." The youth, in his baptism of fire, has acquired self-knowledge and experience, but a radical change has not taken place within him: he remains, in his heroic pose at the end, just as grotesque as the fearful "little man" he was at the beginning. The dialogue he has been carrying on with his own conscience often contains overtones of legalistic chicanery: it is a constant search for excuses to justify his cowardly conduct. Occasional flashes of inner sincerity are defeated by his attempts to demonstrate that what he did was logically and morally valid, but his arguments would fail to convince anyone and only add to his torment. Through a series of excruciating experiences which follow his shameful act he manages to keep his secret and even to rise in stature in the eyes of his regiment. But, instead of closing the book with a reassuring epiphany, the author preserves the ironic structure throughout. Henry's conscience is still disturbed when the book ends, and his concealed guilt spoils "the gilded images of memory."

The Red Badge of Courage contains the account of a half-completed conversion. It is only in a satellite story entitled "The Veteran" that Henry pays the full price for his "sin" and goes through the final stage of his itinerary of redemption. Then, by belatedly but unequivocally confessing his lack of courage on the battlefield, he purges himself of his former lie. In the last scene of "The Veteran," determined to save two colts trapped in his burning barn, he plunges into the flames never to come out, thus making a gesture of genuine and unconventional bravery. Rejecting his previous irony, Crane presents here a real conversion, grounded on cool, selfless determination and not on spurious enthusiasm as was Henry's sudden reversal of mood on the battlefield.

In Crane's war novel religious imagery prevails, centered on an itinerary of spiritual redemption which leads not to eternal salvation but to a blissful impasse. Alone in the middle of the forest the hero discovers the imaginary "chapel" with its "columnlike" trees where a "hymn of twilight" is heard. When the "tall soldier" dies, wildly gesturing in his final agony, he seems to resemble "a devotee of a mad religion"; most significant in the same creative process is Henry's illusion after his cowardly flight: he looks for "a means of escape from the consequences of his fall" and, unable to reach redemption through mere introspection, returns to "the creed of soldiers." But his final charge does not purge him of his guilt in spite of a temporary exultation due to the repression of his fear; "the ghost of his flight" and "a specter of reproach" born of the desertion of "the tattered man" in his sorest need keep haunting the youth at the close of the book. Some obvious similarities with the theme of concealment in Hawthorne's fiction can also be noted: "veil" metaphors and similes clustered around the character of Henry Fleming keep recurring in the narrative. In Chapter I the hero "wish[es] to be alone with some new thoughts that [have] lately come to him"; in Chapter VII he "cring[es] as if discovered in a crime" and, under the burden of his hidden guilt, soon feels that "his shame [can] be viewed." But an ironic glimmer of hope reappears in his consciousness when he imagines that "in the battle blur" his face will be hidden "like the face of a cowled man."

Beside this procession of religious images there appears here and there a scattering of scenes with animal characters which seem to be fables in miniature. The style abounds in symbolic rabbits, squirrels, horses, cows, and snakes which form a conventional bestiary by the side of a Christian demonology swarming with monsters directly borrowed from Biblical literature.

Another facet of this book is its consistent use of legalistic terminology. A dossier is being minutely, if inconclusively, revealed to us: the youth of this story approaches his problem of fear in a logical manner and determines to "accumulate information of himself"; at first he tries to "mathematically prove to himself that he [will] not run from a battle." Then, after experiencing his shameful flight, he acts as his own lawyer and attempts to present a convincing defense of his case: "He had done a good part in saving himself, who was a little part of the army. . . . His actions had been sagacious things. They had been full of strategy. They were the work of a master's legs." A strong ironic coloring, one of the main characteristics of Crane's style in the whole book, can easily be detected here. Henry is constantly trying to show his actions to advantage; when he returns to his regiment after his cowardly escape, he even considers using the "small weapon" — a packet of letters — which Wilson in a panic had left in his hands before the battle. This "exhibit" would, Henry thinks, "prostrate his comrade at the first signs of a cross-examination."

The mechanistic imagery of *The Red Badge of Courage* already adumbrates the development of Crane's war motif in his writings after the Cuban conflict of 1898, and serves to highlight the complexity and destructiveness of modern war: "The battle was like the grinding of an immense and terrible machine to him. Its complexities and powers, its grim processes, fascinated him. He must go close and see it produce corpses."

If military courage had been one of the values pitilessly probed in *The Red Badge of Courage*, it also furnished the central topic for a satellite story entitled "A Mystery of Heroism." Private Fred Collins ventures into no man's land under the pretext of procuring some water for his company; but in fact his action has been prompted by the desire to prove to himself that he is not "afraid t' go." After being "blindly . . . led by quaint emotions" he returns unscathed to his lines, but the author wastes no sympathy on his "heroic" deed. "Death and the Child" deals with the same theme, the scene being now the Greco-Turkish War of 1897; the central character, a war correspondent, soon sees his battle fury die out and, instead of fighting by the side of the soldiers of his mother country, flees and encounters a child who asks him this embarrassing question: "Are you a man?"

In his reporting of the same war and of the Cuban conflict Crane fell in with the conventions of his time and did not aim at more than ordinary journalistic style. But when reworking his factual accounts of battles and recollecting his war experiences in tranquillity he achieved the spare and severe economy of *Wounds in the Rain*, a moving and realistic adaptation in fiction of his own adventures with the American forces sent to Cuba in 1898. His protagonist then ceased to be a dreamy amateur like Henry Fleming in *The Red Badge* or Peza in "Death and the Child," and the figure of Private Nolan, the regular, as anonymous and unromantic as any true regular, stood out in the foreground. Crane was now dealing with war as a special trade, and his soldiers at work were shown to be "as deliberate and exact as so many watchmakers." In "The Price of the Harness" he went beyond the phantasmagoria of his early definition of war and made of "a great, grand steel loom . . . to weave a woof of thin red threads, the cloth of death," the essential metaphor of his battle symbolics. Henceforth, in the logbook of the war correspondent, what had been in *The Red Badge* a "monster," a "dragon," or a "blood-swollen god," gradually came down to the lowly estate of "death, and a plague of the lack of small things and toil." Crane could not have gone any further in deglamorizing that image of "vague and bloody conflicts" which had once "thrilled [Henry Fleming] with their sweep and fire."

A gradual reduction of the concept of war to the archetype can be found in Crane's later stories, if we leave aside as mere potboiling and unoriginal work his *Great Battles of the World*. It is in the "Spitzbergen Tales" that the war metaphor is suddenly brought down to its essentials, the taking of a coveted hill, the storming of a redoubt, or a burial scene on the front line. The typical hero of most of these stories is no longer a private but a noncommissioned or low-ranking officer, the problem of conduct being then studied in an almost abstract context and the main issue being the duty of the responsible professional toward his command. Primarily concerned with war as a personal test, Crane avoided the approach of the historian, that of the strategist, and deliberately worked out that of the moralist.

To him war, in its various manifestations, was the alpha and omega of human life, essentially a testing ground, but adventure could be a fair substitute. Sent to the West and Mexico by the Bacheller Syndicate as a roving reporter early in 1895, he drew upon his tour for a few outstanding stories. His shipwreck off the coast of Florida in January 1897 furnished material for "The Open Boat," a tale which won immediate recognition and found in Conrad and H. G. Wells two faithful admirers. The latter even went so far as to say about it: "[It is], to my mind, beyond all question, the crown of all his work."

Stephen Crane depended on adventure, vicarious or real, as fodder for his imagination. He had to *feel* intensely to *write* intensely. As soon as the pace of his life became relaxed because of illness and a general weakening of his spiritual energy, he was compelled to turn to his childhood reminiscences, also fraught with intense emotions, or to an archetypal war metaphor in order to write successfully.

The short stories "The Blue Hotel," "The Bride Comes to Yellow Sky," and "The Open Boat" outline his personal attitude toward the literary utilization of experience. Although fond of exotic settings and people Crane is not a local colorist. The colors of his adventures are the colors of his soul. For example the real fight that he saw in a saloon in Lincoln, Nebraska, which is supposed to have been the germ of "The Blue Hotel," was transmuted by him into a moral study on the theme of collective and individual responsibility. The narrative in this tale is conducted on two levels, straight storytelling and ironic counterpoint. A Swede who has lived for ten years in New York and is now traveling in the West experiences forebodings of violent death and is eventually justified in his fear, since he meets his doom at the hands of a professional gambler. Crane, however, succeeds in keeping up the suspense by leading his main character into ominous situations at the Palace Hotel which are ironically deflated and prove harmless to the frightened hero. Once the latter feels that all danger is over and is about to celebrate his escape from the hotel in a neighboring saloon, he is stabbed to death by a gambler whom he wanted too insistently to befriend. Crane here comes back once again to an analysis of fear. In the Swede's mind this feeling follows a pattern similar to that of Henry's itinerary in *The Red Badge*: from timidity to unrestrained arrogance. Both Henry and the Swede are intoxicated, the former with a belatedly discovered battle fury, the latter with repeated drinking. Crane also explores the comic overtones of violence, and notes the grotesque fall of the Swede's body, "pierced as easily as if it had been a melon." The protagonist obviously brought about his own destruction, but the writer is not just censuring one man's attitude, and the easterner, Mr. Blanc, who acts as point-of-view character, declares: "'We are all in it! . . . Every sin is the result of a collaboration.'" Once again the creator of *Maggie* stigmatized the unpardonable sin, indifference: no one had done anything to prevent the final denouement from taking place. The hotelkeeper and the bartender had provided drink; the other "collaborators," Johnnie excepted, since he had been most active in arousing the Swede's anger, had each exhibited a different form of passivity.

"One Dash — Horses" is another study of fear, this time in a Mexican setting. In its gaudy and alluring garb this tale reads like a direct transcript of experience, but the narrative is not limited to the account of a thrilling manhunt; Crane is more interested in exploring the psychological springs of fear and the power of illusion. The young American and his guide are afraid of the Mexican bandits, and the latter are terrorized by the thought of the mounted police — the "rurales" — but it is an abstract stereotype of the traditional enemy which causes this feeling in both cases. The Mexican bandits prove to be playthings in the hands of the gods, and the arrival of a group of prostitutes scatters to the winds their plans of murder and plunder; later on, when their lust has been appeased and they have resumed the chase, a detachment of rurales frightens them away without firing a single shot. The real power of the story lies in its subtle use of irony and in its cascading evocations of fear in a western-style pursuit.

In "The Bride Comes to Yellow Sky" Crane reached a peak in his exploration of the humorous overtones of fear. A favorite of the author himself and of many of his admirers, "The Bride" raises the western story to the level of the classic by consistently applying to a trite but dramatic situation the powerful lever of irony. It deals with a very unromantic event, the homecoming of a town marshal after his wedding with a plain-looking and timid bride. This town marshal is afraid of nothing except public opinion and, since his marriage was secretly arranged, he fears the hostile reaction of the inhabitants of Yellow Sky, an obvious projection of Crane's own predicament in his life with Cora. When, after walking through the deserted town, the couple reach the door of their home, they meet Scratchy Wilson, the local outlaw. A bloody encounter to come, we might think, but in fact nothing happens: the outlaw is defeated by the mere sight of the town marshal seen for the first time as a married man and walking home unarmed. "Defeated by a woman's mute presence" might have been the headline for such a story if it had been printed in a "yellow" newspaper. Crane thought that "The Bride" was "a daisy," and he was right. From beginning to end this charming tale proves that the whole mystique of the wild West was for him nothing but a game, and he enjoyed watching this game in its closing stages.

But no judgment of Crane's ability as a storyteller can be reached without a proper assessment of "a tale intended to be after the fact" entitled "The Open Boat," which relates the concluding phase of an adventure almost fatal for him. The newspaper report he sent to the *New York Press* in January 1897, immediately after his shipwreck, gave a detailed account of every episode excluding the "thirty hours" spent in an open boat. It took a few weeks for the definitive story to crystallize in his mind as a parable of human existence. We follow the ordeal of four survivors during their long wait in a lifeboat, their desperate attempts to reach the shore after their ship has sunk. Finally the captain decides to risk steering the frail dinghy through the breakers: the four men — the captain, the cook, the oiler, and the correspondent — have, each of them, felt the "subtle brotherhood" born of their shared distress and struggle. Once in the breakers the boat is overturned and the oiler is killed. The other three set foot safely ashore. Crane never wrote a more orderly tale: the correspondent, acting as point-of-view character — although he is also a participant — helps to bring the main facets of the story into focus. We learn much about the transformation of his mind in the crucible of experience. This shipwreck is for him a journey leading from cynicism to humility. But here again Crane retains the ironic approach, especially when he shows the correspondent's indignation leveled at the serene indifference of God. "Shipwrecks are *apropos* of nothing" puts into a nutshell the meaning of the whole story. There is the world of facts on one side and the world of ideas and literature on the other, but facts as such do not exist to *prove* anything. However, some lessons can be drawn from the chaos of experi-

ence if men manage to be "interpreters." Crane's message here is
one of endurance, brotherhood, and stoic acceptance of man's
fate; his vision of the universe is one in which man appears frail
and insignificant when isolated but surprisingly strong in a united effort. Ruthlessly debunking all the conventional views
about heroism, he seems to imply that the only courage worthy
of esteem is unobtrusive, silent, and more self-denying than
self-assertive.

The true power of this story comes from a style which, in
descriptive passages, is almost that of a prose poem. The
dialogue, spare and accurate, gives balance to the general tone.
According to Edward Garnett, Crane's art at its best was "self-
poising as is the art of the perfect dancer." Joined to the grace of
the dancer we find in this tale of human frailty a superb control
of emotion which makes it a masterpiece of classical art, the epic
flow of the narrative being constantly tempered and toned down
by gentle touches of irony.

There always remained in Crane, as Alfred Kazin has pointed
out, "a local village boy." Essentially American in his stance,
although a rebel against many things American, he willingly
spoke about his experience of the small town. Far from idealiz-
ing his vision, he set it against the background of his urban and
cosmopolitan environment and judged it unemotionally.

The Crane brothers loved the countryside of Sullivan County,
New York, where they fished, hunted, rode horses, and camped
during the summer months. The hills, mountains, and valleys of
this still rather wild area form a recurrent image in many of
Stephen Crane's stories, poems, and prose poems. Although he
used this background indirectly in his fiction, he made of it the
infrastructure of his vision of the world.

The Third Violet reflects a deep attachment to the colors and
shapes of Sullivan County. It exploits both the popular theme of
the "summer hotel" and Crane's own experience at the Art Students' League in New York. In this novel the author has captured some of the flavor of bohemianism, but his treatment of
this subject lacks originality. The Third Violet, which won very

little applause from critics except for Ford Madox Hueffer, is
saved from mediocrity by contrasting vignettes of rural and
urban life. This book hints at the difficult struggle of young
artists with the commercial values of their age: Hawker, a young
painter, goes to Sullivan County where his farmer parents live;
he is merely in search of peace and inspiration but, in a neighboring hotel, the summer has brought adventure in the shape of
a rich New York heiress, Miss Fanhall. It is love at first sight and
the novel abounds in meetings and vapid conversations between
the two lovers and a few other characters, a "writing friend" of
Hawker's called Hollanden, a rival in love, named Oglethorpe,
who is the irresistible rich suitor, and a group of irresponsible
young artists belonging to Hawker's circle in New York. Among
the latter stands out a rather colorful young model in love with
Hawker, Florinda. We close the book unconvinced by the plot
which, with the gift of a final violet symbolizing the reconciliation of the two lovers, seems to be heading for a conventional
epilogue. Crane did not want his novel to end tragically as his
real-life romance with Nellie Crouse had done.

"The Monster," a story set in a rural background, can be regarded as one of the most important of his short works. It is
centered on the disastrous consequences of a generous action: a
doctor's son has been rescued from his burning house by a
Negro servant, Henry Johnson, whose face is "burned away."
Out of gratitude the doctor decides to nurse his heroic servant
and insists on keeping him in his reconstructed house, but the
sight of the "monster" frightens everyone in the neighborhood;
the doctor soon becomes an object of opprobrium and loses
much of his practice. A deputation of influential citizens tries to
persuade him to compromise with public opinion and asks him
to turn Henry over to an institution, but the doctor remains
adamant. The last scene shows him returning from his rounds
and finding his wife crying over the teacups of guests who have
not come. This brilliant exposition of village mores is enhanced
by symbolic touches which, in the laboratory scene during the
fire, reach a climax with the lurid vision of threatening and

fantastically colored shapes. Besides the fear born of physical danger, the author probes the blind unreasoning panic generated by the sight of the harmless and horribly maimed Negro, and the many anxieties caused by public opinion. He has also, by the very choice of his protagonist, indicated that true heroism is not the privilege of the whites alone.

Crane began reminiscing about his early youth when he had used up the store of material born of his adult experience. Port Jervis, New York, was the nucleus around which *The Whilomville Stories* took shape. It is "any boy's town" but also a very specific one within easy reach of New York City, yet quite provincial and sleepy with its backdrop of fields, rivers, hills, and forests, a place where boys and girls can roam at peace except when under the ferule of their school or Sunday school teachers. The fields are close by and the farmers' slow and benevolent manner offers a sharp contrast to the "barbarous" habits of the villagers who give tea parties, launch into charitable campaigns, and, in the summertime, entertain relatives from the city.

The rural life depicted by Crane is more civilized than that Mark Twain had evoked before him; it is less sentimentally reconstructed than the *Boy's Town* of W. D. Howells. Abhorring as he did the "Little Lord Fauntleroy" craze which had swept his country in the 1880s, Crane did not hesitate to show us real children. He is aware of their tastes and distastes and conscious of their cruelty — at times they appear to him as "little blood-fanged wolves." In fact, more than a picture of childhood, he gives a picture of town life, since the children project an image of their parents' world stripped to its essentials. Although fond of the company of youngsters and a great favorite with his nieces, Crane was not holding a brief in favor of youth. To quote Robert Frost out of context he "lov[ed] the things he love[d] for what they [were]"; his children were, like their adult counterparts, charmingly deluded in their vision of the world, and we can safely smile at their innocent pranks, for Crane did not allow them to give free rein to their worst instincts. At the critical moment something happened: a bully relented or an adult came into view, and none of these little backyard dramas turned into a real tragedy.

By profession a journalist and a writer of fiction, Crane had a higher regard for his poetic endeavors than for the rest of his literary work. He preferred his first volume of verse, *The Black Riders*, to his *Red Badge of Courage* because "it was a more ambitious effort. My aim was to comprehend in it the thoughts I have had about life in general while 'The Red Badge' is a mere episode in life, an amplification."

But he did not observe the traditions and conventions of poetic expression respected by most of his contemporaries, except isolated rebels like Walt Whitman and Emily Dickinson. Alfred Kazin has called Crane "our first *poète maudit*" and such a label fits him to perfection, for he regarded poetry, more than prose, as a vehicle for ideas generally unconventional or iconoclastic. It is easy to find models for the patterns if not for the tone of Crane's early verse. He had obviously read Biblical parables, and some of the work of Emily Dickinson, Whitman, Ambrose Bierce, and Olive Schreiner, but his poetry remained essentially the expression of his own vision.

The sharpness and brevity of the sixty-eight pieces forming his *Black Riders* remind many readers of Emily Dickinson's great verbal economy. Like that of the recluse of Amherst his voice was one of protest. His own rebellion went against the God of the Old Testament, and he strove to debunk a cluster of false values, especially ambition, conformity, worldly wisdom, military glory, and traditional religion. The universe pictured by Crane in his poetry has elements of pessimism which have caused some critics to regard it as naturalistic, but the poet also exalts the positive virtues of love, endurance, and self-reliance. Crane feels a great admiration for the "little man" who keeps facing the mountains fearlessly, for the lonely individualist who "sought a new road" and "died thus alone," for "they said he had courage." The first themes of his poetic vision radiate from a central concern, the problem of man's relation with God. Even earthly love can be poisoned by the idea of sin and man must free himself from his obsessive fear of God and from the network of illusions woven by his imagination. Crane's rebellion was sound but the occasionally crude phrasing of his protest and the printing of the volume in small capitals made it fair game for the parodists.

His second book of poetry, *War Is Kind*, contained thirty-seven poems: fourteen of these had already been printed between 1895 and 1898; a group of ten love poems called "Intrigue" and some of the remaining pieces belonged to a second poetic output. The iconoclastic note had not died out and the author went on debunking the outward forms of religious ritual:

> You tell me this is God?
> I tell you this is a printed list,
> A burning candle and an ass.

But his poetry gradually became more concrete and more socially oriented. Instead of dealing with abstract imaginings, vague and remote parables, it drank deep from the fountain of experience. His bitter satire on the popular glorification of military courage in such a poem as "War Is Kind" (which, although the initial piece in the second volume, belongs to the first period) had been expressed along general lines. With "The Blue Battalions" and the poems inspired by the Spanish-American War, Crane did not hesitate to present war as the utmost form of God's playful fancy and violently denounced the exploitation of "patriots" by "practical men" as well as the imperialistic overtones of America's help to the Cuban rebels.

Several poems stigmatized other forms of exploitation of man by man. The gaudy and showy splendor of the mansions of the new rich aroused his metaphoric ire with a vision of

> . . . a crash of flunkeys
> And yawning emblems of Persia
> Cheeked against oak, France and a sabre,
> The outcry of old beauty
> Whored by pimping merchants
> To submission before wine and chatter.

And he ironically rejected the basic injustice of laissez faire economics:

> Why should the strong —
> — The beautiful strong —
> Why should they not have the flowers?

If the theme of love had, in the poems of the first poetic manner, taken on few romantic dimensions except in the sheltering gesture of a woman's "white arms," the second volume of verse and some posthumous poems enable us to probe deeper into Crane's house of love. "On the desert" and "A naked woman and a dead dwarf" fly the banner of Baudelairean decadence most clearly and remind us of "La femme et le serpent" and, as has been recently pointed out, of a prose poem by the French symbolist entitled "Le fou et la Vénus." "Intrigue," the last section of *War Is Kind*, represents Crane's attempt to bring into focus the many components of his love poetry: sensuality, sin-consciousness, and jealousy form the dark side of man's central passion, but Crane's bitter lyricism is spoiled by hackneyed romantic imagery, skulls "with ruby eyes," cracked bowls, castles, temples, daggers, and specters.

He discovered a better instrument for his highly sensitive nature in the prose poem. "The Judgment of the Sage" and "The Snake" are true fables and the same ingredients are found in them as in his verse; but, whereas the verse rejects all traditional rules (rhyme, regular meter, and very often stanzaic form), the prose poems retain a classical mode of expression. They remind us of Baudelaire's utilization of the same medium, but here again Crane's manner remains distinctly his own. He thus studied some archetypes, those of charity, material success, earthly conflict or cosmic battle. "The Judgment of the Sage," which raises the ghost of a Kantian dilemma, briefly tells us the story of a vain quest, that of worldly wisdom. Should we practice charity "because of God's word" or because the beggar is hungry? Crane does not solve this riddle; God seems to play with man his eternal game of hide-and-seek and keeps him on the run. "A Self-Made Man" parodies the Horatio Alger type of success story. "'To succeed in life . . . the youth of America have only to see an old man seated upon a railing and smoking a clay pipe. Then go up and ask him for a match.'" "The Voice of the Mountain" and "The Victory of the Moon" are focused on the conflict between man and a mysterious cosmic power which can occasionally be defeated by "the little creature of the earth." With "The Snake" the inevitable fight for survival is brought to its emotional climax: the two most antagonistic creatures in the world, man and the snake, confront each other in a ruthless duel in which the principals fight with equal arms, the snake with its venom and man with his stick. If the snake is defeated it is not for lack of courage. Thanks to a clever manipulation of language Crane combines in a unified whole the simplicity of the fable, the logical structure of the sermon, and the raciness of the folktale.

His poetry at times foreshadows imagism, as Carl Sandburg pointed out in his "Letters to Dead Imagists," but some pieces of the second volume of verse show a tendency to explode the small abstract capsule of the early poems. It is difficult to say where Crane's real poetic genius lies, whether in his spare, concise parables, in his longer symbolistic compositions, or in his prose poems. He worshiped brevity as the first tenet of his literary creed, but he was also touched by the wave of decadent aesthetics that Copeland and Day, his publishers, who were also the American publishers of the *Yellow Book*, had helped to introduce into the United States. There was, however, too much love of moral integrity in Crane for him to become a true decadent. In his verse he often displayed the pathetic agony of a fallen albatross, but the prose poem was perhaps the literary instrument whose scope and subtle rhythm best suited his genius.

Crane's style has a certain number of idiosyncrasies: it is primarily the language of a writer in transition betraying an inner conflict between a romantic tradition and realistic impulses. He began with what he called his "Rudyard-Kipling style" and the "Sullivan County Sketches" contain the germs of most of his future work, displaying as they do a love of abstraction and a systematic use of color, patterning the narrative with structural irony, and building up an oneiric atmosphere laden with threat. It is a gradual mastery of form that we witness in the passage from the style of the early years to that emerging between 1894 and 1898.

Impelled by a desire to control the deep stirrings of his soul, he soon declared that he wished "to write plainly and unmistakably, so that all men (and some women) might read and understand." Crane's literary aesthetics was close to that of the French master of the short story, Guy de Maupassant. According to the author of *Pierre et Jean*, "Les grands artistes sont ceux qui imposent à l'humanité leur illusion particulière." Such a position might very well have been defined by Stephen Crane who wanted the writer to tell the world what "his own pair of eyes" enabled him to see and nothing else. Maupassant's universe, however, differed significantly from Crane's: whereas the French writer often indulged in an excess of sensual evocations, Crane preserved throughout his writing career the viewpoint of the moralist and usually conveyed his ethical comments by means of ironic counterpoint.

He was deeply conscious of man's littleness and of God's overbearing power. Man's wanderings on the earth were pictured by him as those of a lonely pilgrim in a pathless universe. Crane's phraseology comes directly from the Bible, the sermons, and the hymns which had shaped his language during his youth. The topography of his stories, where hills, mountains, rivers, and meadows appear under symbolic suns or moons is, to a large extent, an abstraction fraught with religious or moral significance. With its "monsters" of various kinds and its "dragons," the demonology of *The Red Badge of Courage* evinces a truly apocalyptic quality. In Crane's best work the imagery of the journey of initiation occupies a central position and reaches a climactic stage with some experience of conversion. He did not accept, it is true, the traditional interpretation of the riddle of the universe offered by the Methodist church. Nevertheless he constantly used a Christian terminology, and the thought of "sin" inspired his characters with guilty fears and stirred up within them such frequent debates with a troubled conscience that it is impossible to study his achievement outside a religious tradition.

But he did not remain a prisoner of the stylistic patterns which he derived from his revivalist heritage. New York street life very early made an impact on his language, which thus acquired its liveliness and its ability to picture violence in colorful terms. Crane's dialogues abound in expletives, in stereotyped phrases, in phonetic transcriptions of common verbal corruptions and dialectal idiosyncrasies. Yet they never fall into the trap of over-specialization. His ear was good, whether he listened to Irish, German, Italian, or Cuban immigrants in New York, to farmers in Sullivan County, or to Negroes in Port Jervis, but he never tried to achieve a perfect rendering of local dialect. In *The Red Badge of Courage* he used dialogue to introduce some degree of differentiation between Henry Fleming and his comrades but, on the whole, Crane's characters all speak one language which is Crane's own, a youthful and casual version of the American vernacular of the 1890s often heard in artists' studios and among students.

Language is in the mouths of his central characters a stylized medium carrying universal overtones, and this trait reveals an essential aspect of his fictional techniques, namely the dramatic approach. He tried his hand several times at playwriting and, although his various attempts in this literary genre were of modest stature, he was naturally inclined to work out his tales and some of his verse in terms of stage stylistics. He completed three very slight plays. *At Clancy's Wake* (1893) is a one-act sketch which brings to life the hilarious moments of an Irish wake in New York; *The Blood of the Martyr* (1898) satirizes in three brief acts German imperialistic policies in China. Another attempt at playwriting was his "Spanish-American War Play," unpublished in Crane's lifetime but included in *The War Dispatches of Stephen Crane* (1964): this two-act drama gives a mildly amusing but superficial picture of stereotyped national traits against the background of a real conflict that the author had seen at first hand. Only a fragment of the text of "The Ghost" — his English play — has reached us so far and it is difficult to take seriously what was meant to be a mere Christmas entertainment. All his other attempts at playwriting were abortive.

What remains most striking in Crane's style considered as a whole is a concern for brevity and a constant use of irony which serves a twofold purpose: it provides his best work with tightly knit thematic structures and reveals his tacit belief in a rigid set of values which condemns indifference and conformism, and extols moral courage and integrity.

Seen in the perspective of the years which have elapsed since his death, Crane's work is surprisingly modern. His influence on the war literature of the twentieth century in England and America has been very significant. Many of Hemingway's novels and short stories disclose a similar preoccupation with "the moral problem of conduct" and obvious stylistic affinities; distinct echoes of *The Red Badge* can be heard in *A Farewell to Arms*. In England we could trace recurring correspondences in the work of Joseph Conrad and Ford Madox Ford. Ford, like Conrad, had been a good friend of Crane's during the last three years of his life, and both defended his literary and moral reputation in magazine articles or prefaces after his death. The plight of the isolated hero, which became a favorite theme of Conrad's, stemmed directly from *The Red Badge of Courage*. Obsession with the fear of showing a white feather haunted the soul of the author of *Lord Jim* as much as that of the creator of Henry Fleming. In his own fiction Ford Madox Ford used complex techniques and mixed many strands of life, but some of the most dramatic scenes in *A Man Could Stand Up*, which are mere vignettes of life at the front, remind us in their bare and rugged prose of deliberately unpoetic descriptions of war in *The Red Badge*. Like Crane, Ford emphasized "the eternal waiting that is War" and the crippling effects of noise on a battlefield. And, in order to describe the subtle change taking place in a soldier's mind, he used almost Cranean terms.

Among the pioneers of the "free-verse army" Crane is often neglected by anthologists or literary critics. Yet he gave to the poetry of his country the patterns and rhythms of an "exasperated prose" that foreshadows modern poetic expression.

Carl Van Doren wrote in 1924: "Modern American literature may be said, accurately enough, to have begun with Stephen Crane." This statement needs to be qualified, but Crane was one of the leading figures of protest of his generation and thus showed the way to American liberalism. His influence in the field of the novel has affected a mode of thought rather than literary techniques, if we leave aside his synaesthetic use of imagery which survives almost intact in F. Scott Fitzgerald. Crane's impact has been felt mostly in the genre of the short story, for which he displayed a personal preference. "The Blue Hotel," "The Bride Comes to Yellow Sky," and, above all, "The Open Boat" are some of the finest models of American literary achievement in this genre, and the greatest successes of Faulkner, Sherwood Anderson, Hemingway, Fitzgerald, and other modern American short-story writers hark back to these models. Accuracy in details, conciseness, and effective rendering, framed and supported by an ironic structure, are now frequently regarded as essential requirements by American practitioners of the short story.

Most of Crane's work could be explained in terms of his religious background and he always betrays, even in his most sportive mood, the serious preoccupations of the born moralist. However, his slum stories, instead of aiming to move the reader by exaggerated pathos and convert him to the cause of reform, wish to convert him to the cause of psychological truth; social implications are left for the reader to discover but are not explicitly stated. When dealing with his main theme, war, he gradually worked out a revolutionary stand, doing away with externals and reducing human conflict to a classic drama of internal forces struggling with elemental powers. From Henry Fleming in *The*

Red Badge to Timothy Lean in the "Spitzbergen Tales" the itinerary of heroism evolves from a path sprinkled with doubtful victories to a road doggedly followed with a sturdy and silent acceptance of personal responsibility; diseased and action-hampering introspection eventually gives way to selfless and un-assuming patterns of affirmation. "The Open Boat" contains a plea for human solidarity and *Wounds in the Rain*, in spite of a persistent and depressing background of military servitude, dis-creetly affirms the superiority of collective to individual prowess. A subtle feeling of warmth and brotherhood pervades the later studies of Crane on war; even "The Upturned Face," a macabre piece which describes a burial scene on the front line, places the reader in the midst of an ultimate manifestation of soldierly brotherhood.

It is in the novel of manners that Crane's achievement is at its lowest ebb. He did not try to study complex human relationships born of urban settings but dealt with a few basic themes, rivalries between lovers, or conflicts between generations and social class-es. Often unable to provide his puppets with life, he proved his mastery in the art of reproducing informal dialogue. He ex-perimented in the field of the picaresque novel — a medium he had already used in several short stories — but *The O'Ruddy* cannot be regarded as a genuine offspring of his mind since Robert Barr gave this novel its conclusion and ultimate form.

Crane's identity runs no risk of being drowned in a backflow of imitators, because his style remains his own. His unerring eye for color, his brilliant use of synaesthetic effects, his love for the potent metaphor made him controversially famous in his lifetime and now stamp him as a truly original artist. His some-times erratic grammar no longer shocks us, while his cinematic techniques have come into their own.

It was his aim to underline elements of absurdity in human life, and his work contains disquieting overtones for sedate minds. His was a voice of dissent which rejected the ostensibly impregnable soundness of historical Christianity, the conven-tional vision of a well-ordered society, and that genteel tradition of culture which never left drawing rooms and libraries. Crane inherited the New England habit of individual assertion. He fits well into the American liberal tradition and can, in some respects, be regarded as a spiritual son of Emerson. Any form of dogmatism in any field of human life seemed to him both childish and harmful to what he valued above everything else, the integrity of the human soul. No problem could, according to him, ever find a definitive solution and he had certainly listened to Emerson's advice: "Congratulate yourself if you have done something strange and extravagant, and broken the monotony of a decorous age." This sentence adorned a beam in one of the studios of the old Art Students' League building in New York where Crane lived sporadically in 1893 and 1894. Above and beyond this cult of nonconformism is another idea of Emerson's which involves the deeper regions of the soul: "Always do what you are afraid to do." Crane put this motto into practice so consistently that he wrecked his health and seriously endangered his moral reputation in his own country.

His recent popularity, essentially due to a revival of critical interest during the 1950s, should help prepare the ground for a clearer assessment of Crane's achievement. To our generation he can still teach moral integrity, a revised conception of courage, and psychological truth, all the more effectively because he did not resort to traditional didactic devices. He can also show modern prose writers the flexibility of the English language and encourage them to make linguistic experiments and create a language free from any excessive tyranny of the past, perfectly in tune with the spirit of the age and yet retaining the robust vitality which is the trademark of the classic.

FRANK NORRIS

Frank Norris's name is much better known today than anything he ever wrote. The manuals of American literature bestow measured praise on *McTeague* (1899) and *The Octopus* (1901), note that *The Pit* (1903) was a relative failure, and mention the posthumous *Vandover and the Brute* (1914). They go on to report that Norris introduced French naturalism into American fiction, discovered the talent of Theodore Dreiser, and influenced legislation designed to curb the railroad monopolies.

A more complete account would have to include a long, pseudoromantic narrative in verse called *Yvernelle: A Legend of Feudal France* (published in 1892 while Norris was an undergraduate), a sheaf of short stories, enough literary criticism to fill a volume, and three more novels: *Moran of the Lady Letty* (1898), *A Man's Woman* (1899), and *Blix* (1899). No more can be said for *Moran* than that it is as entertaining as many of Jack London's stories, and no more implausible; even less can be said for *A Man's Woman*; but the total achievement is considerable for a writer who died at thirty-two. He did not exert the general influence on American letters of a Howells, and his work has attracted no circle of admirers like Stephen Crane's, but in spite

of certain lurid flaws his best writing remains immensely effective.

The circumstances of his life had much to do with the eventual
nature of his writing, and even explain some of the variations in
its quality. His father, Benjamin, a self-made Chicago businessman, was gifted at making money; his mother, Gertrude, had at
one point flirted with a stage career, and had cultural tastes that
made the money welcome. From his birth, in Chicago in 1870,
Norris had what were known as the "advantages." When the
family pulled up roots and moved to San Francisco, in 1884,
Benjamin Norris went into real estate and did even better. But
San Francisco was not to be enough for the children of Gertrude: in 1887, after vicissitudes that included the death of a
brother, and a brief and unsuccessful stay in London, young
Norris found himself studying art at the celebrated Académie
Julien, in Paris. He was barely seventeen.

How much of the lush Paris of those years Frank Norris saw is
problematical. For a year his family was also in the city; then they
returned to the States and for a few months young Frank was
alone — until his practical father, discovering that his son was
writing tales of medieval knights instead of working at his art
classes, summoned him home. The son obediently matriculated
at the University of California.

He seems to have learned little about French literature during
his stay in Paris. Instead, he had been intensely caught up by a
sort of romantic medievalism: the lore of chivalry, armory, and
the antique hardware of the Musée de Cluny. The writing that
had displeased his father had been sketches concocted for his
younger brother. Nothing shows that he read, say Zola, let alone
any representative of the then flourishing French symbolists.
But at least he must have learned to read French.

At the University of California he assumed the role of a
boulevardier, but not so thoroughly as to separate him from the
somewhat strenuous undergraduate life of the Berkeley of that
time. He joined a fraternity, and sometimes took part in the
hazings and rushes he would later defend as proper training for

muscular and blond young Anglo-Saxons. It appears that a chronic estrangement from the most elementary mathematics prevented his taking a degree, but he did, during his college years, pick up the ideas about human evolution, more Spencerian than Darwinian, that are reflected in his novels.

Meanwhile his parents had divorced, so that Norris was relieved of all pressure from his father to take up a business career. He went east, entered Harvard as a special student, and came under the benign influence of Lewis E. Gates. The Harvard English Department was ambivalently disposed toward the teaching of "creative" writing. Some members, Gates among them, obviously believed that the subject could be taught. Others followed Irving Babbitt (whose appointment was actually in French) in declaring that teaching men how to say things before they had anything to say was so much poppycock.

Norris was grateful for Gates's encouragement, and doubtless also for the incentive to work regularly. He had already begun to write: his stories had appeared in the undergraduate magazine at Berkeley, and he had had a contribution or so in the San Francisco *Wave*. More important, he had been working on the opening chapters of *McTeague*. Gates, who was familiar with Continental literature, was in a position to see what he was trying to do. Clearly the stay in Paris was belatedly having an effect: Norris had been reading Zola. *McTeague* showed the influence, as did *Vandover and the Brute*, which Norris began work on in Cambridge. Although he would finish neither during the year in Cambridge, he appears to have kept both novels going at once.

Norris was taken far more by Émile Zola's individual example than by French naturalism as a whole. Although he later professed enthusiastic admiration for Flaubert, the naturalistic current that originates in the latter's *Education sentimentale*, and is transmitted by the Goncourt brothers to writers like Joris-Karl Huysmans, apparently left him untouched. Doubtless he was temperamentally unable to accept Flaubert's principle that the essence of most lives is their sheer monotony. All Norris's own novels are so full of action that one can hardly imagine his grasp-

ing the notion that monotony can be the matter of fiction. He had
no perception of the great truth, so clear to all the naturalists
including Zola, that both monotony and horror are mitigated by
the presence of a style.

Americans rarely perceive the stylist in Zola, and Norris was
no exception. The creator of the Rougon-Macquart series spent
hours listening to the speech of working people, learning their
special vocabularies and the unique language of each trade.
Hence the rare quality of the *discours indirect libre*, or "reported
speech," in which he makes his characters think. Norris, on the
other hand, merely makes his characters sound ignorant, without catching the flavor and quality of what they say that would
do so much to admit the reader to their lives.

He was more aware of the theoretical background of Zola's
naturalism, but can hardly be said to have been impressed by it.
Positivistic determinism, and the influence of heredity and environment, play only a small role in *McTeague* and a yet smaller
one in *Vandover*. Norris does remember, in *McTeague*, to attrib-
ute his hero's regression to a strain of alcoholism in the family,
but there is not even this to explain the decline of Vandover,
whose trouble would be described by any puritanical moralist as
a weakness of character.

There are grounds for wondering whether Norris ever really
understood the nature of French naturalism at all. Naturalism,
he argues in one of his later critical pieces, is the opposite of
realism. The latter, he says, is occupied with the everyday behavior we encounter in our usual lives, whereas naturalism is
concerned with the unusual and extraordinary, with life on a
social level unfamiliar to us, or with happenings unlikely to
occur in life as we know it. The formulation sounds strangely
like Hawthorne's famous distinction between romance and
novel, but Norris is thinking here of Zola: he cites as an example
the incident in *La débâcle* where a soldier discovers that he has
bayoneted his old and dear comrade in arms. Norris simply
mistakes Zola's idiosyncratic penchant toward melodrama for
the characterizing trait of naturalism as a whole.

Yet if Norris had not read Zola, *McTeague*, *Vandover*, and, later, *The Octopus* would surely not be the novels they are. If the manuals are stretching a point in making him the prime importer of naturalism into America, it is still entirely true that he is the link between our local naturalism and one of the great exponents of the French variety.

In college he had been exposed to a peculiarly American version of the theory of evolution. Starting from the brute beast, man has risen to the level where he now is, civilized, capable of intellection, possessing what may be thought of as a soul. There is reason to hope that he will continue to evolve, always upward, toward new heights. But this applies to man in the mass. In each individual there is something of the primordial beast, latent but still alive, and if anything goes wrong evolution may easily reverse its direction and the civilized being regress toward the original, brutal condition of the race. This is what happens to McTeague and Vandover.

The theory is alien to Zola's determinism; its optimism — man is headed for a greater good, while at the same time evil in individuals is explained and justified — is more intense than any that Zola or his contemporaries ever achieved. But at the same time it lends itself to the adoption of Zola's favorite literary techniques.

Minute scholarship has revealed numerous incidents and scenes in Norris's novels that are suggestive of Zola, and more particularly of *La terre* and *La bête humaine*, which were the novels Norris particularly preferred. But Norris's debt is greater than the total of reminiscences and borrowings. The shape of his best novels, taken as wholes, suggests that Zola's practice was never far from his mind.

The plot of *McTeague* conforms to the traditional naturalist pattern. All the needed data are given at the start, and the main action — except the ending — flows out of the data; no fact is withheld to allow the story to take an unexpected twist, and the facts given mean what they purport to mean.

McTeague would be an ordinary working man except that he

has learned dentistry by watching an itinerant charlatan. He sets up his "parlors" in San Francisco, falls in love with one of his patients, and shortly marries her, but in getting Trina he makes an enemy of another suitor, Marcus Schouler. The latter reports him for practicing without a license and the state shuts his office. The loss of his livelihood sets off a decline; he takes to drink; a streak of sadism comes to the fore; he tortures his wife to make her tell him where she keeps the $5000 she has won in a lottery. She refuses, having herself become a victim of the avarice that has always been her great weakness. Finally McTeague kills her, takes the money, and returns as a fugitive to the mining country in the Sierras where he started life.

Nothing in all this seems unlikely; the story was in fact suggested by newspaper accounts of a particularly squalid murder in a poor section of San Francisco. Less likely are the two prominent subplots. In one of these a man who has married a crazy Mexican girl for the totally imaginary gold plate she keeps saying she has inherited finally slits her throat in a fit of lust for gold. And all the while an elderly couple who live in the same lodging house as the McTeagues and the other pair indulge in a somewhat mawkish, evening-of-life romance. But these are minor, and detract less from the main story than from Norris's reputation for good taste — unless, indeed, the old-age idyll is in the novel as a propitiatory sop to the bad taste of the novelist's contemporaries. The main line of the story, in any case, is up to the naturalist standard of plausibility.

The characters of *McTeague* are working people and the life Norris paints is that of the working class. Like Zola he has documented his work by direct observation; his book is not only a "novel of San Francisco" but more specifically one about life on Polk Street. He knows his Polk Street well enough to give the effect of telling the truth about what one of his successors in naturalism, James T. Farrell, calls "the exact content of life in given circumstances." The story moves in and out of the eating joints, bars, and houses, among a mixed population of poor wage-earners, some of whom are underprivileged immigrants like the girl McTeague marries.

Such a world encourages violence. Two messy murders, sundry beatings, a case of mayhem, McTeague's torturing of Trina, and the fight in the desert that ends in the death of both McTeague and Marcus combine to make *McTeague* a much more violent book than many produced by Norris's French model. And in contrast with his American contemporaries, Norris is quite willing to show his reader physical damage. There had been violence, and to spare, in earlier American writing, including *The Red Badge of Courage*; but whereas a writer like Crane tends to deflect his reader's eye from the effects of violence — the most we know of Jim Conklin's mortal wound, for example, is that it looks as if he had been chewed by wolves — Norris resolutely shows us what has happened.

Sex, on the other hand, he treats with a reticence that Zola would hardly have understood. In one episode McTeague kisses Trina "grossly" on the mouth while she is anesthetized in his dental chair; later in the book, Trina spreads her hoard of gold pieces on her bed and lies down naked on the coins; but having made clear that his characters are moved by powerful, and sometimes perverse, sexual drives, Norris is content to let the matter rest. This was doubtless as much as the American public would have permitted. The changes in taste that have intervened in the last seventy years should not be allowed to obscure the fact that even this incomplete explicitness, like indeed his finding the materials of a story in the life of the working class, was new and bold.

In making *McTeague* a case history, also, Norris was not necessarily following his French masters. Even though Zola and the Goncourts exploited this pattern repeatedly, it is also implicit in the notions of evolution he picked up in college: something goes wrong in the individual's life, the beast within emerges, and regression is inevitable. Norris did not need Zola to tell him this, and it may even be that encountering an already familiar idea when he turned his undergraduate attention on French naturalism merely deepened an existing commitment.

Nothing, of course, inhibited his following Zola closely in the use of symbols. The outsize replica of a tooth McTeague hangs outside his parlors plays the same role as the still in *L'assommoir*, the coal-pit tower in *Germinal*, or the locomotive in *La bête humaine*: it sums up and interprets his life. He has wanted the tooth obsessively, and is completely content once he has got it; having to give it up again represents the total shock of his catastrophe, whereas the gilt that covers it symbolizes the consuming greed for money that grows on all the principals as the story moves toward its end.

By and large Norris was right in inscribing his wife's copy of one of his novels "from the boy Zola." By itself, *McTeague* would justify the quip. Yet if there is much of Zola in this story there is even more of Norris. Between the son of the real-estate magnate and the poor mine-boy who turns dentist the social gap is wide. However interested Norris may be in such characters, they are not his kind of people. He is incapable of the sympathy that so often allowed the socialist Zola to see life as it looked to his characters; and the benign detachment of the Goncourts, explicable only by their unthinking, perhaps totally unconscious acceptance of European class distinctions, is unavailable. In America all men are created equal, but all men are not equally admissible to membership in a fraternity on the Berkeley campus. His preference for white and Protestant, Anglo-Saxon characters, almost blatant in his later novels, is already in evidence; his treatment of the ways and speech of Trina Sieppe's German immigrant family sounds at times like condescending parody.

Yet at the same time, a number of the changes Norris made in his manuscript before publication seem intended to increase his reader's liking for McTeague. Particularly in the last few chapters, when the murderous brute has become a pitiable, hunted creature, our sympathy is intended to reach out to him. And he is never mean or treacherous. Norris does not excuse his weaknesses by a sentimental appeal to overpowering environmental circumstances, but he does not condemn him, either. The trouble is that the part of the story where we are most expected to feel sympathy is also by far the one hardest to believe. The attempt fails, in large part because *McTeague* is the work of an inexperienced and still clumsy writer.

The clumsiness and inexperience show up even in passages of undeniable power. In the following, the dentist and his friends have been out on a picnic, and what began as a friendly wrestling match between McTeague and his one-time crony, Marcus, has suddenly turned into a real fight, with Marcus biting through his opponent's ear.

Then followed a terrible scene. The brute that in *McTeague* lay so close to the surface leaped instantly to life, monstrous, not to be resisted. He sprang to his feet with a shrill and meaningless clamor, totally unlike the ordinary bass of his speaking tones. It was the hideous yelling of a hurt beast, the squealing of a wounded elephant. He framed no words; in the rush of high-pitched sound that issued from his wide-open mouth there was nothing articulate. It was something no longer human; it was rather an echo from the jungle.

Sluggish enough and slow to anger on ordinary occasions, McTeague when finally aroused became another man. His rage was a kind of obsession, an evil mania, the drunkenness of passion, the exalted and perverted fury of the Berserker, blind and deaf, a thing insensate.

As he rose he caught Marcus's wrist in both his hands. He did not strike, he did not know what he was doing. His only idea was to batter the life out of the man before him, to crush and annihilate him upon the instant. Gripping his enemy in his enormous hands, hard and knotted, and covered with a stiff fell of yellow hair — the hands of the old-time car-boy — he swung him wide, as a hammer-thrower swings his hammer. Marcus's feet flipped from the ground, he spun through the air about McTeague as helpless as a bundle of clothes. All at once there was a sharp snap, almost like the report of a small pistol. Then Marcus rolled over and over upon the ground as McTeague released his grip; his arm, the one the dentist had seized, bending suddenly, as though a third joint had formed between wrist and elbow. The arm was broken.

The young novelist's inexorable repetitiousness is part of a consciously adopted technique. From the beginning the motifs of physical size, blond or yellow hair, huge hands, strength, and subhuman stupidity have been constantly present. The passage merely expands the subject of his overwhelming animality. This insistence, rather than the occasional remarks about a theoretical determinism scattered through the early chapters, is what prepares us for McTeague's eventual reversion to the brute.

To other, more sophisticated techniques, Norris is almost aggressively indifferent. He is not in the least interested in "showing" as opposed to "telling." His immense willingness to comment on the action, to explain the cause of everything that happens — as when he tells us what the man's voice sounded like — is more pronounced here than it will be in the later novels, although he will never rid himself of it entirely. The same is true of his use of a third-person, omniscient point of view, giving himself a clear view into the mind of any character he likes and thus putting himself in the perilous position of reporting the motivations of conduct that the reader might better be trusted to deduce from behavior.

It has probably required little more than this to undermine Norris's reputation among twentieth-century critics. The enormous weight of preference for the novel according to Henry James, with its severe restriction of point of view to the "central moral consciousness," has put older and simpler procedures in a poor light. Everything in the complaints of adverse judges like Lionel Trilling and the late Joseph Warren Beach in their dismissals of the novels of Dreiser is equally applicable to Norris. The particular impact of *McTeague* cannot be accounted for by the Jamesian calculus, nor will it be admitted by critics who do not concede the occasional aesthetic effectiveness of massive accumulations of detail.

McTeague opens with a typical Sunday afternoon in the life of the hero — his dinner, his pitcher of steam beer, his nap in his own dental chair. Then comes a turn-back to his youth in the mines and to his time with the charlatan who taught him his trade. Next there is a minute description of his physique, and another of his office, including a first mention of the symbolic gilded tooth. Only after this does the novel move outside for a description of life in Polk Street. Finally, McTeague spots his chum and future nemesis, Marcus, and the first episode, the taking of a dog to a veterinary hospital, ensues. The reader has, so to speak, been given a detailed view of the habitat and the habits of the animal McTeague, and been prepared to watch the animal perform.

Such procedures may properly be called Zolaesque, since Zola used them, but they are not necessarily naturalistic in every case. Norris learned much from Zola that Zola had learned from his own predecessors. It is a naturalist strategy to give the reader all the necessary data, as *McTeague* does, at the beginning and then let the ensuing action flow out of these data, withholding nothing that could allow the story to take an unexpected twist, and making the data mean exactly what they purport to mean. But the device of showing the animal in his minutely described habitat was standard literary technique; Zola doubtless learned it from Balzac. Consequently it is fair to say that *McTeague* is a naturalistic novel, but in the sense that Zola's novels are naturalistic: an excellent example of nineteenth-century realism, but with special emphasis on the biological and the deterministic. Through Zola Norris got the instruments for attempting a slice of American life, seen steadily and whole. Historically, the fact that it was offered to a public whose pabulum consisted of romances like *When Knighthood Was in Flower* and the output of F. Marion Crawford imparts an additional significance.

Vandover and the Brute must be judged with greater caution. The manuscript came to light well after Norris's death. Norris may have been unwilling to publish it, or, more likely, may have been unable to find a publisher. His brother Charles revised the manuscript, although qualified opinion today holds that the latter probably did not supply the ending, as was once thought to be the case. What Norris's own feelings about the book, as we know it, would have been is a matter for speculation, at best.

Yet Norris's hero, this time, is remarkably like the author, and whereas the things that befall McTeague could not conceivably happen to people of the novelist's own kind, what happens to Vandover certainly could do so. This novel attempts a study of a representative of the San Francisco middle class, and for his naturalistic documentation Norris appears to have turned to his own autobiography.

Young Vandover returns to San Francisco with a Harvard education of sorts and the intention of developing his talent in painting. Somehow he never gets started, and the tendency to frivol away his time grows on him. He becomes more and more devoted to "vice" and "bestial pleasures," and at length seduces a girl who offers little resistance but who commits suicide when she finds herself pregnant. This event sets off a chain reaction: Vandover loses the "nice" girl he has never quite got round to marrying; Vandover's father dies; the dead girl's family brings a suit; the distraught Vandover allows himself to be cheated out of his property by an old friend of Harvard days; he gambles away what little is left, and finally his sanity wavers and collapses; he becomes a case of lycanthropy.

Lycanthropy is a mental condition in which a man thinks that he is a wolf, and behaves like one. The state is relatively rare, although well enough known to have appealed to the imaginations of certain French romantics like the poet Pétrus Borel. Few of Norris's readers can ever have seen a case, and doubtless some learn of the disease by reading his story. But the lycanthropic state, as Vandover experiences it, sounds hideous, and we cannot help wondering just what depths of vice, debauchery, and bestial pleasure brought it on.

Vandover's essays in sin seem, on the whole, rather mild and even timid. One can imagine the memory of them making a tenderly nurtured individual somewhat neurotic and guilt-ridden, but hardly anything worse. We must, of course, allow for the inhibitions imposed by the taste of the moment. The record shows, for instance, that Norris's publisher, Doubleday, wanted him to rewrite the passage in *McTeague* where "Little Owgooste," forced to sit too long while his family watches a variety show, wets his pants. If current notions of delicacy made this humble incident unpalatable to cultivated taste, what chance would there have been of describing explicitly any sort of riot among the fleshpots?

Norris's difficulty was that he was trying to follow a French model in a climate where it was impossible to do so. Zola, like the Goncourts, had been devoted to case histories of the more picturesque sort, and Norris's choice of lycanthropy is surely worthy of the master. But although Zola may have put off some readers by creating, for example, a character whose major accomplishment was the loudness of his farting, he clearly did not alienate the reading public at large, or dismay his publisher. And the direct picturing of monumental debauches in novels like *Nana* being permitted, the decline and fall of characters like Nana herself is fully motivated; the reader is not left casting about for the reason. This fact measures the distance then separating Paris from New York.

But why should Norris himself not have seen the disproportion between sin and retribution? One can only propose a plausible hypothesis. Vandover's trajectory is remarkably like the young novelist's own: origins in San Francisco; sojourn in the more sophisticated East; return — imminent in Norris's case when he was starting *Vandover* — to California with the intention of living a life that by local standards was abnormal. Whereas Vandover will paint, Norris intends to write, and neither will involve himself in ordinary ways of earning a living. If, when he got home, Norris should be unable to settle down and justify his mother's faith in his talent, then what disaster might not lie ahead? If *Vandover and the Brute* is read as transposed fantasy of this sort, the issue of plausibility does not arise.

Such a reading, on the other hand, is an invitation to the amateur psychoanalyst. What was the effect on Norris of being brought up by this strong-willed woman whose commitment to the life of the spirit — even though it took the genteel form of organizing Browning Clubs — was real enough so that she

would let him live a writer's financially precarious life? And
would not an explicitly documented career in sin reveal a knowledge that might desecrate the relationship of mother and son?
Such questions have their special interest, even their fascination.
But answering them would be an exercise in pure speculation.

Norris's biographer, Franklin Walker, was persuaded that beneath his superficial sophistication, Norris had a strong streak of
puritanism in him, that within the morally noncommittal
naturalist there lurked a hidden but severely disapproving
moralist. This is not impossible. And the preference Norris
shows in his less serious fictions for clean-minded, two-fisted,
asexual but vigorous heroes tends to support the view. He was,
after all, the contemporary of the founders of Boy Scouting and
of the hit-the-line-hard ethics of the first Roosevelt. *Vandover* has
moments when it sounds like *Stover at Yale*.

The most alert of Norris's interpreters, Donald Pizer, proposes an even simpler solution: lycanthropy is a possible stage on
the way to paralytic insanity related to paresis. Pizer may be
right. Paresis results from the presence of spirochetes in the
bloodstream. Assuming that Norris knew this fact, he may have
been trying to say, as plainly as the prevalent taboo on mention-
ing syphilis would let him, that his hero's escapades had left him
the victim of venereal disease. But if this was what the novelist
intended, all literary difficulties are not automatically removed.
If Norris is saying subtly that his man is syphilitic, it must also be
admitted that such subtlety is anything but characteristic. In fact,
it would be hard to catch Norris being so subtle anywhere else in
his collected works. And even if this instance is the exception
that proves the rule, so far as the technique of fiction is concerned, it leaves Norris still in the predicament of having obscured the pivotal motivation of Vandover's story. Easiest of all
the explanations to accept would be precisely that Norris did not
publish the book — except for some isolated chapters — because
he felt that the problem had not been solved.

Vandover is thus a flawed book; it is not an uninteresting one
and has a charm unexpected in naturalist fiction. The opening

descriptions of life at Harvard are worthy forerunners of classics, some of them forgotten, like George Weller's *Not to Eat; Not for Love*. And there are period pieces, picturing the gay blades of the nineties, that stand by themselves. If Vandover's downfall could only have been made more convincing this novel might not have been dwarfed, as it is, by *McTeague*.

Norris was not so persuaded, it must appear, as we are today that in *McTeague* and *Vandover* he had found his natural manner. He went through a brief period when he abandoned his first, instinctive ways in an effort to please the genteel. But eventually, late in 1899 — thus after *Moran of the Lady Letty*, *A Man's Woman*, and *Blix* — he returned to "straight naturalism with all the guts." The expression is one he used in a letter to his friend Isaac Marcosson to tell him about his "Epic of the Wheat," of which the first volume would be *The Octopus*.

The example of Zola shows up as plainly in *The Octopus* as it does in *McTeague* or *Vandover*, but in a different way. The earlier novels had each focused on one character and the vicissitudes he passes through when his congenital weakness becomes dominant. In this respect, they suggest the relatively unadventurous Zola of novels like, say, *Son Excellence Eugène Rougon*. The wheat trilogy, on the other hand, recalls the Zola of the great social frescoes like *Germinal* and the sprawling poems of fecundity like *La terre* and *La faute de l'Abbé Mouret* — the militant enemy of social abuses who combined his crusading prose with a deeply neo-pagan poetry in praise of elemental life.

Norris had planned a cyclical work, with three stories less closely interrelated than those in the Rougon-Macquart series, but treating closely related subjects. *The Octopus* describes the raising of the grain; *The Pit* continues with the buying and selling of it; and the third volume was to have been devoted to its distribution overseas. Norris died (in 1902) before he could start the third. We have only *The Octopus* and *The Pit*; and by common consent the former is greatly the better of the two, because Norris's knowledge of the machinery of business was too small, or else his feeling for business as an epic force was not intense enough. *The Octopus* may also be a better job than *McTeague*, because of its superiority in design and in articulation, but this is not generally conceded. And yet, for a number of years, *The Pit* consistently outsold these other novels and presumably had more readers. This may be for no more obscure reason than that *The Pit* has a tycoon for a hero.

In the center of *The Octopus*, like the mine in *Germinal*, is the railroad, pushing out its tracks like tentacles across California and squeezing to death everything it touches. The story is based upon an actual incident in the history of the Southern Pacific, and denounces an abuse that really existed, a system of preferential freight rates designed to extract every penny the traffic would bear.

Yet although Norris met people like Ida M. Tarbell during his months in New York, he hardly qualifies as a dedicated muckraker. He is not against Big Business on principle, and he seems even to have admired the successful business figures of his time. His disposition is more reminiscent of American Populism: when respectable, middle-class people like himself are suddenly required to wrestle with a colossus, his sympathies are on their side.

The country people in *The Octopus* have been farming land leased from the railroad, with the option eventually to buy, and have made a profit up to the time when the railroad first raises rates and then calls in the options; the price charged for the land, out of all proportion to its value at the time the farmers originally took over, is based on the value of the property after it has been improved by the farmers themselves, at their own expense. The wheat ranchers finally revolt, meet the posse sent to evict them in a pitched battle along an irrigation ditch. Those who are not killed are ruined.

The other major force in the story, along with the soulless and inhuman corporation, is the wheat itself. In a way, the heroine is the fecund American earth. Norris's long descriptions of the sowing, germination, cultivation, and harvest are without parallel in American literature; one has to go to Tolstoi for anything to rival them. Not even the bad agricultural methods of the ranchers — whom Norris does not defend for having taken too much from the earth too rapidly and without putting enough back — can exhaust this natural wealth. And in a sense the real crime of the railroad is to have frustrated nature by making it impossible for men to go on feeding other men with the wheat. By its neo-pagan adoration of nature as force, no less than by its broad canvases, the size of its landscapes and of the events that take place in them, *The Octopus* is a very Zolaesque book.

That this has not been fully recognized simply attests that criticism has been more attentive to Zola's theoretical utterances than to his practice, and is relatively unaware of how much more Zola owed to the causal theories of Hippolyte Taine than the debt he acknowledged. Zola's pronouncements sound as if the whole key to his notion of the "experimental" novel were Taine's Introduction to his *History of English Literature*, in which Taine posits a narrowly biological basis for his determinism. It happens that this Introduction was meant to catch the attention of a general reading public, at the cost of being relatively sensational in the statement of Taine's beliefs, and is peppered with such dicta as "Vice and virtue are chemical products, like sulphuric acid and sugar." In a letter written somewhat later in life, Taine remarked that he wished to God he had never written some of these capsule formulations.

Earlier than the Introduction he had written a much less flamboyant and sensational statement of his theory in a book called *Les philosophes classiques*. Here he outlines a system of causality in which the essential notion is one of impersonal forces underlying the working of nature. Although his illustrations are biological — as they are in the Introduction — it is clear that forces of another kind, for example social or economic, are not logically excluded. With respect to this fundamental perception, the famous formula of heredity, environment, and historical moment that Taine propounds in the Introduction constitutes a grouping into categories of certain impersonal forces. Later in Taine's career, especially after 1870, he tends to emphasize forces that are social or even political. In Zola's novels, though not in his theoretical declarations, fascination with impersonal force is recognizable everywhere.

Seen in this perspective, the central subject of *The Octopus* is one that Zola would not have disowned. Mere men are powerless to change the course either of the growth of wheat or of the economic operations of the railroad. Both are impersonal, and both obey their own internal laws. (Hence the argument of one of the railroad officials that a corporation operates according to laws that cannot be changed, or their effect mitigated, by the members.)

But an impersonal force in itself is difficult to deal with in a work of literature. It must be concretized, either in a representative character or in a transparent symbol. One cannot well hate or love a legal entity, but one can discharge all kinds of emotion upon the figure of S. Behrman, the crass and repulsive agent of the carrier who also personifies the evil within it. And one can be frightened and revolted by an octopus.

The locomotive that nearly hits the young poet, Presley, in the opening chapter, is less a machine than a symbol of malevolent power.

He had only time to jump back upon the embankment when, with a quivering of all the earth, a locomotive, single, unattached, shot by him with a roar, filling the air with the reek of hot oil, vomiting smoke and sparks; its enormous eye, Cyclopean, red, throwing a glare far in advance, shooting by in a sudden crash of confused thunder; filling the night with the terrific clamour of its iron hoofs. . . .

Then, faint and prolonged, across the levels of the ranch, he heard the engine whistling for Bonneville. Again and again, at rapid intervals in its flying course, it whistled for road crossings, for sharp curves, for trestles; ominous notes, hoarse, bellowing, ringing with the accents of menace and defiance; and abruptly Presley saw again, in his imagination, the galloping monster, the terror of steel and steam, with its single eye, Cyclopean, red, shooting from horizon to horizon; but saw it now as the symbol of a vast power, huge, terrible, flinging the echo of its thunder over all the reaches of the valley, leaving blood and destruction in its path; the leviathan, with tentacles of steel clutching into the soil, the soulless Force, the iron-hearted Power, the monster, the Colossus, the Octopus.

This passage could be used to show that Norris was not an accomplished stylist. The metaphors, in particular, will not survive even the friendliest scrutiny: the leviathan does not have tentacles, and the octopus, who does have them, does not use them for clutching the soil; the whistles of steam locomotives did not bellow. This frightening Thing undergoes too many metamorphoses in a brief space just so that we will be frightened by it. But it is less important that he should be denounced for straining after effect than that he should have felt the straining necessary. The symbol must be established, by all the resources of rhetoric he can muster. This is the elevated style of a period that found its models in the emphatic improvisations of political and pulpit eloquence, but it is nonetheless an elevated style. Norris is calling upon it to confer importance upon a symbol which will give us something we can really hate.

By a similar process, S. Behrman, the agent, is made similarly useful. There is no causal connection between Behrman's job and his insensitiveness, his grotesque taste in dress, his crude manners. He could serve the company as well if he were blessed by the opposite qualities. But the reader can detest this man, with his varnished straw hat and his vest covered with embroidered horseshoes, and through him the organization he serves. There is supposed to be poetic justice in the accident at the end of the story, when Behrman is killed by the wheat. He personifies a force, and must be killed by a force. His presence, like the recurring symbol of the locomotive, connects the principal line of the story with the tradition of naturalism.

Just as in *McTeague*, however, Norris's naturalism is not unrelieved. Interwoven with the main action are a number of subplots that cannot by any stretch be called naturalist.

Presley has come to the wheat-growing San Joaquin Valley to write a long poem about the land and its Spanish past. Before the year is out he gives up the project in favor of a poem about the here and now, and the realities of life in the Valley; it attacks the trusts. His role in the novel is to provide the point of view of an educated and refined sensibility. Norris does not use him, as Henry James would have done, as the consciousness through whom all the action is refracted. We see the events from his angle only upon occasion. But his sensitive responses to them allow Norris to avoid some of the commentary he might otherwise have felt impelled to insert, and at the same time the story of what happens to his poem forms an implicit commentary on the conflict between the major forces in contention.

Presley's friend Vanamee, the sheep-herding mystic, has little connection with the principal thread of the novel except that his sheep are the ones run down by the locomotive in the first chapter. He prefers solitude and stays aloof from the concerns of the ranchers. Years before, his one true love had been brutally raped by some unknown, and then died after childbirth. By some extrasensory means that is never explained beyond calling it a concentration of mental energy, he believes that he can bring her back. Vanamee, rather than the Mexican parish priest who is included only for local color, appears to represent the spiritual in a situation where the other characters are overwhelmingly preoccupied with the material: for the farmers, engrossed in their struggle for life, a devotion like his would be unthinkable.

For us, on the other hand, the event it produces is unbelievable. Feeling that his dead fiancée is drawing nearer, Vanamee takes to waiting for her in a mission garden, and finally she does indeed come, over the new wheat — in the person of the now-grown child who looks exactly like her. The reader is expected to believe that she has lived in this country neighborhood since her birth without Vanamee's having heard the least rumor of it.

In another subplot, the rancher Annixter, a crabbed health-faddist with marked misogynistic leanings, is attracted to the young and wholesome Hilma Tree, the dairymaid. When she rejects the chance to become his mistress, Annixter discovers that the strange stirrings within him must be love. He proposes marriage and is accepted; they spend their honeymoon in San Francisco, and by the time when, after their return, Annixter is killed in the battle by the irrigation ditch, we have been persuaded that love of a fine woman has made him a better man. The touch of Dickensian sentimentality is less obtrusive than the idyll of the old couple in *McTeague*, probably because Annixter is one of the harried ranchers and thus plays another role in the story besides that of hero in a love affair.

A fourth subplot involves one Dyke, an engineer who loses his job with the railway, then finds himself forced off his farm, tries to meet his desperate need for money by robbing a train, kills a trainman, and is finally hunted down as a fugitive. All Dyke has ever wanted is to give his little daughter a decent education in a seminary for young ladies.

Thus while in its main lines *The Octopus* has much of the typical naturalist novel, much else in it does not conform to the naturalist pattern. From episode to episode the railroad wins and the farmers lose; force crashes against force with the inevitable outcome. Courts, legislature, posses combine to crush the hopeless individuals. And when all is finished we are shown examples of the wrecked lives of the dispersed farmers. But this in itself does not account for the subplots to which Norris has clearly given much attention.

After *The Octopus, The Pit* is a disappointment. Norris did not know Chicago as he knew the land and people of California, and what he knew about trading in wheat futures was not enough to fill a book. The second installment of his epic accordingly shrinks to the dimensions of a domestic love story.

The hero, Curtis Jadwin, has made one fortune in real estate and appears about to make another in wheat. He marries a genteelly cultivated girl from New England and installs her in a luxurious mansion near the Lake. They move in a society that justifies Henry James's complaint that America is socially too poor and thin to support a novel. Laura Jadwin's efforts to refine her husband do not succeed, and his success at the Exchange enflames his gambling instinct. While he is busy trying to corner the world's supply, she is very tempted to run off with a former suitor, the effete aesthete Corthell. Jadwin is ruined when his corner breaks. The marriage barely survives.

Norris revives his usual devices. The book is built around the familiar recurrent symbol — in this case the metaphor of the Wheat Pit as a gigantic whirlpool — shored up by his most ambitious prose. He invokes the economic law of supply and demand, and the natural law that when men are hungry more food will be planted, to play the roles of impersonal forces. Although *The Pit* is not so complex and heavily populated as *The Octopus*, he is still working in broad, panoramic frescoes. There is even a hint of Jadwin's decline under adversity, but its course is arrested by the presence of a good woman.

For once a Norris novel has a fully realized, if not completely winning, heroine. One suspects the brunette and slight Laura Jadwin is a composite of his mother, Gertrude Norris, and Jeannette Black Norris, his wife. She is, in any case, no mere love-object of a muscularly masculine hero, but is treated as interesting in her own right: a very considerable share of the novel is given over to her story, from Massachusetts to Chicago and from girlhood through marriage to neglect, temptation, and final reconciliation. Unfortunately, Norris also makes her self-centered and occasionally downright selfish. But despite her shallowness she is real and, in Norris's world, new.

Jadwin, on the other hand, is a close relative of McTeague. A tycoon born on the farm, one of the generation whose wealth did not inhibit their liking to sit out on the "front stoop" on warm spring evenings, he has the powerful muscles, awkwardness, and ineradicable lack of polish of the working man. With him is contrasted Corthell, who represents "art" while Jadwin represents "life"; there is no doubting Norris's preference for the energetic and still primitive philistine over the pallid man of refinement.

For Norris is faithful to the clichés of his age. A man who gets to the top of the pile does so by virtue of superior qualities of energy and strength. Social Darwinism here supports the Protestant ethic. Society is not inherently bad, but it encourages frivolity and the cultivation of the less virile qualities of character. Cities are interesting but corrupt, while strength of character comes from contact with the land and the elements.

Norris's critical essays, perfunctory and sketchy as many of them are, reveal a hard core of anti-intellectualism, with the characteristically American contradiction that consists of respect for and, simultaneously, suspicion of education. They contain no seriously articulated notion of the purpose and value of the literary activity to which he has nonetheless committed his own life, but declare repeatedly that "life" is better than "art." Jadwin is the kind of hero he could, and did, admire.

This is why Jadwin is not a very convincing Titan. If this fundamentally simple and uningenious man could corner the world's wheat, it is hard to see why any reasonably shrewd though not especially intelligent character, given enough money, could not do the same thing — and why, indeed, it is not done with distressing regularity.

There is no escaping it: *The Pit* reveals Norris's great weakness. An inadequate understanding of human character is intimately related to the defect in his style that vitiates even the central metaphor of his book. The image of the great whirlpool strikes us as vastly overwritten simply because Jadwin's accomplishment is not so great as Norris thinks. Jadwin, himself, is not big enough and words alone will not make him so. It would not be unjust to say of his performance in *The Pit* what Lionel Trilling says of Dreiser in all his novels: he does not write well because he thinks poorly.

Hence a survey of his contribution to American naturalism must conclude that it is indeed right to call him a naturalist but that calling him one does not account fully for the whole nature of his talent. There is another, nonnaturalist side to him even in his best work. When one turns to the rest, what this side was becomes unmistakable. Most of Norris's critics have dutifully noted the strain of melodrama that persistently turns up in his stories, but usually to minimize it as perhaps regrettable but not particularly important. Yet it is a constant factor in his successes (except *Vandover*) and his failures (except, perhaps, *Blix*).

Norris had gone home from Harvard, in the summer of 1895, with two unfinished novels and no immediate intention of going on with his writing. Before the year ended he was in South Africa reporting for one of the San Francisco papers on the unrest that preceded the Boer War. He was present at the fiasco of Jameson's raid, saw such excitement as there was to see, was under fire at least once, and caught a fever that put an end to any thought of further African adventure.

There followed two years of sporadic writing and journalism in San Francisco. He resumed writing for the San Francisco *Wave*, turning out sketches, essays, and some of the short stories that were posthumously collected in *The Third Circle* (1909). With renewed health came a certain tendency toward dissipation — of a rather mild sort from all appearances — and the renewed discovery that writing can be hard work. During 1897 he seems to have gone through a period of marked depression.

But in 1896 he had met Jeannette Black, and the progress of the courtship coincided with a return of creative energy. Early in 1898 Norris was writing an adventure story for publication by installments in the *Wave*. This was *Moran of the Lady Letty*. In New York, S. S. McClure had been reading Norris's incidental writings in the *Wave*, and, with the first installments of *Moran* in print, invited Norris to come to New York and take a job. McClure had joined forces with Frank Doubleday, in the house of Doubleday, McClure, and Company, by the time Norris got there.

This was how Norris came to be the editorial reader who drew the firm's attention to the manuscript of Dreiser's *Sister Carrie*. Meanwhile Doubleday and McClure published *Moran of the Lady Letty* in 1898 and *McTeague*, at last completed, in 1899. *Moran* went largely unreviewed, and *McTeague*, though praised by Howells, stirred considerable protest — there were cries of "stamp out this race of Norrises" — without raising the kind of scandal that sells books in quantity. Even Howells had suggested that Norris might do well in future to avoid the extreme realism for which we read *McTeague* today. Doubtless convinced that Howells was right, Norris went to work on *A Man's Woman*, a novel incapable of shocking any taste at all other than the purely literary. His letters show that he found the book disastrously hard to write and was perfectly aware of not having brought it off. He published it, even so, in newspaper installments during 1899 and in book form in 1900.

His one other excursion outside naturalism was *Blix*, a transposition into fiction of his romance with Jeannette Black. The hero, Condy Rivers, is a young writer who falls in love with a well-bred girl—he nicknames her "Blix"—who has little patience with the frivolity of contemporary San Francisco society. Condy has most of the amiable characteristics of a young college graduate, including a tendency to fool away time and money gambling at his club. Blix learns poker and beats him consistently, until he finally gives up the pastime. Being autobiographical well beyond the degree reached in *Vandover*, this love story adds an interesting sidelight on the latter novel: the suggestion is strong, in *Blix*, that Norris entertained private worries about going to the dogs. In the novel, as in real life, he does not do so: Blix eventually leaves for the East and Condy receives a providential invitation from an eastern publisher that will enable him to follow her.

Some critics, including the late Lars Åhnebrink, have found this novel "charming." Its accounts of the couple's walks along the edge of the Pacific, and one of a fishing expedition to an inland lake, are in fact informed by a kind of heartwarming felicity. But more significant for the present purpose are the chapters in which, on their walks, the couple fall in with the keeper of a life-saving station who has knocked about the world extensively and has a fund of stories to tell. These Condy drinks in, to store against the day when he will need them for his books. This is "material" and also contact, albeit at second hand, with "life." Condy's cultivation of this parasitical relationship suggests the importance for Norris of his own conversations with one Captain Joseph Hodgson of the Fort Point Coast Guard station.

Books of action and adventure were selling well, but Paris, Berkeley, and Harvard had prepared Norris poorly for such enterprises. However convinced he was that "life is better than literature," in this sense he had not lived. He was entirely willing to be a romancer as well as a novelist, but the competition was stiff: Stevenson, Richard Harding Davis, Kipling, and Joseph Conrad had all gone places and done things.

So had Norris, briefly. Like so many others he had been an accredited correspondent in the Spanish-American War and had seen some of the fighting, but, like his trip to South Africa, this expedition seems to have given him little to use in his fiction. Condy's attachment to "Captain Jack" suggests strongly that he felt a kind of poverty of invention in himself. Did Norris entertain the same feeling? His willingness to work with secondhand materials, like the delight he took, according to one of his letters, in the writing of *Moran*, excites suspicions of his seriousness. Was he a writer with "something to say" that gave him trouble in the saying, or was he merely a rather talented young man who wanted terribly to be a writer?

Alternative answers may be proposed. His early commitment to naturalism may have been only experimental. Or it may be that he was short of money, wanted to marry, and loved Jeannette Black more than he did any special literary mode. What is certain is that *Moran of the Lady Letty*, and even more so *A Man's Woman*, attest the fallibility of a method that capitalizes upon vicarious experience.

Moran has the distinction of being one of the best yarns about salt water and derring-do ever written by an author who knew nothing firsthand about either. Even while his novel was coming out in installments, Norris was hearing from knowledgeable friends about his howlers in nautical terminology and procedures. He seems to have listened unperturbed and was perhaps right in doing so: reviewers of his finished book were much more critical of the superabundance of unnecessary incident than of bloopers about the art of navigation. But his ignorance of his subject was not, of course, unrelated to the proliferation of episodes.

Of these there is surely God's plenty. Ross Wilbur, a San Franciscan, Yale graduate, and dedicated ladies' man, happens into a dockside saloon to while away the time between a tea and a debutante party, drinks a Mickey Finn, is dropped through a trapdoor, and finds himself shanghaied aboard a disreputable schooner manned by a Chinese crew and commanded by a white thug. They drop down the coast looking for anything they can scavenge or salvage, and meet the derelict *Lady Letty.* Aboard the drifting hulk is one living soul, a somewhat postadolescent Norse goddess, big, blonde, beautiful, and profane, but absolutely unfamiliar with men. An accident leaves her and Wilbur to command the schooner and its Chinese crew through a series of wild adventures. These include a night battle on the shore, against the crew of a marauding Chinese junk, for the possession of a piece of ambergris. Excited by the fighting until she does not know who is her enemy, the girl Moran throws herself upon Wilbur in berserk rage. He subdues her by physical force — and as he holds her helpless Moran learns to love the man who has mastered her.

When, after other and no more credible adventures, they bring their ship back to California, Wilbur has become another man. He has killed an opponent in armed combat. His muscles are hard. And at the same time he has been regenerated by the primitive maiden, and the once effete Yale man is now thoroughly out of patience with the social whirl, to which he cannot think of returning. Similarly, Moran has been changed by her contact with a cultured and civilized man into a charmingly feminine, though incompletely tamed, young woman.

At this point Norris played with the idea of sending them on another voyage, this time around Cape Horn to join the filibusterers drawn to Cuba by the approach of war. This he renounced, however, in favor of having Moran murdered by a skulking Chinese crewman she and Wilbur had protected from the vengeance of an enemy tong. The choice had the obvious merit of ending the yarn and getting an inconveniently antisocial heroine off Norris's, and his hero's, hands.

Moran easily sustains a first reading, though most readers would require a special incentive to undertake a second: the strain of suspending disbelief is simply too great.

A Man's Woman is no less demanding, and offers even less in the way of reward. The story involves an Arctic explorer who comes home from an expedition to the northern wastes, where most of his companions died, to claim the love of a rich woman who has turned her back on an empty social life, founded a nurses' home, and herself become a nurse. Later he forces her to abandon nursing his closest friend — a survivor of the expedition — just as the latter is at the crisis of typhoid, because he objects to her endangering herself. The friend dies, but the couple marry — and after some months the hero renounces his bliss to depart on a new expedition to the North Pole.

The heroine, Lloyd Searight, is another Moran in physique and pale Nordic beauty, but has wealth, education, and unmitigated idealism in addition. Ward Bennett, the explorer, is a McTeague in a Brooks Brothers suit: he even has the same jutting jaw and somewhat neanderthal brow. Well-born, educated, intelligent, but at the same time full of uncontrolled brute energy, he is devoted to getting exactly what he wants — the love of a woman, one last exhausted effort from companions dying on an ice floe, or the assent of his fiancée to desert a man who will perish without her aid. In the Arctic he proves himself capable of any extreme — and is no less so when he returns to civilization. When Lloyd's horse threatens to run away with her, for example, he kills the beast with one blow of his geologist's hammer.

The book presents the reader with more psychological improbabilities than he can easily tolerate. Would any man, in the name of love, insist on leaving his friend to die wretchedly for lack of nursing? Would a woman of Lloyd's alleged intelligence and pride have accepted being forced into such a situation?

Would any woman with a minimum of self-respect have fallen in love with this educated gorilla in the first place? The difficulty of belief was already great in *Moran*; here it is insuperable.

The important truth about *A Man's Woman* is not so much that this novel is melodramatic as that the melodrama taken as such is of low quality. *Moran of the Lady Letty*, even more shamelessly devoted to a world divided without nuance into bad people and good people, inattentive to proportions between cause and effect, subordinating motive to action, caring little if anything about probability, and depending heavily on the reader's overlooking its defects in his eagerness to learn what happens next, is far less offensive. Norris has poor Moran murdered in cold blood simply to be rid of her. Wilbur has left her aboard the schooner moored just offshore while he does an errand in San Francisco; the one Chinese remaining with them attacks her with his knife; love has civilized her to the point where she cannot use her strength to resist; the murderer leaves her body aboard, slips the cables so that the schooner will be wrenched free at any strain, and swims ashore; the captain of the lifeboat station finds her dead and brings the news to Wilbur just as the *Lady Letty* breaks away; Wilbur can only helplessly watch his schooner standing out to sea bearing the body of his beloved into the sunset. We do not greatly object, possibly because we know that Norris, himself, did not take the book very seriously and had a huge good time writing it.

But the final chapters of *McTeague* are not just an expedient for breaking off a yarn; from the sketches submitted as "themes" in Lewis E. Gates's writing class, it is clear that they were in the original plan. His delay in finishing the book is evidence that he was not entirely sure of their fitting with the rest.

He makes poor McTeague take flight back into the Sierras, looking for safety in the scenes of his boyhood, lets him find gold he will never be able to spend, endows him with a special sixth sense that infallibly warns of danger. As the posse approaches, McTeague takes flight again down the Panamint Range and into the desert. His implacable enemy, Schouler, insists on following him alone, after the posse, which he has now joined, turns back. The chase continues through the desert, which Norris widens beyond its geographical dimensions for the purpose, until the inexorable pursuer catches up. They fight; and McTeague kills Schouler — but only after the latter, in one last surge of strength, shackles himself to McTeague with handcuffs for which there is no key. They are miles from the nearest water.

Few, even among Norris's enthusiastic admirers, argue that this abrupt change in modes of fiction enhances *McTeague*. Nevertheless, the common judgment is that the turn to a flight-and-pursuit pattern does not impair the quality of the earlier part of the novel. They are perhaps right, but the same plea cannot be made in favor of *The Octopus*, because this whole novel is structured on the principle of melodrama, and one's final judgment depends on how well one feels the melodrama succeeds.

The essence of melodrama is violent contrast, and *The Octopus* is built of violently contrasting scenes. The slaughter of Vanamee's sheep, in the opening chapter, follows the scene of quiet conversation in which the sheepherder reveals so much of himself to Presley. The arrival of the bad news that the railroad has called in its options comes directly after the pages about the merriment of the whole ranching community at Annixter's barn dance. The sequence on Annixter's honeymoon with Hilma in San Francisco is sandwiched between accounts of how Dyke has been starved off his own land, and of how he robs the train — which happens to be the express that is bringing the couple back to the ranch. The episode of the great jack-rabbit drive and its attendant slaughter ends with the word that a posse is coming, and the ranchers hurry home to be slaughtered themselves.

There is thus no change in method toward the close of the book, when Norris adopts a technique of alternating fragments of pieces of dissociated but contrasting action. In the penultimate chapter, after disposing of various minor characters — Minna Hooven, for example, is driven to prostitution — Norris picks up, first, a dinner party at the home of one of the officials of the railroad, and, second, the wanderings of old Mrs. Hooven and six-year-old Hilda, penniless and looking for a place to sleep. The night is cold, and the woman and child are desperate; the dinner, at which Presley is surprised to find himself a guest, is elaborate and succulent. The camera switches back and forth between the dinner and the waifs in increasingly rapid rhythm, with each shot briefer than the one preceding. Finally we see the couple sink down under a bush. We return to the dinner:

Just before the ladies left the table, young Lambert raised his glass of Madeira. Turning toward the wife of the Railroad King he said:
"My best compliments for a delightful dinner."

Then back to the bench:

The doctor, who had been bending over Mrs. Hooven, rose.
"It's no use," he said; "she has been dead some time — exhaustion from starvation."

These last pages are not only immensely effective in themselves but also entirely appropriate in the structure of the novel: they accelerate the rhythm that the reader has felt from the beginning. The rapid and incessant reversals of fortune are rushed to a kind of climax. The technique is the one that would be adopted, a decade or so later, for the wordless narrations of the early movies. To describe it one is almost forced to fall back upon the vocabulary of the cinema.

The final chapter moves in a much slower tempo. The hated S. Behrman has come to watch the lading of a ship that will carry some of the railroad's surplus wheat to the starving Orient. The operation is automatic. No one else is about. By itself the golden stream pours out of a hopper and falls into the hold. Behrman loses his balance, lands in the hold with the flood pouring in upon him. He struggles against it, tries to find a ladder, screams. The wheat mounts inexorably. His struggles weaken. At the end of the sequence one sclerotic hand sticks out above the rising surface of the grain. Then the hand, too, disappears beneath the flowing gold.

This ending is almost obligatory. The logic of *The Octopus* requires this last, crowning contrast, emphasized by the slowness of the pace and the fadeout at the end. It returns us to the conflict of the great, elemental forces: the railroad has won its battle on the purely human plane; nothing can be done for victims; but in the titanic struggle in which they have been pawns the scapegoat representing the force of the corporation is overwhelmed by the force of the wheat, which is the force of nature itself.

And at the same time, Behrman's end satisfies another compelling need. The villain must not be allowed to prosper from his misdeeds. That everyone else should suffer without his being punished would violate the fundamental law of melodrama. Also, as befits melodrama, the punishment has to be ironic; it is right that Behrman should die under the weight of the wealth he has helped accumulate.

The reader has been prepared for this crowning irony from very early on. The principle underlying the contrasts of events that determines the structure is basically an ironic one. We learn very soon that whenever anything seems to be going well for any of the characters he is merely being deluded and that new misfortune will shortly come upon him. We know what the character does not — that no matter what he does to avoid it, trouble will come.

Of course, there is nothing inherently melodramatic in such irony in itself. It frequently appears in the most respected tragedy, for example the *Oedipus*. But in tragedy it is an aspect of the human condition and its presence is inevitable, whereas in melodrama it is present because someone has stacked the cards.

At his best, Norris is not greatly worried about credibility, and coincidence is endemic, not only in *Moran* and *A Man's Woman* but in the novels he took more seriously as well. McTeague's carrying his poor canary in its gilded cage through weather that would have killed a gamecock, Norris's extending the boundaries of the desert so that McTeague can get too far away from water, like Vanamee's not knowing — for all his supersensory powers — that the lost fiancée's daughter has been right there in the neighborhood, appear not to have disturbed him, and are unlikely to disturb a present-day reader. And one finds no disabling defect at the beginning of *The Octopus* when, to introduce his dramatis personae and finish rapidly with the exposition, he arranges for young Presley to meet practically every important character in the book, and hear all the local news, in the course of one afternoon's bicycle ride down the valley. But elsewhere he rigs the game precisely for the sake of irony. Bad news, we have noticed, always arrives *after* moments of joy or jollity. And of all the trains poor Dyke could have chosen to rob, he must fall on none other than the one carrying the Annixters home from their honeymoon. In such instances the relationship between cause and effect is, to say the least, incoherent.

Once the first excitement of reading has worn off, one wonders even if the death of S. Behrman was not contrived, also. The holds of ships are normally equipped with ladders. Behrman is not so stunned by his fall that he is unable to flounder about. Yet he does not flounder along the bulkhead, where the wheat would be less deep and where, even if blinded by dust, he would know that he could find a ladder by groping with his hands. Did Behrman truly die an ironic death, or was he, like Moran, simply murdered by his author?

Seen in the light of his most successful novel — which after all we must take *The Octopus* to be — Norris emerges as an instinctive melodramatist working with naturalist materials. The formula may be extended to describe the author of *McTeague*, and, in some degree, of *Vandover* and *The Pit*. It accounts for the nature of his successes and at the same time for his characteristic awkwardness in dealing with such problems as the elementary one created by the fact that a novelist is supposed to deal with live men and women.

In especial, women. Apart from the heroine of *Blix* (which, as an idyll, belongs to a special critical category) and Laura Jadwin in *The Pit*, his women are either kept in auxiliary roles, like Trina and the other feminine figures in *McTeague*, and presented in

terms of one or two simple character traits, or else handled with
extraordinary gingerliness. The reader would be at a loss to say,
for example, what the "fast" Ida Wade, whom Vandover
seduces, actually looks like. She is hardly more than an object for
the momentary attention of Vandover. And Moran, although
described much more completely, impresses much less as a
human female than as a wish fulfillment.

Moran's long hair, statuesque body — she stands six feet, with
broad hips and deep breasts — and blonde complexion may
have been meant to make her look like a seagoing Brünnehilde,
and his point is clear; but in her ignorance, innocence, and sexual unawareness she seems even more a statue come to life — the
Galatea of a timid erotic fantasy. As a story, *Moran of the Lady
Letty* needs little more than she provides, however; complexity of
character, or depth, would make her presence inconvenient for
the hurried romancer.

Hilma Tree, in *The Octopus*, has a much more important literary function: she is the young woman for whom Annixter, one
of the central figures in the book, makes over his life. She is
another tall, blonde, and opulent woman, and more amply described than any other woman in the book. But Norris simply
refuses to let the reader look at her. The dominant adjectives in
the descriptions — "sane," "honest," "strong," "alert," "joyous,"
"robust," "vigorous," "vibrant," "exuberant" — indicate only
Annixter's responses to her. Doubtless the reader is expected to
respond in the same way, but his impression is more likely to be
that Annixter, still eccentric, has gone off the deep end for a
country wench who washes her face and knows how to milk a
cow. Of Lloyd Searight, the heroine of *A Man's Woman*, there is
little more to say.

But while what the critics commonly report about Norris's
women is undeniable, reports on his men are easily overdone. It
is true that several of his heroes run to a type: evolution has
produced, if we judge by them, nothing finer than the blond,
strong, somewhat prognathous, perhaps a bit dumb but never
inactive, Anglo-Saxon. In comparison, other races are inferior;

white supremacy is axiomatic. Orientals are treacherous by nature; other foreigners can hardly be taken seriously and at times are simply comic. McTeague is a brute, but occupies a place on the evolutionary ladder on which Ross Wilbur occupies a higher rung; the latter needs only to have the social veneer worn away, and the muscular primitive beneath brought out, by a few months of buccaneering. Ward Bennett is, in Norris's eyes, the complete "man's man." Beside men like these, intellectuals and persons of advanced aesthetic taste show up badly. Even emotional sensibility seems a bit suspect: Norris is all admiration when Bennett leaves old companions to die disabled on the Arctic ice, and shows no indignation when Jadwin shrugs off the thousands who will have no bread because he has forced up the price of wheat.

Yet, especially in his later novels, a very considerable number of male characters do not conform to pattern. Aside from Jadwin himself, most of the men in *The Pit* have little of the Nordic superman about them; in *The Octopus* there are none. Annixter is a man of action when need arises, and shoots it out with the drunken cowboy Delaney when the latter tries to break up the barn dance, but as a group, he, the Derricks, and their friends are ordinary citizens. Toward the end of his life Norris may have been coming around to the idea that the common American man can be something of a hero.

Critics have been at pains to show that Norris meant to reveal, discreetly, the sexuality of his characters in such incidents as McTeague's kissing the anesthetized Trina. They are quick to concede, however, that the attempts are very discreet indeed, that at most the novelist intended only to implant the idea of sexuality in the reader's mind and leave the rest to his imagination. But, on the whole, this is not convincing. Norris not only shies away from sex, but also from most aspects of private, domestic life. One remembers only one pregnancy in his novels, that of poor Ida in *Vandover* — of course a bad thing that brings its own punishment. Among Laura Jadwin's complaints, which after several years of married life are not few, there is no mention of her being childless. One is left with the uncomfortable conclusion that these women were not real enough to have children.

In any event, the population of Norris's world is too unvaried, and perhaps his understanding of life itself was not deep enough, to permit writing the kind of social and psychological novels that Henry James has taught us to prefer. Possibly because his understanding of life itself was also melodramatic, so that he saw men and women only in melodramatic relationships, he did not feel the need. Something of the sort seems to have been his great limitation. It was only when he could bring the techniques of melodrama to deal with a subject adapted to and tolerant of the limitation that he wrote enduring work.

He had planned another "epic," which would have retold the story of Gettysburg, with one volume for each of the three days. For the ultimate judgment of his talent, it is a pity that he did not live to write it. That he was thinking of a subject that, by its nature, did not involve women suggests at least faintly that he had discovered where his bent lay. He might have suffered from the inevitable comparison with Stephen Crane, but even this would have been revealing.

Today, his novels reveal their weaknesses more strikingly than their strengths. Henry James has reformed our notion of the novel. Psychoanalysis has changed our understanding of human personality. An intervening generation of stylists and technicians — Hemingway, Wolfe, Fitzgerald, Faulkner — has given us a new respect for the word, and perhaps also a new suspicion of the word used carelessly. We have come to expect that a novel will offer us the spectacle of "ethics in action," and at the same time the vectors of stress in our ideas of social and personal morality point in totally different directions. Even the country Norris was writing about has changed beyond recognition. It follows that we cannot appreciate Norris's achievement unless by a vigorous, and sympathetic, effort of the historical imagination.

His better books insisted, by their example, that literature was a serious matter — in a time which, to judge by its recorded preferences, had not granted this point. His blend of naturalism and melodrama was, as Dreiser's career also testifies, as much as the country could take before the great expansion of tolerance in taste that came, not without resistance in many quarters, after 1918. We think today that it opened the way not only for Dreiser but for all the novelists who, without professing the naturalist faith, have needed the freedom in choice and treatment of subject that the naturalists were the first to claim.

In France and elsewhere, naturalism aimed to produce a kind of shock effect: the exposure of the animal behavior of the human animal was not expected to be accepted with tranquillity. Naturalism was working with a new dimension of humanity, and offering a new explanation of certain puzzling aspects of human behavior. Not that Norris was, by nature, animated by a desire to shock people. But the testimony of contemporary critics of *McTeague* is convincing; their genteel rejection of the novel is evidence that it did, in fact, shock. The shock had to be achieved, and its first effect dulled, before the American novel could move into the wide field it occupies today. We can measure its potential for shock by the fact that even now, in spite of our habit-induced dullness, Norris's picture of life as actually lived in a given time and place has retained some power to shock.

Meanwhile, what V. L. Parrington called critical realism aimed, more or less consciously, at exposing imperfections and abuses in society and in the political structure, often by making the reader identify himself with the victims. To the extent that *The Octopus* still arouses our sympathies for the wheat ranchers, even though the depredations of the railroads have long since become an academic matter, we have to call this novel a success.

And further, in spite of his penchant for melodrama, Norris's better novels played their part in substituting flesh and blood people for the myth-figures — the Sheriffs, Rangers, Cowboys, and such — in the literature of the American West. If we honor writers like Stephen Crane for their part in this achievement, we can hardly deny Norris the credit he, too, deserves.

W. M. FROHOCK

THEODORE DREISER

In addition to his eight novels, Theodore Dreiser's work includes four books of short stories and sketches, four about travel, two of autobiography, one of poems, one of plays, and four, best described as miscellanies, in which he mixed science, more autobiography, politics, and social problems. But we read the rest of his writing mostly because it illumines the novels. They are his claim to greatness, and it is on them that any attempt to assess his achievement must fix attention. Current criticism tends to honor him most for *Sister Carrie* (1900) and *An American Tragedy* (1925), assigning second best either to *Jennie Gerhardt* (1911) or to the first two parts of his "Trilogy of Desire," *The Financier* (1912) and *The Titan* (1914); much less is said in praise of the third part of the trilogy, *The Stoic* (1947), or of *The Bulwark* (1946); and of *The "Genius"* (1915) more critical evil has been spoken, probably, than good. We have only recently begun to concede what the Europeans have told us for years, that the achievement these novels represent was truly a major one.

Current manuals credit Dreiser with "power" and "compassion" and they are right, just as they are right in adding that often the power is "crude" and the compassion "mawkishly sentimental." But such formulas label without explaining. The

source of his originality was a trait of character: he was constitu-
tionally unable to say he saw what he did not in fact see, what
wasn't there to be seen. His drafts show him trying to restrain
this gift—for example, in revising *Sister Carrie*, to avoid offend-
ing current taste he worked to make his heroine less promiscuous and less willing to be kept than he had originally conceived
her — but such attempts failed because the gift was instinctive
and visceral. This naive innocence of vision in his novels made a
shambles of the public moral assumptions of his time.

People were supposed to be guided by conscience, but the lives
he observed, including his own, were shaped by the blind, incomprehensible "forces" of nature. Everyone agreed that success came from grit, enterprise, honest industry, and clean living, but in his experience the successful were those who combined the most ruthless wheeling and dealing with great good
luck. Happiness was supposed to reward deep love and devotion
to one woman — with book, bell, and candle — but he learned
for himself what his heroes confirm, that the woman we love
today may become tomorrow's millstone. Unselfish devotion and
kindness were recommended to all women, but he couldn't see
that they had lightened his mother's burdens, and they bring
little but grief to Jennie Gerhardt, whereas the girl who keeps
her eyes open doesn't necessarily come to a bad end because she
goes to bed with other women's husbands; witness Carrie
Meeber. Such discoveries may strike us today as rudimentary,
but the point is that in Dreiser's time no one was supposed to
make them. Hence the impact of his novels.

American mores have changed so much that our cultural history seems unreal. It is hard for us to believe that the so-called
genteel tradition was not a cynical conspiracy among an established elite to legitimize their fortunes and justify the society
they headed. Thinkers like Max Weber and Thorstein Veblen
have persuaded us so thoroughly that the ethic of the rising and
expanding middle class was what the middle class needed to
believe that we forget that millions of people did in fact believe
in it as they believed in the gospel from which they thought it

derived. For many readers, even so late as the Coolidge administration, Dreiser was denying the meaning of their lives.

The fairy tale doesn't report that the child who dared speak of
the emperor's nakedness became a popular hero; and although
the moral and religious issues that once made dispassionate discussion of Dreiser's work difficult have long since disappeared
with the cant that surrounded them, our praise is too often
limited to the niggardly admission that he "told the truth" about
American life as he saw it. Yet a reader who believes that a
characteristic function of the novel is to penetrate appearance
and reveal the reality beneath is in no position to dismiss Dreiser
so summarily. And if he also agrees that when the reality revealed is important ethically, socially, or culturally, the novelist
who reveals it must be granted a kind of importance also, then
he must concede a certain stature to Dreiser. The reality itself
may be unpalatable — although this is less likely today than
when the novels were new. And we may have little taste for the
ways and means Dreiser used in the revelation — as is more than
likely since we have become so aware of fictional technique in the
interim. The achievement isn't thereby explained away.

No one contests that Dreiser knew the kind of American life
he wrote about at first hand. Few novelists have written their
own experience into their novels with so little transposition, or
made it so clear afterwards (see *Dawn*, 1931) that they have done
so. (He had to abandon an early draft of *An American Tragedy*
because he had poured so much of his youth into that of his hero
as to knock the story out of proportion.) Life in America, as he
knew it, was absorbing but also rough, harsh, and often nasty.

His father, John Paul, had immigrated from Mayen on the
German Moselle, not far from Coblenz, and moved across the
country from job to job, doing reasonably well at the weaver's
trade until fire destroyed his woolen mill in Sullivan, Indiana,
and he was injured by a falling beam during the rebuilding.
Nothing he touched thereafter prospered long; he devoted the
rest of his life to paying his debts, and retired into what the
younger Dreiser considered a very superstitious and bigoted

Catholicism. Responsibility for the family, which increased with dreary regularity, fell largely on Sara Maria Schänäb Dreiser, the Moravian farm girl John Paul had married on his way west. The children were Paul, the minstrel and hoofer, who changed the spelling of his last name to Dresser and wrote songs like "On the Banks of the Wabash" and "My Gal Sal"; Rome, who became an alcoholic bum; Emma; Sylvia; Mame, who like Emma got an early reputation for promiscuity and, later, ran a whorehouse; Theresa; Al; Theodore, who was born two years after the father's accident, in Terre Haute, on August 27, 1871; Ed; and Claire. With such help as she could get from the older ones as they left home, the mother dragged her brood from Sullivan to Terre Haute, to Vincennes, back to Sullivan, to Evansville, to Warsaw (Indiana), and to Chicago, according to where chances looked best of keeping them fed, clothed, and alive. These wanderings assured Theodore an insecure childhood.

The family was never in one place long enough to establish itself, even had it had money to do so. The behavior of the older sisters rapidly earned it the kind of name that meant exclusion from the society of such rural, or semirural, communities. Schooling was erratic: Dreiser saw enough of parochial schools to leave him with a lifelong aversion to nuns and priests, and had one experience of a public school that was luminous by comparison. Later, one of his teachers paid his way through a year at Indiana University. He had few friends and few ways of making any. The first volume of his autobiography, *Dawn*, pictures an uncertain, rather unhappy little boy, and then a sensitive, awkward, and no happier adolescent, "on fire with sex."

His novels would be the richer for this life. His uninhibited sisters were material for *Sister Carrie* and *Jennie Gerhardt*. The weak failure of a father and the courageous, responsible, and drudging mother recur in *Jennie Gerhardt* and *An American Tragedy*. The uneasy, unhappy boy, ashamed of his parents and of the way the family lives, and deprived by birth of the pleasures other children seem born to, is embodied later in Clyde Griffiths, the hero of *An American Tragedy*. In addition to such easily recognizable patterns, the fear of poverty and failure that pervades the novels comes straight out of an underprivileged midwestern childhood.

Once he was old enough Dreiser was off to Chicago on his own, employed at first at such jobs as dishwashing in a greasy restaurant or driving a laundry wagon, but in time finding newspaper work on the *Daily Globe*, where he began what turned out to be a long and slow apprenticeship. Wherever he went more experienced hands taught him what they knew. From Chicago he moved to St. Louis and jobs on the *Republic* and the *Globe-Democrat*. Then he drifted slowly eastward, looking for a place to settle down, with stops in Grand Rapids, Toledo, Cleveland, Buffalo, and finally Pittsburgh, where he found a job on the *Dispatch*.

He was training his eye. His early pieces were not momentous journalism, but they show an alertness to the picturesque, especially as it emerges from a drab urban background. He was as fascinated by what goes on in back streets and alleys, away from the glare and glitter, as by the lives of the wealthy under the bright lights. He learned what a newspaper writer so rapidly learns: not to trust his reader's power of inference or his ability to understand what he isn't told explicitly. Less rapidly he learned the value of feeding his reader a diet of concrete facts.

In the Pittsburgh Public Library he read Balzac, who gave him an example of what the novel could be, and a model from which his own fictions would rarely depart. In *Dawn* he regrets that the discovery didn't come sooner, at Indiana University, but one wonders whether Balzac's great value for Dreiser would have been available except for the latter's own previous experience with writing. The Balzac he discovered was clearly not the visionary, "metaphysical," author of *Seraphita* and *Louis Lambert*, but rather the one most apt to teach a feature writer what to do with his material — whose long, factual, third-person narratives, told by a narrator who sees and knows everything, could be accounts of real lives in the jungle of contemporary society. Novels like *Lost Illusions* are built from accumulations of detail that sounds as if directly observed, with the flow interrupted only by essay passages in which the novelist impenitently breaks off the story to explain motives and comment on the action. Elaborate techniques are absent, or else hidden; and Balzac often appeals to contemporary scientific theory to illumine the ways of his characters. Years later, sophisticated critics like Joseph Warren Beach, mindful of the divergent ways of Balzac and James, would reproach Dreiser for being too like his master. They were entirely right in identifying the relationship: Dreiser owes far more to Balzac than to Zola or the other French naturalists, for example. But was Balzac such a bad master to adopt?

After Pittsburgh he joined his brother Paul in New York. In 1894 newspaper work was hard to find. He caught on as a "stringer" with the *World*, but found that the money paid per inch of space wouldn't keep him alive, and moved to a staff job on *Ev'ry Month*. Plainly he had become a hack, and as a hack he soon took to free-lancing articles for periodicals like *Success* — a curious publication dedicated to fostering the great American cult. His interviews with tycoons follow a required format such that one wonders why Dreiser, himself, wasn't embarrassed. The facts are that he wasn't, that material success would never cease fascinating him, and that what he learned at this time would be most useful when he came to write his novels about Frank Algernon Cowperwood.

In 1898, to his permanent chagrin, he married. Sara White was attractive, somewhat older than he, like him from the Midwest, but unlike him disposed to social conformity. Dreiser says that after his first ardor he cooled rapidly but married her anyhow; the union was doomed from the start. They separated after a few years, but even after the separation became permanent, Sara White — "Jug," as he called her — would never consent to divorce and the marriage stayed on the books until her death. In his novels, Eugene Witla (the "genius"), Cowperwood, Clyde Griffiths, and — seen from another angle — Lester Kane in *Jennie Gerhardt*, all commit themselves to women and repent at leisure.

Meanwhile, early in 1900 he finished *Sister Carrie*. Frank Doubleday, the publisher, heeded the enthusiastic recommendation of his editorial reader, Frank Norris, to accept the manuscript. What happened next has been disputed. Dreiser's prefatory note in later editions says that Mrs. Doubleday was so shocked by the story that she urged her husband to withdraw from the contract and that when Dreiser held him to their agreement Doubleday honored it in the letter only, printing and binding the book indeed but making no effort to promote it.

Recent studies find Dreiser's account somewhat one-sided. Doubtless the Doubledays did discover that they had taken on a shocking book, and quite possibly Mrs. Doubleday was no woman to approve of Carrie Meeber, but they may also have had second thoughts about what the public would accept and buy and simply decided to cut losses. In any event, the record shows that they did publish the book and sold, in 1901–2, about 900 copies. It was, at the time, a failure.

Failure haunted, just then, this author of success stories. His marriage was going badly; he was restless and depressed; he worried about his health and even his sanity. In 1902 he got so low that his brother Paul stepped in and sent him to a rest camp operated by William Muldoon, a reconditioner of businessmen, trainer of boxers, and figure in the New York sporting world. Muldoon's rigorous discipline and some fresh air eventually got Dreiser back to a point where he could cope with life. But he left the camp only to find a job at hard, physical labor on a railroad crew, and not until late December 1903 did he return to his familiar setting — and then not as a writer but to fill a series of editorial jobs.

Successively he was on Frank Munsey's *Daily News*, *Smith's Magazine*, and the *Broadway Magazine*, of which he was briefly managing editor. Finding that he was better at editing than at managing, he moved in 1907 to the *Delineator*. There he was well paid, and apparently found work and surroundings congenial. When his hero, Witla, in *The "Genius"* reaches a similar point, Dreiser clearly thinks him a success. Some even feel that, if

Dreiser had remained so comfortably situated, he might never have finished another novel.

But, in 1910, the mother of Miss Thelma Cudlipp objected so vehemently to Dreiser's attentions to her daughter that she packed the daughter off to Europe and got Dreiser fired from the *Delineator*. In the same year he and Sara White completed their separation. The year following he published *Jennie Gerhardt*. The next fifteen years were to be his period of incessant productivity.

After *Jennie Gerhardt* came *The Financier*, *The Titan*, *The "Genius,"* the short stories, plays, essays, one of the autobiographies, and finally, in 1925, his fifty-fourth year, *An American Tragedy*. Dreiser didn't write easily, and his drafts show that he labored over the revisions. These must have been years of unremitting work. The reward wasn't, perhaps, the literary equivalent of the success he had admired, studied, speculated about, and doubted in other men, but he had reached material security, his books were read—perhaps more often read than admired—and he had become a visible public figure. He had also forced the reading public to accept serious, grim realism.

Sister Carrie is undeniably a serious and grim story. Carrie Meeber finds life in Chicago as harsh as it ever was back in Wisconsin, and learns that no one cares much whether she starves on what she can earn in a factory. Money and commodities are what count, and the men she meets teach her that physical attractiveness is a commodity, fully negotiable. There is no moral conflict and she isn't bright enough to be cynical; she just exploits the one commodity she has.

She lets Charles Drouet, the salesman she meets on the train from home, set her up in an apartment. She quits him for Hurstwood, the manager of Fitzgerald and Moy's prosperous saloon, who steals his employer's funds, abandons his wife and family, and runs away with her to New York. While Hurstwood's fortunes decline, she parlays her small talent, and her good looks, into a career on the stage, and eventually cuts him loose. He goes downhill to a suicide that is literally a pauper's death, while

Carrie, when last seen, is on her way to further fame and fortune.

If Dreiser had made her a calculating little vixen who stopped
at nothing to get what she wanted, the story would not be half so
effective. In the finished version she isn't even really promiscuous, and none of her moves toward secure ease is really planned.
She moves in with Drouet because she doesn't want to go back to
Wisconsin, and leaves him again because she suspects that he
won't ever put through the "little deal" that would let them
marry: Hurstwood has something more substantial to offer. Her
conscience nags her, but never loudly enough. She drops Hurstwood, in turn, when she sees the luxuries other women enjoy.
She is not even particularly shrewd.

Her men are almost as passive as she. Drouet picks her up on
the train because it isn't in him not to try to pick up a pretty girl.
Having a pretty mistress, and being known to have one, flatters
his vanity. But he is nowise disposed to entangle himself permanently, so that the same instinct that made her attractive to him
in the first place now warns him off. Poor Hurstwood is also a
creature of circumstances. His marriage has cooled, and his wife
is dominating, grasping, and shrewish. Naturally — as Dreiser
knew from experience — he is drawn to any girl who promises to
renew his youth, and can be had. Yet he sees the attendant
inconveniences, and blind luck makes his crucial decision for
him: he is still not sure that he will abscond and take Carrie with
him when, as he is closing his firm's safe for the night, he is
tempted by the sight of so much money and takes out a sheaf of
bills to fondle it; he is still listening to an inner voice telling him
to put it back when the door of the safe snaps shut.

Chance plays a similar role in *An American Tragedy* when the
accident the hero has planned to bring about takes place without
his actually causing it. In both novels the protagonist's responsibility is incomplete; and in both what Dreiser thought of as
natural "forces" push them into the situations where they are so
vulnerable. Luck combines with nature to determine their fates.

One can see how Frank Doubleday may have despaired of

selling *Sister Carrie* in a country where belief in moral responsibility was fundamental. Yet Dreiser was working from life. His sister Emma had come from the country to Chicago, and had formed a liaison with one L. A. Hopkins who, like Hurstwood, had stolen money so that they could run away to New York. Emma hadn't had Carrie's subsequent success, but in other respects Carrie is no more an invention than is his picture of the mean life of poverty she wants to avoid at any cost. The life of the urban poor he knew at first hand; he had been jobless in Chicago himself and knew the skid rows of a half-dozen cities; some of the pages in *Sister Carrie* are lifted almost verbatim from Dreiser's early newspaper sketches of more or less picturesque misery. A strict moralist could condemn Carrie and Hurstwood, and also condemn Dreiser for not condemning them, but he could hardly deny the authenticity of their story.

His reading had convinced Dreiser that there must be "laws" by which the "forces" governing our lives may be seen to operate, and these laws must be open to scientific explanation. Hence a basic determinism in human affairs. Yet at the same time, we mush have some degree of free will, at least a limited liberty of choice, or else life is meaningless. He pondered the dilemma for forty years without reconciling the opposites to his final satisfaction.

At this point the difference between his naturalism and that of Zola and the French is fundamental. Zola felt that he was demonstrating the applicability of established scientific law. As he had gotten it from Taine, heredity, environment, and the historical moment determine human behavior, so that he could write, case after case, the "natural history" of two interrelated families under the Second Empire. The formula was already in existence when he began writing, and was entirely familiar to his audience, so that however monumentally wrong Zola may have been in accepting it, he had the advantage of not having to explain it in his fictions. He could take it as a datum.

Dreiser is in exactly the opposite position. He is demonstrating nothing. From *Sister Carrie* to *The Stoic* he pictures life with all the

faithfulness he can muster, but casts about gropingly for explanations. They are often inadequate, to a point that such notions
as his theory of the "chemisms" that determine personality, or of
the electricity that passes from one person in love to the other,
are best taken as metaphor. And because he often seems unaware of the inadequacy, his disquisitions may strike an irritable
reader as pompous ignorance.

If a naturalist is a writer who treats humans as products of
nature, and nature in turn as the seat of the "forces" that shape
life, and if in doing so he leaves the impression that nature
means more to him than art, then Dreiser was indeed a
naturalist. Taine had written that vice and virtue are chemical
products like sulfuric acid and sugar; and Dreiser says in *Dawn*
that with a slight change in the mixture of body chemicals his
brother Paul would have been a great man. Such parallels are
endless, and make the point irrefutably. But it is not from a
theoretical naturalism that Dreiser's novels derive their power.

Once the reader of *Sister Carrie* has seen the characters and
knows their situation, he knows what will happen. Even before
Hurstwood's luck snaps shut the safe door, we are sure that he
will steal the money and that from that point we shall be following the trajectories of two lives, one still climbing, the other
always pointed downward. The inevitablity of the outcome is in
the characters themselves: Carrie will go on being Carrie, and
Hurstwood has already made his own ruin. There is no tragic
acceleration of events. Time, as measured by the clock and the
calendar, will be inexorable.

Sister Carrie may be classified as objective realism, but beneath
the surface one suspects a basic personal fantasy. In Hurstwood,
but for luck, went Theodore Dreiser — and who knew how long
luck would hold? Dreiser had not exorcised the memory of his
unhappy, ineffectual father. Attentive students have detected
symptoms of fundamental insecurity even in his endless pursuit
of women, believing that he was really looking for the warm
protection against the consequences of failure that one woman,
his mother, had once given him. The articles written for *Success*

are implicit reminders that success does not exist unless its opposite exists also.

Carrie Meeber's success must be compensated by Hurstwood's decline. He must lose his investment in the saloon he has bought into in New York, must try only feebly to find other income, must sink to living on the twelve dollars a week Carrie earns as a chorus girl, must grow shabby and old before our eyes, must go from one mean job to another meaner one, and finally to wretched illness and suicide. One remembers that at that moment Dreiser was headed for a nervous breakdown of his own.

Thus his sympathy for Hurstwood — the first manifestation of his celebrated compassion — may be interpreted, and perhaps discounted, as indirect self-pity. In any event, it differentiates him at one more point from the European naturalists, whose dispassionate detachment was their hallmark. In *Sister Carrie* his pity is muted, but Dreiser is already the man who years later, when he saw the 1931 film of *An American Tragedy*, burst into tears.

Most of the perennial objections concerning technique apply as well to *Sister Carrie* as to any of Dreiser's later novels. His omniscient point of view permits him to tell us what kind of people his characters are instead of letting us see them in action and decide for ourselves. Too often he characterizes them by describing externals, as if all one needed to know about a person were revealed by his dress. Sometimes he puts a terrible strain on credibility: how, for example, can Carrie be so dumb as to want Hurstwood to marry her when she knows that he is already married? What the characters say reveals little that we do not know already; he reports the event and then what was said during the happening, so that the dialogue doesn't, as (say) Hemingway's dialogue does, advance the story.

Much of this kind of criticism boils down to saying that Dreiser was blissfully unaware, in 1900, of the prescriptions that Percy Lubbock would propose as precept, in 1921, following the example of Henry James in *The Craft of Fiction*. Just how does it happen that a novel written without benefit of such wisdom can affect its reader so deeply? One possible answer could be that in the house of fiction there are several mansions.

Jennie Gerhardt again draws upon Dreiser's family. Jennie's father is a poor, disabled, aggressively religious (but Lutheran, not Catholic), unassimilated immigrant. A drudging mother courageously struggles to keep the family going. Jennie, as passive a character as Carrie Meeber, and not half so lucky, is modeled upon the sisters Mame and Emma.

Working with her mother in a hotel in Columbus, Jennie catches the eye of George Sylvester Brander, the junior senator from Ohio, who is moved by her sweetly simple ways and good looks. He helps her bedraggled family, overrides her father's surly objections, and says he intends to marry her. More out of gratitude than love Jennie goes to bed with him. Then, before he can make good his promise, the bad luck that besets Dreiser's protagonists intervenes: Brander dies suddenly. Jennie finds herself pregnant, has her baby secretly, and in time goes to work as a maid in an important Cleveland family.

A friend of her employers, Lester Kane, son of a rich Cincinnati manufacturer, finds her compellingly attractive, but has no intention of marriage. From love, this time, Jennie accepts a liaison and lives with Kane in Chicago for a number of years. Even after he learns that the child she has been providing for is her own, Kane seems perfectly satisfied, but Jennie's peace is troubled by the disdain of neighbors who detect her status. Then Kane's father dies, and he learns that to inherit his share of the business he must end the liaison. In time Jennie persuades him that he should do so and he subsequently marries a widow of his own social status. One sorrow is heaped on another when her child dies of typhoid. And then Kane himself dies, and Jennie last appears, unrecognizable through heavy veils, following his funeral at a distance from the legitimate mourners.

This is what the poor may expect of life. In all senses but the technical, Jennie is a good woman — kind, loving, loyal: she has been helpful to an unresponsive family; she even takes in and cares for the old father who once wanted to put her out of the house; she is a good mother to her child, and devotedly faithful to Kane. The latter does not leave her in want, but otherwise her goodness has to be its own reward. Like the heroine of Flaubert's *Simple Heart*, she has loved without return.

Perhaps she is too good to be true. She learns little from experience, and, the complete opposite of Carrie Meeber, she lacks all instinct of self-protection. Her beauty and charm must be taken on faith. (They captivate Senator Brander, but thanks to Dreiser's preference for telling us about character instead of exhibiting it in action, we aren't prepared for his being swept so easily off his feet.) Poverty and bad luck don't embitter her as they do her brothers and sisters. Dreiser was probably combining certain traits of his sisters with some of his mother's in an idealized portrait. In any case, it is certain that Jennie, in his eyes, is an innocent victim of life's injustice.

Here another American myth is punctured: not only do girls like Carrie sometimes not have to atone, but sweet and kindly girls like Jennie can suffer just because they are too poor to protect themselves. Is it possible to be poor and moral, too? The question dogged Dreiser all his life. The impulses that in his later years involved him in such liberal causes as those of Tom Mooney, the Scottsboro boys, and the striking miners in Harlan, Kentucky, go back to his instinctive hatred of poverty. It seems clear that even his joining the Communist party, shortly before he died, was not based on conversion to a theory. He was not a systematic social thinker, and there is much to suggest that his espousals and allegiances were more emotional than rational. He simply disliked seeing strong people push weaker people around.

As Walter Allen insists in a famous study of English fiction, it is characteristic of the novel to protest against the abuse of power. For Dreiser as for Dickens, power and wealth are synonyms, and poverty exposes people to coercion. The poor man has fewer social and moral options: Jennie's brother Bass lands in jail for stealing coal from the railroad — but the alternative would be to let his family freeze. It is a measure of Hurstwood's degradation that he scabs in a motormen's strike because he has no other means of earning two dollars a day. Jennie has the looks and good nature to make Kane an attractive mistress, but not the culture and education to make her accepta- ble to him, and his family, as his wife. Very little, here or else- where in Dreiser's writing, is revolutionary. The word "equity," which he uses so frequently, means little more than that ex- tremes of poverty and wealth are unfair, and that a society that tolerates them should be reformed.

Jennie Gerhardt is not, however, a social tract. Dreiser's aim is less to stir indignation than to evoke pity, and to do so simply by drawing the contours of a life. As in *Sister Carrie*, the structure of this novel is the simplest possible, following the lines of a biog- raphy. Time is again treated as rectilinear, the mere unwinding of the years. He feels no need of sophisticated craftsmanship.

He is relatively indifferent to writing in "scenes," and entirely capable of using an entire chapter to discuss what has happened earlier, without advancing the action a step. A more typical pro- cedure starts a chapter with a discussion of a situation or the state of a character's mind; then may come the narration of a new event, perhaps followed by the dialogue that accompanied it; finally there may be summaries of the effect of the event on one or more characters. In terms hallowed by recent use, "re- port" often replaces "dramatization," and the "authorial voice" is persistently audible, while the "point of view" is entrusted to one character or another to suit the novelist's convenience.

It is in the discussions, where he speaks in his own voice, that Dreiser most clearly confirms the criticism that he writes "like a rhinoceros." The following, from the opening of Chapter 11 of *Jennie Gerhardt*, is not an unfair example: "It is curious that a feeling of this sort should spring up in a world whose very es- sence is generative, the vast process dual, and where wind, water, soil, and light alike minister to the fruition of that which is all that we are. Although the whole earth, not we alone, is moved by passions hymeneal, and everything terrestrial has come into being by the one common road, yet there is that ridiculous tendency to close the eyes and turn away the head as if there were something unclean in nature itself. 'Conceived in iniquity and born in sin,' is the unnatural interpretation put upon the process by the extreme religionist, and the world, by its silence, gives assent to a judgment so marvelously warped."

Such a mixture of circumlocution, inversion of adjective and noun, uncertainty in vocabulary, and burdened syntax identifies the self-taught writer. Dreiser tells us that in childhood he had read whatever he could get his hands on, but the English and American romantics he goes on to mention, especially when not offset by generous amounts of the English Bible such as sustained Crane, Norris, and even Sherwood Anderson, could be bad models for a style. In addition, the son of an immigrant workman and a Moravian farm girl who learned to write from her children's copybooks can't have heard simple, idiomatic English at home. Dreiser writes an acquired language. So did Joseph Conrad, but it is one thing to write an acquired language, as Conrad did, after having mastered another in the natural way, and something quite different to write one starting as Dreiser did, so to speak, from zero.

The critical moaning over the defects in Dreiser's English can be overdone. His barbarisms are notorious, and it is quite true that he is at times embarrassed to find what Flaubert called the *mot juste*. But it will be noticed that the passages most often quoted to discredit him are those in which he speaks directly to the reader, in his own voice. At the worst they show him being overelaborate, wordy, perhaps pompous, sometimes even arch. In other words, he shared the difficulty with elevated style that characterized his generation. Even Stephen Crane was forced to fall back upon the treasury of pulpit oratory and Fourth of July cliché for the loftier passages of *The Red Badge of Courage*. Dreiser's style was formed in the climate of the "Cross of Gold" speech, as the least respect for historical contexts obliges us to remember. He was born too soon to belong to the generation who solved the problem of elevation by avoiding it and adopting the tones and rhythms of *Huckleberry Finn*. And even where his prose offends he is never frivolous; his seriousness and sobriety are evident; however awkward, he means what he says.

Pity is the presiding emotion in *Jennie Gerhardt*, and the emotion is unmixed. The uncomplicated nature of his disposition toward his heroine may indeed explain why this novel should be so simple in outline and, except for the curiously blurred final chapter, so relatively rapid in the narration. On the twin patterns of success and failure, which he had adumbrated in *Sister Carrie*, his feelings were far more complex, and his subsequent novels dealing with them become correspondingly more deliberate in their pace.

Dreiser did not equate success with the mere jingling of millions. Even in his hack-writing days he had included among the specimens he interviewed for *Success* a few who, like John Burroughs, had reached the top without amassing money. In *Sister Carrie*, young Bob Ames, who speaks for Dreiser, explains to Carrie that some satisfactions are not for sale. In various novels Dreiser disdains a number of cautious, conservative, upward-bound types who devote their lives to making as much money as possible at the least possible risk. Lester Kane's brother who runs their family business, Clyde Griffiths's cousin waiting to inherit his father's factory, Orville Barnes in *The Bulwark*, with his fears that his sister's behavior will compromise his own career, are treated without sympathy. Dreiser's aversion to such fellow travelers of capitalism was total.

What interested him was the uninhibited, freewheeling paragon of unleashed energy, the "buccaneer" capable of taking whatever he wanted against any opposition. For such men success is a kind of game played as much for the mere winning as for any tangible prize. In that this figure obeys no rules but those he makes for his own convenience he has something vaguely Nietzschean about him; he also has some of the lineaments of a romantic hero, condemned to operate in the world of business. Some critics argue that this ultimate descendant of the

Romantic Outlaw appealed to Dreiser because the novelist could easily identify with him, as he had for opposite reasons with Hurstwood and as he needed to do with all his heroes. They point out that after *Jennie Gerhardt* Dreiser devoted his life to variations on the rags-to-riches formula, and view his tycoons as examples of wish fulfillment. The argument is plausible: day-dreaming has served many novelists well. But it is also true that Dreiser used the success-failure patterns for exploring character in a way that transcends the interest of success and failure in themselves.

Charles E. Yerkes had been a traction magnate who, after making and losing fortunes by manipulating the finances of street railways in Philadelphia and Chicago, had narrowly missed taking over, just before his death, the underground tube system of London. He had bounced back to relative respectability after a term in prison, had been as flamboyantly spectacular in love as in finance — he had retained a law firm to come to terms with his abandoned flames — and might also have gone down in history as a great philanthropist if death had not interrupted his public benefactions. Yet if Yerkes is remembered today it is because Dreiser took him for the model of Frank Algernon Cowper-wood. He researched Yerkes's biography with great care, and the trilogy parallels it closely.

Cowperwood is not, surely, a human type found only in America, but just as surely he is one that flowered to fullest perfection in the favorable climate of the expanding American economy. He grows up around Philadelphia, exhibiting all the thrift and industry recommended by the Quaker tradition but untouched by the corresponding moral restraints. His eye for the main chance discovers an opening in street railway stocks, and before he is out of his twenties he is a man of substance, with wealth, a wife who is a cut above him socially, and a lovely home. But his acquisitiveness, which is the expression of his restless energy, is unsatisfied and as his sophistication grows with his wealth he develops a knowing eye for art and women. He takes for his mistress a young and beautiful girl, Aileen Butler.

Trouble comes when a crash in the market following the Chicago fire catches him short and he is unable to cover his losses. He serves a prison term for embezzlement, and gets out, wiser and cannier but fundamentally unchanged, in time to pull together his fortunes by taking advantage of another crash — Jay Cooke's. He resolves to make himself a new life in the West.

At the beginning of *The Financier* the youthful Cowperwood stops to watch a lobster in the tank of a fish market window eat a live squid. This, he realizes as he meditates the revolting performance, must be the law of life: the lobster eats without compunction and will in turn be eaten by a creature further up the scale. Cowperwood's subsequent career bears out the law. Dreiser does not make him a wittingly cruel man, but one whose instincts will not let him be bested in the struggle for survival. Latter-day readers may feel, more simply, that Cowperwood has the personal and social morals of a lobster, but in Dreiser's perspective he is only obeying the law of his own nature, which derives from the law of nature herself.

In *The Titan* Cowperwood has left Philadelphia for Chicago, where Aileen marries him as soon as his first wife agrees to the divorce foreshadowed at the end of *The Financier*. New operations in public utilities — first illuminating gas and then traction once again — multiply his wealth. He collects art and women, the latter recklessly: an unbroken succession of mistresses includes wives and daughters of close business associates. Aileen, whose social inadequacies have made her a liability anyhow, discovers Cowperwood's philandering, beats up one lady in a vulgar brawl, and eventually drifts into affairs of her own. Finally, knowing that they will never crack Chicago society, Cowperwood installs her in an ostentatious mansion in New York.

Meanwhile, Cowperwood's stock-watering, sharp dealing, keen foresight, and sheer nerve make him a national power. He squeezes adversaries, bribes politicians, and buys elections until he seems ready to get control of all the surface transport of Chicago. But at last he comes up against a man of principle who won't be bought, and who is the governor of Illinois. He vetoes the bill that would grant the long-term franchises Cowperwood needs to consolidate his holdings — and the legislature fails to override the veto. Although still enormously wealthy, Cowperwood has to give up Chicago as a bad job.

This "Trilogy of Desire," as Dreiser called it, was to be completed by *The Stoic*, but he delayed too long in reviving his hero, and the novel, published posthumously, can't be judged as one would judge a finished work. Cowperwood's last foray is his try to take over the London underground. Bright's disease interrupts it and he comes back to New York to die. The museum and hospital he had planned as his memorials are not realized, and a flock of legal vultures rapidly pick his fortune apart.

The Stoic further complicates the moral ambiguities of an already ambiguous story. The rapid crumbling of Cowperwood's fortune suggests that Dreiser may have come to feel that his tycoon's whole life illustrates the vanity of vanities. In addition, the concluding chapters increase the uncertainty by following Cowperwood's last mistress to India in search of a guru who can tell her the meaning of life. What the lesson is can be the object of disagreement, but this unworldly man surely does not tell her that the good way to live is identifiable with Cowperwood's.

James T. Farrell, an admirer of Dreiser and one of his literary executors, reports that Dreiser was so uncertain about *The Stoic* that he asked Farrell to read the manuscript and advise him. Farrell attributes the move to the old man's doubting the survival of his talent, and doubtless this was most likely. But one wonders also if Dreiser, in later years, hadn't lost some of his sympathy and admiration for his hero, and perhaps his taste for the values Cowperwood represents. Had he become aware of the moral ambivalence of the earlier sections of the trilogy?

For Cowperwood is, clearly, a malefactor of great wealth. In his private life he pulverizes the Decalogue — except that he does not commit murder—and gets away with doing so because he is rich. In the public sphere he is indefensible: ultimately his dividends could only come from the pockets of the little people who paid more than the ride was worth to get back and forth between home and work. But Dreiser's eye is resolutely turned away from the social damage a man like Cowperwood causes.

Dreiser sees him covered with glamour, richly dressed, handsome in a "leonine" way, and somewhat bigger than life. Cowperwood's great moment comes when, having brought a financial crisis on the other traction enterprises in Chicago, he confronts a meeting of the bankers who have supported them. Thinking that he is short of liquid funds, they tell him that they will call all his loans. But he has foreseen exactly this move, and his position is completely solid. He faces them down, saying that he is ready to pay every penny if they insist. But, he adds, if they do insist, he will "gut every bank from here to the river." Dreiser's admiration here seems complete.

One obvious explanation is that during the years after he left the *Delineator* to return to writing, Dreiser was privately trying the mantle of success for size. This is inescapable in the case of Witla, in the autobiographical *The "Genius." The Titan* and *The Financier* may be read as a portrait of the artist as a success of another kind. For Cowperwood forces his way over the "moralists and religionists" who exist to frustrate the superior individual.

Cowperwood wins through by doing what Nietzsche calls becoming what he is — as much a product of nature as the lobster in the tank. So much the worse if this makes him one of the strong who push about the little people whom Dreiser momentarily forgets. Cowperwood can't imagine failure, and doesn't know what insecurity means. When he wants a woman he takes her, and the women are happy to be taken. He refuses to let marriage become a trap, and summarily unloads women who stale on him. Friends he doesn't need, so long as he can pay lieutenants who are faithful through self-interest or fear. What luxury he wants he simply buys. He even ends by finding the perfect mistress for an old man in beautiful, young, clever, charming, educated, and above all devoted Berenice Fleming. These are, one notes, rewards nature hadn't lavished on the novelist, but just as, but for luck, he might have been a Hurstwood, so also, with a slightly different mixture of chemicals in his body, he might have been a Cowperwood. Even a self-proclaimed realist may dream occasionally, especially if, as Dreiser does in *Dawn*, he proclaims in the same breath that he is a romanticist by temperament. Few of us feel responsible for the morality of what we dream.

A reader brought up on more recent fiction may feel the defect of the trilogy to be one of technique. As always, Dreiser is following the example of Balzac — but, in this instance, somewhat inattentively. Balzac is perfectly relentless about stopping his narrative to tell his reader in advance what the character on display is going to be like. But when Balzac arrests the narrative flow of, for example, *Le curé de Tours* to give us the "physiology" of the Old Maid, and tell us what to expect of Sophie Gamard, Mlle Gamard goes on to do exactly what we have been made to expect. "Action is character," wrote Scott Fitzgerald in one of the notes found with the manuscript of *The Crack-Up*. "A man is what he does," echo the existentialists, following André Malraux. The obligation a novelist incurs, when he discusses a character with his reader, is to remember that what the person does characterizes him also, and the two ways of characterization had better not contradict each other. Quite simply, what one sees of Cowperwood in action disagrees with Dreiser's estimate of the manner of man he is.

The fault is not completely Dreiser's, however. Cowperwood may be fascinating as a full development of the potentials of a certain human type, but culturally he is a museum piece. Little could be more foreign to us now than his world of unregulated business, and few or no inhibiting taxes, where the public conscience was less offended than overawed by the Robber Barons. The best part of the trilogy is set in the time of Dreiser's own youth; the streetcars Cowperwood modernizes are still drawn by horses and the big deals he brings off are of the gaslit, horse-car era. A time that prefers security to free enterprise must read these novels as historical fiction, or else out of interest in Dreiser.

Interest in Dreiser is necessarily the best reason for picking up
The "Genius." Whereas the Cowperwood story is fictionalized
biography — the kind of fleshing out of verifiable fact with
unverifiable, imagined detail that the French call *vie romancée* —
the life *The "Genius"* puts on public display is his own. An element of self-justification, as in most such more-or-less veiled
confessions, creeps in, along with a tendency to touch up and
correct the details of his own destiny.

Eugene Witla grows up in a midwestern town, but in a family
less desperately poor than Dreiser's and not driven to the grim
expedients his own adopted. The boy is sensitive and shy, but
not made to feel painfully excluded from the life around him.
His sisters don't embarrass the family, and his father, though not
an imposing figure, isn't a bigot or a walking ruin. In other
words, Dreiser makes Eugene's a less special case than his own.

Young Witla drops out of school, where he has not done particularly well, works awhile for the town newspaper, and then
moves on to Chicago. There his lessons at an art school bring out
the wisp of talent he has suspected in himself, and determine his
vocation. There also he has his first experiences with women,
including an easygoing model at the school, and then Angela
Blue, an attractive, farm-bred girl, somewhat older than he and
a deeply conventional nature. When he leaves Chicago for New
York he and Angela are somewhat vaguely engaged to marry.

Marry her Eugene finally does, but after his work has begun to
attract attention, and after he has come to know young women
more cultivated and interesting as well as less conventional than
Angela. His early success in painting continues, but he becomes
weary of the conformity of his bride. Angela Blue is Sara White,
of course, and the story continues to parallel Dreiser's own —
though with certain adjustments — through breakdown, temporary loss of belief in his gift, increasing estrangement from his
wife, a job on a magazine, and dismissal from the job when he
becomes too attentive to the daughter of an influential family.

The "Genius" isn't one of those novels in which the protagonist
learns the difference between appearance and reality, and

finally comes to some triumph of self-understanding. Witla seems no wiser about himself at the end than at the beginning. His feeling — clearly Dreiser's also — that an artistic temperament entitles him to exemption from the rules of normal decency and fairness that ordinarily govern conduct, not only in sexual behavior but in social and business activities also, is hard for the reader to share. There is something too self-centered and priggish in the callous way he terminates his liaison with the model, and not much less in his relations with Angela. One gets a feeling that where there is so much ego there should be more talent.

Dreiser wrote most of *The "Genius"* in 1911, while his mind was also occupied by Cowperwood. (His publisher of the moment advised delaying publication.) Cowperwood is as exempt from the rules as Witla, so far as actual behavior is concerned, but he asks for no special treatment beyond what he can force the world to give him. The closest he ever comes to self-righteousness is when, in *The Titan*, he tells Aileen, who has caught him red-handed, that he can't change what he is and that she had better put up with him. The quotation marks in the title of Witla's story may be ironic, but the irony isn't based on a perception that Witla's values are rather confused. As a self-portrait, *The "Genius"* is too self-indulgent.

For the satisfactions Witla wants from art are those that Cowperwood wanted from business: money, luxury, women, position, perhaps even power. On this scale, Witla's gift for painting comes perilously close to falling in the same category as Cowperwood's proficiency in watering stocks.

Outside the context of its moment, *The "Genius"* doesn't seem a particularly subversive book or one to endanger public morals. But on the eve of World War I disquieting reports were abroad that revolt against the reigning mores was sweeping such bohemias as Greenwich Village. Young-lady poets were writing poems about burning candles at both ends, and young artists, back from Paris, were full of new and alien ideas. Very naturally, Dreiser's novel came to the attention of John B. Sumner and the other custodians of virtue. Probably no novel in which sex played such an important role could have escaped, but *The "Genius"* was only the more challenging because it was so serious. Dreiser was no smart aleck to be dismissed as merely frivolous. Such a book had to be suppressed. The total effect of suppression was, of course, to advertise the novel and increase the notoriety of its author.

Thus *The "Genius"* is a modest part in the history of the conflict between Artist and Philistine, American style. Despite its defects it does reveal the awkward situation of the painter or writer — at a point in history when "alienation" had not yet become a cliché. Subtler minds than Dreiser's, from Veblen on, had made many of the same points and analyzed the causes more deeply, but no one else had made such an attempt to show what could be the consequences on an individual life.

Meanwhile the conception of art that emerges from Dreiser's discussion of Witla's work adumbrates the aesthetic of his own fictions. Witla's preferences attach him to the Ash Can school. He likes subjects suggestive of the color, roar, and rattle of the great city, such as earlier painters avoided as inherently ugly — streets on rainy nights, the clutter of crowded squares, freight yards with massive cars, glistening rails, and mighty locomotives. He goes in for strong, if not violent, color, broad and sweeping effects, and the feeling of motion and activity. In brief, as Dreiser puts it, he painted "Life." With due allowances for looseness of language, the identification of art with life is the basis for a realism from which the picturesque is not excluded. There is much talk about "the beauty of life," also, in his autobiographies, as well as the assumption that the power to feel this beauty marks the "poet." In Dreiser's literary practice this can be reduced to the statement that the observation of life as actually lived can be the source of strong emotions. The formula suggests that his realism, as he remarked himself, was romantic.

Only a romantic realist could have written *An American Tragedy.*

Critics agree generally that out of all Dreiser's novels this is the one with which we are most obliged to come to terms. It is either a literary monument or a monumental failure. Over the years readers have come to perceive that *An American Tragedy* is a shrewdly planned structure of calculated effects, that Dreiser knew what he was about, and that little if anything gets into it by chance. It is immaterial, for example, whether or not he borrowed the questions and answers of an actual courtroom dialogue for the trial of Clyde Griffiths; what is material is that the pages sound, and are meant to sound, like a transcription. They have the exact value of an account based on a stenographer's record. Either one grants the validity of the technique or one doesn't. Whichever the decision one's grounds will be ultimately aesthetic: what one wants of a novel is either life, in Dreiser's sense, or what art makes of life. Dreiser imposes the decision on us.

For years he had been collecting news stories about young men who had tried to extricate themselves by violence from transient love affairs like his own with Sara White. He was particularly fascinated by the case of one Chester Gillette, who, back in 1906, had chosen to murder rather than marry his pregnant working-girl sweetheart. Current newspapers had followed Gillette's capture, trial, appeal, and execution industriously. A general outline of events and no little detail were there for Dreiser to appropriate.

World War I appears to have deferred the start of the writing. Like many Americans of German blood he was disturbed and uncertain of his sympathies; his participating in the debates between intellectuals that preceded the entry of the United States into the war suggests the extent of his preoccupation. He could, and did, bring together and publish collections of short stories, plays, and essays, but it is reasonable to assume that he had no stomach for undertaking a long piece of work. He waited until 1919.

The procedure could not be quite the one he had used for Yerkes-Cowperwood, since this time he needed some changes in the central character: the Gillette of the newspapers had to be made more passive, less decisive and brutal; incident had to be manipulated so as to intensify the tragedy; the hero had to dream of success but be frustrated by nature, weakness of character, and sex.

Not that Clyde Griffiths's dream is at all complex. He is not bright enough to think out what he wants. In its elementary form, the dream consists of rising in business until you can have the money, luxuries, pleasures, and, especially, women you want — "a good time," as Clyde thinks of it; "the better things," according to Dreiser. Clyde would like to be like his uncle, who owns a factory in Lycurgus, New York, or like his cousin, who will one day inherit it and meanwhile drives a car of his own. He would like to sport about with a wealthy, glamorous girl like Sondra Finchley. For wanting nothing better than this he ends in the electric chair.

His parents are street preachers who run a "mission" in Kansas City, and who live a grubby and mean life; they are rigidly religious and dirt poor. He leaves school as soon as he can, and eventually gets a bellhop's job in a flashily luxurious hotel. The glamour he sees about him is everything home isn't. Dimly he wants something like it for himself, just as he wants to play about with the other bellhops and their girls. The fun ends abruptly when a group of them make off with a car for a joyride and manage to run down a small child. Clyde has to disappear.

The early version in which Dreiser drew so many details from his own youth had to be abandoned, but the finished text reveals all the familiar patterns of his family life. In addition to the parents, the pregnant sister, and the rest, there is especially the boy who wants something better than he has been born to. After Dreiser-Hurstwood, Dreiser-Cowperwood, and Dreiser-Witla, now comes Dreiser-Clyde — but for luck and a few chemicals.

Working in a club in Chicago, Clyde meets his father's successful brother, whom he persuades to try him in a job at the factory in Lycurgus, near Utica. In Lycurgus the Griffithses are people of standing; they do as little for this unimpressive relative as decency requires. Clyde lives in drab lodgings, works at a monotonous job, watches his young cousins and their friends from a distance, and learns how wide a gap money can create. He is desperately lonely, but determined to win acceptance.

Here the story falls into another familiar pattern. Loneliness prevails over ambition, and he begins what he intends to be a passing affair with Roberta Alden, a farm girl who has come to work in the factory. She is his reality; the dream remains one of sharing the life of the local smart set and having a girl like glittering Sondra Finchley. By the time he learns that the group is beginning to accept him because Sondra finds him interesting, he learns, also, that Roberta is pregnant.

When she insists on marriage, Clyde panics at the loss of his evaporated dream. Other expedients failing, he forms a half-baked plan of contriving an accident and lures her to a lonely lake in the Adirondacks. Actually the accident that occurs is genuine: Roberta rises in their rowboat and lurches toward Clyde; he hits her unintentionally with his camera; they overturn; a gunwale strikes her on the head and she drowns. Clyde leaves her in the water, wanders about the country awhile, and then joins his rich friends at their summer resort.

His movements have been so inept that the law traces him easily to Lycurgus and back, turning up new evidence at every stop. Clyde is held for murder. An ambitious district attorney has done his work well: letters Clyde has forgotten to destroy, marked travel folders, his behavior where the couple stopped on their way to the lake, what he took with them in the rowboat, and the transparent falsehood of the story Clyde's lawyers cook up for him combine to hide the one fact that might save his life: that he had lost the will, or the nerve, to kill her before Roberta stood up in the boat. The jury finds guilt in the first degree. When both his appeal and a plea to the governor fail, Clyde is executed.

Many readers have complained that Part III of this novel, devoted to the events that follow the drowning, is too long and too painful. But given Dreiser's intention, what else was possible? As is entirely clear at the end, everything in the story is

pointed, from the beginning, toward the electric chair. Clyde i
caught by his family's circumstances, by his ignorance and inex
perience, by his unintelligence, and most of all by his dream o
success. Roberta's pregnancy is almost an afterthought of fate
This trap is a machine, and it is of the essence that its movemen
should not accelerate: it needn't hurry for fear of losing its vic
tim. It is in Part III that we realize fully how unaccidental th
seeming accidents of Clyde's life have been.

Actually the trap is life itself. For some years Dreiser had bee
deeply interested in the work of Jacques Loeb, the physiologis
whose studies of elementary forms had led him to the conclusior
that any life is a simple matter of mechanics. Expose a flower t
light, a chemical change takes place within the plant tissues, an
the flower turns its head. Dreiser not only read Loeb's writing
but also corresponded with him, and with passing time turnec
from the determinism of "laws" and "forces" he had learnec
from the nineteenth-century British toward a mechanistic posi
tion of his own. If life in a plant or a fruit fly can be explained a
the functioning of a machine, then why not the more comple
forms of life and ultimately the universe as a whole? Loeb him
self had recommended to psychologists that they investigate th
chemical bases of behavior. Years afterward Dreiser was stil
warmly interested in what Loeb had done. It would be hard t
doubt that the theory of mechanism stirred his imaginatior
when he was writing *An American Tragedy* and affected his basic
visceral feeling of life. Not only is Clyde Griffiths caught in a
machine, he is a machine — or part of a universal one.

The paradox of *An American Tragedy* is, of course, tha
machines do not weep over their condition.

Henry James complains because Flaubert confided the role o
"central moral consciousness" to such "mean" and uninteresting
characters as Emma Bovary and Frédéric Moreau. Obviously th
same criticism would apply to Dreiser's novel — if it were indeec
true that the only people with a story worth telling are those
gifted with intelligence fine enough to understand the mora

implications of what happens to, and around, them. Clyde
Griffiths is just not morally conscious. Like most of the population of Dreiser's novels, he lives on a plane where moral alternatives aren't visible. He never perceives the tawdriness of his
dream of success. In a sense, Dreiser manages to place the moral
consciousness not in a character, and not in the omniscient narrator, but in the reader.

However repellent a free animal may be, in a trap it becomes
an object of pity. Pity is the dominant emotion of *An American
Tragedy*, not for Clyde alone, but for the mother who writes
sob-sister reports of his trial so that she can earn the money to be
there and goes on an improvised lecture tour to raise more
money for the appeal; and for the poor, ignorant farmers who
are the parents of Roberta Alden; and for Roberta herself; even
for Clyde's weak, incompetent father; and for the poor, dumb
victims of the American Dream, everywhere.

The nice critics who complain that to win us over Dreiser has
to appeal to the morbid fascination that keeps us panting over
the daily accounts of sensational murder trials may not be wholly
wrong. But what has Clyde done worse than believe, however
dumbly, what he has been taught to believe, and want what he
was supposed to want: money, the kind of life one sees more
fortunate people lead, love? His excuse is Eugene Witla's: if
American life had proposed less sleazy satisfactions he would
have aimed at them. In this sense only, the title of this novel is
appropriate. Clyde may be cubits beneath the stature of a tragic
hero, but America is big enough to have a tragic flaw.

Judged by standards much less stringent than we apply to
James and Flaubert, *An American Tragedy* is not a well-made
novel. Even H. L. Mencken, for years Dreiser's stout supporter
— and who had vigorously defended the earlier novels — found
it too long and rambling. It puts many burdens on its reader; the
dialogue is awkward; the pace is slow. In contrast, the other
great American novel whose hero is killed by his dream of success is written in neatly constructed scenes, and has Nick Carra-

way in it to judge it for us and to tell Jay Gatsby that he is finer than the Buchanans. But one doesn't finish *The Great Gatsby* with sorrow in one's heart. Neatness may not be the ultimate criterion.

Actually, Dreiser's craftsmanship is of a higher order than his critics willingly admit. His basic procedure has to be situational irony, since so much of the effect depends on the reader's understanding better than the characters do what is happening to them. Hence the value of a structure of parallel incidents: the pregnancy of Clyde's sister in the early part and Roberta's pregnancy; the accidental death of the child the joyriders run down and the accident on the lake; the similar scenes with which the novel opens and closes, with the Griffiths family out evangelizing on the sidewalk. Such examples can be multiplied indefinitely. Other ironies are produced by Clyde's wrong estimates of people: his models among the bellhops in Kansas City, whom he takes for experienced men of the world, the reader recognizes as uncouth louts; the uncle he considers a tycoon is in truth a timid small-town businessman somewhat overawed by big-city surroundings; Sondra, his dream woman, actually expresses the full content of her mind in the most repulsive baby talk. For the sake of irony Dreiser is even willing to stretch credibility severely: the farmer from whom Clyde asks directions when he is out driving with his rich friends turns out to be the father of Roberta. With these he devises parallels of language and echoes, such that his reader is reminded of earlier incidents when he learns of later ones, which create something like a fabric of constant cross-reference. How carefully Dreiser planned his work must be obvious. A novel about confused characters, as one critic has said of this one, is not necessarily a confused novel.

At fifty-five, Dreiser had become a public figure. His attitude toward any matter of general interest became news. He had never been one to avoid exposure. The essays of *A Traveler at Forty* (1913), the miscellany called *Hey Rub-a-Dub-Dub* (1920), and *A Book about Myself* (1922) had exhibited his personality, directly or indirectly, from various angles. Now *Dawn* revealed the story of his youth, with great frankness and occasional charm, but also with perceptible self-indulgence. Over the years he had inclined increasingly toward socialism—which may be why society seems more clearly at fault in *An American Tragedy* than in the earlier novels — and he now became repeatedly involved in conspicuous liberal causes.

Few seem to have found his personality a winning one. He made heavy demands on his friends and was easily hurt by them, even when they had been as generous as Arthur Henry and H. L. Mencken. Dreiser and Henry had met in Toledo, where the latter was on the staff of the *Blade*, and the friendship had blossomed rapidly. Henry invited Dreiser and Sara to spend the summer of 1899 in Maumee, where, with Henry's encouragement, Dreiser began *Sister Carrie*. Henry helped revise the manuscript; scholars even believe that some of the holograph is in his hand. Later he aided Dreiser to find work in New York and advised him in his dealings with Doubleday. Relations remained warm until 1904, when Dreiser spent part of his vacation as Henry's guest on an island in Long Island Sound. Henry was between marriages, and Dreiser may not have taken to the new lady. Whatever the cause, he became an awkward companion and put a grave strain on his welcome. Henry, doubtless annoyed, made him a character in a novel, *An Island Holiday*; Dreiser recognized the unflattering portrait and the friendship ended for all time.

With Mencken his relationship lasted longer — from 1907 until Mencken reviewed *An American Tragedy*—and the rift between them was later patched up, but the pattern is similar. The men corresponded cordially for years. Mencken was generous with advice and helpful with ideas. He praised Dreiser's books privately and in print, and stormed at the critics who neglected them. But one unfavorable review was enough to cancel everything. As still other friends, like the British publisher Grant Richards, had learned, the kinder one was to Dreiser the easier it was to wound him.

His stands on foreign affairs were timed as if he wanted them to be unpopular: he delayed condemning the Nazis until after his countrymen had done so almost unanimously; he persisted in trying to join the Communist party — which rejected his applications so long as Earl Browder had a say in its affairs — years after the Russo-German nonaggression pact of 1939 had disabused American liberals about the idealism of the Kremlin. Even favorable critics thought him wrongheaded.

Abstract thinking had never been his forte. His year at Indiana University had not taught him to read critically. He never learned to distinguish science from pseudoscience. Students detect echoes of Herbert Spencer, for example, in his novels, mixed with fragments of psychological theory according to which dwelling on pleasant or unpleasant thoughts induces the formation of corresponding "anastates" and "katastates" in the psyche. This he had culled from the writings of a certain Elmer Gates, who practiced "psychology and psychurgy" in Chevy Chase, Maryland. As he grew older his respect for science seems only to have increased, but what he said about it only added to his reputation for confused thinking.

The truth was that he had grown old. His friends were dying off. His own health was failing. He was no longer sure of the quality of what he wrote. Yet, almost despite himself, he would finish *The Stoic* and *The Bulwark*.

The story of *The Bulwark* had been in his mind since 1912, when a Pennsylvania Quaker girl, Miss Anna Tatum, had told him about her father's grief over his children's departure from the strict Quaker faith. He had drafted occasional bits of it, but invariably put the drafts aside to work on more pressing subjects. Now in old age he took it up again, turning out a novel that may betray some loss of powers — it is briefer and less loaded with detail than his other stories — but is probably his neatest and sharpest, and humanly a very touching one.

Solon Barnes is a Quaker and follower of the Inner Light who comes from humble beginnings on a Maine farm to a place of power in a Philadelphia bank, acquiring without loss to his integrity the wife, home, family, and respect of his neighbors which are the fruits of success. A crisis comes when he sees that his colleagues in the bank are following practices which, while within the law, remind Dreiser's confirmed readers of Cowperwood. Guided by the Inner Light, and firm in his principles, he resigns from the bank and retires to his family. But the very principles that have sustained him have opened a gulf between him and his children. He has been rigid and authoritarian. One daughter, embittered by her physical homeliness, finds what satisfaction she can in being an assistant to a professor of psychology at Llewellyn College for Women. The other, like Miss Tatum, abandons the quiet Quaker life for the bohemia of Greenwich Village. His son Orville turns into one of those cautiously conservative success seekers Dreiser could never abide. His second son, caught in an escapade that results in the death of a girl, commits suicide in jail. Then his beloved wife, who has stood by him through everything, dies. Seeing how old he is and in what wavering health, and how much he needs them, his daughters come home to be with him — and discover that he has become a man at peace. He has learned to accept his virtues and his faults in humility. When he dies the Quakers call him the Bulwark of their faith.

On one of his last walks through his rural property, Barnes comes on a small puff adder which, in its fright, rises up like a small cobra. He talks quietly to the tiny snake and it relaxes. Later it slithers fearlessly away across the toe of one of his shoes. The old man is deeply stirred, as his daughters see when he tells them of what happened. Barnes, and Dreiser, have moved out of the world of Frank Cowperwood and his lobster into one where the ultimate verity is not that each order of life preys on the one below it. Life does live on life, he muses as he watches an insect eat a leaf, but this must be part of a universal plan — an order in another sense, corresponding to the feeling of order within him.

That Dreiser's mind dwelt much on such ultimately religious questions in his last years would be clear in any case from the concluding pages of *The Stoic*, where Berenice listens to the teaching of the guru. But whereas in that novel the pages come as a puzzling intrusion, *The Bulwark* is something very rare, especially in American literature — a religious novel of impressive dignity and power.

Thematically, the materials of *The Bulwark* are not new: the family that becomes oppressive, the effect on the children of the father's religious inflexibility, the conflict of moral systems, the meaning of success and the values that constitute it. Three of the children also renew character types that are already familiar. But Dreiser has reversed or displaced his values. Material success is no longer a synonym for success in life. Peace of mind, internal harmony, and love are prime satisfactions. The role of the family is not necessarily to frustrate. Nothing can stop the changes brought by passing time, but time itself can bring the understanding that certain fundamental virtues survive.

On December 28, 1945, Dreiser himself died.

Published a year after his death, *The Bulwark* did little to change critical opinion. It was an old man's book, and perhaps a book for old men. And his voice came from a remote past.

Broad sectors of American criticism had resisted him for years. The "New Humanists" of the teens and twenties had deplored what they called his "determinist naturalism" and kept up a defense of established morality that frightened off several publishers besides Doubleday. The James revival of the thirties had attached supreme value to the kind of novel Dreiser was least able to write. His old-fashioned technique didn't lend itself to the vivisection of the New Criticism. The metropolitan "Liberal Intellectuals" had small patience with a novelist who, they held, wrote poorly because he thought poorly. In the two decades between *An American Tragedy* and *The Bulwark*, a generation of technicians like Faulkner, Hemingway, and Fitzgerald had changed ideas about what could be done with the novel as a form. The increasing trend away from realism, beginning at the end of World War II, probably predisposed younger critics to see Dreiser's novels only as vast accumulations of detail, undigested and unformed by any controlling imagination.

The resistance had never been unanimous, of course. From early on there had been Mencken. V. L. Parrington had admired Dreiser, as is evident from an unfinished chapter in the last volume of his influential *Main Currents in American Thought*. Even when Dreiser's stock was at its lowest, the thoughtful and independent Alfred Kazin broke through the clichés of critical disapproval to do him justice in *On Native Grounds* and again in introductions to the reprints of several of the novels. F. O. Matthiessen, after writing luminously about the Jameses, undertook to write a monograph which would offer a balanced view of Dreiser and, indeed, does so, even though left incomplete by Matthiessen's death. And most recently, Robert Penn Warren, with the combined authority of an eminent novelist and a respected critic, marked Dreiser's centennial with his *Homage to Theodore Dreiser*. It should be added that practicing novelists, from Frank Norris to Scott Fitzgerald, James T. Farrell, John Dos Passos, Saul Bellow, and more lately Warren, have always been more generous in praise of Dreiser than have their critic contemporaries.

It would be gratifying to report that at long last Dreiser had had his due. But is this the truth? The case may be that, after the years that have elapsed, only those who value his work write about him, while the rest care too little to break silence. Even today the Dreiser monument in Terre Haute commemorates not the novelist but the brother who wrote "On the Banks of the Wabash" and "My Gal Sal." As one English student of America, Marcus Cunliffe, remarks in his brief history of American writing, Dreiser remains a special problem for American readers.

Yet he upset the dictum of Henry James, that American life is too thinly textured and culturally unvaried to support the novel, and showed, indirectly, that James was merely indicating the limits of the novel of manners. He shared with Edgar Lee Masters and Sherwood Anderson the somewhat elegiac feeling that even the anonymous, average — or perhaps subaverage — American had his own poignant and significant story. The everyday ordinariness of his people makes his so-called naturalism very different from that of Frank Norris. Norris's notion of naturalism emphasized the abnormal character — Vandover, McTeague — treated in realistic detail but seen through the sensibility of the romantic, and thus infallibly as material for melodrama. Dreiser's people have absolutely nothing of "the beast within," and are not monsters: no Dreiser character, for example, has the innate malevolence of S. Behrman, whose ominous shadow darkens the action of *The Octopus*. For Dreiser, human affairs are always of human size, even when they involve the "Titan," Frank Cowperwood. What happens to the people in his novels could happen to anyone.

Consequently he brought our naturalistic novel into closer similarity to European realism than to the theory-bound oeuvre of Zola. For all of Dreiser's interest in science, science has nothing directly to do with the interest of his stories. The physical environments of his characters aren't animal habitats in the biological sense so much as human situations. As he was deeply aware, himself, he looks back to Balzac.

Yet his achievement is different in nature from Balzac's. Dreiser's novels don't attempt to picture a society or account for the way it works. If he was aware of the broad variety of human types that constitute a world, he made no attempt to represent the variety in his books. Even the most indulgent of his adherents must admit that the secondary figures derive their interest less from what they are than from their relationships to the principals. Pushing the similarity with Balzac too far obscures the basic fact that Dreiser was a master of case histories.

Failure to draw some such distinction has led European readers to assume not only that these cases are typically American, and fully representative of American life, but also that there is little more to American life than what they represent. Marxist critics in particular have used Dreiser's novels as a stick for beating their effigy of American capitalism, holding capitalism responsible for the monotonous cultural poverty to which the novels testify. In the eyes of no few serious students of American literature in the European universities, who forget that when

Dreiser finally had some free money, after *An American Tragedy*, he found little better to do with it than play the stock market, he figures among "the artisans of revolt."

Granting that a constant concern with money is an identifying trait of realistic fiction everywhere, Dreiser's realism is set apart by the exclusiveness of the concern. His perspective on life is relentlessly economic: even the artist, Witla, struggles for economic status, and this is true of the rest of his characters whether they concentrate on amassing fortunes or on staying out of the almshouse. Apart from sex, they have few other occupations; they rarely play or indulge in any other gratuitous activity; leisure, to occupy or be bored with, seems foreign to their natures — as indeed does the notion of enjoyment.

The perspective could not but be conditioned by his own experience of life. By birth he belonged to the disadvantaged; in a family that had left an old culture behind without acquiring a new one, and in a rural area, his chances of getting a broader view were small. Nor could such education as he got help greatly. The point is often made that he was among the first American writers whose perspective wasn't that of the East Coast and whose blood wasn't that of the "old stock." This is partly true at best, and perhaps misleading to boot; what is surely relevant is that he grew up in cultural and financial poverty. He tells in *Dawn* of having been sent home from school because the weather was getting cold and he had no shoes.

On this point again he contrasts sharply with Norris, who looks poverty in the eye nowhere in his novels. Vandover loses some inherited wealth, but because of an advancing pathological condition; McTeague's rage for gold is again pathological; the people forced off their ranches are threatened by pauperdom, but we see only two of them suffer its effects, and only briefly, at the very end. At the age when he undertook serious writing, Norris had lived comfortably in London and Paris, and studied at Berkeley and Harvard; Dreiser, at the same age, had barely made it from Terre Haute and Chicago to New York.

By consensus, his most durable novels are those of which he

knew the subjects most intimately: *Sister Carrie, Jennie Gerhardt, An American Tragedy.* Obviously he was just as familiar with the materials of *The "Genius,"* but in this instance the distance between author and subject is wrong. Few critics maintain that the Cowperwood trilogy is of the same quality; one sees so much of Cowperwood, over so many years, and in situations that can't help being repetitious, that unless one shares Dreiser's curiosity about the techniques of fast dealing his hero becomes somewhat too predictable and thus monotonous.

Taken together, these novels don't offer a picture *of* American life so much as pictures *from* American life. The most successful focus on people who start at a disadvantage in the universal competition of a society that substitutes a theoretical social mobility for class distinctions. In this matter of subject Dreiser was not innovating, of course: at least sporadically, the realists of the nineties, especially Crane and Norris, had recognized the interest of such lives as an area for fiction to explore. Dreiser's originality is that, as a native of the area, he could write about life in it without sounding as if he had gone on a slumming expedition. It was in this that he set the example to be followed by the realists of the years between the publication of *An American Tragedy* and World War II — Steinbeck, Farrell, Dos Passos, and the others.

What made him unpopular for a long time was also what made him the kind of novelist he was, that naive innocence of vision that made him report what he saw rather than what he was supposed to see. Good and bad were words; what counted in reality was strength or weakness. Free will was a word; people as he saw them were helpless against external "forces." Morality was a word; the observable reality was nature. He could not resolve such dilemmas, but he could, and did, refuse to sweep them away. Europeans have long been trying to tell us that this kind of novelist should command more than perfunctory respect.

JACK LONDON

Jack London lived (1876–1916) at a time when a dramatically new set of ideas, growing out of the theory of evolution, was changing the course of men's thinking. These ideas stimulated, frustrated, and tantalized London all his adult years. Charles Darwin and Herbert Spencer, messiahs of the new creed, became his intellectual mentors, along with Friedrich Nietzsche and Karl Marx. It might be said that London's very real private struggle with life — which he dramatized in stories so arresting and exciting that they are still read over the world — became for him an epitome of the Darwinian Struggle for Existence, his success an example of the Spencerian Survival of the Fittest.

It is not easy for people today, who have lived with accelerating change through three-quarters of the twentieth century, to grasp how revolutionary and shattering were Darwin's and Spencer's ideas. Before they burst upon the intellectual horizon it was, for example, generally held that the world had been created in precisely the year 4004 B.C. and that the various species of flora and fauna were immutable: a rose, or a horse, or a man had always been the same creature, although variations or developments *within* each kind were possible. Then came Darwin in 1859 to propose that the earth was many millions of years

old and that all extant species had evolved from a common beginning in the sea at some remote moment of time. Design and
order had not presided over this evolution, either; it took place
through the accumulation of infinitesimal and accidental variations. Millions upon millions of individuals (in whatever species)
were wasted in the struggle for existence in which the slightly
superior variation managed to survive and reproduce itself. The
first reaction to this great theory was outrage. Darwin was denounced from countless Christian pulpits by ministers who accused him of maintaining that man descended from monkeys —
although this was one point that he did not urge in his *Origin of
Species*. Even so, the implication was unmistakable, and the very
foundations of religion seemed to be threatened.

If Darwin was the scientist of evolution, Herbert Spencer was
its philosopher. He worked from 1860 to 1903 on the many volumes of his great *Synthetic Philosophy*, a work that undertook a
new synthesis of knowledge based on a new guiding idea, which
was, of course, evolution. Spencer asserted that evolution is the
fundamental law of social as well as physical process: from simple and relatively uniform materials evolve increasingly complex
and specialized structures. He contended that the more complex
forms, whether individual creatures or social organizations, are
the more stable — and thus he saw the social struggle for existence as leading up to the ultimately perfect and stable society.
The evils of child labor, poverty, unemployment, and industrial
warfare which were rampant in Western Europe and America
were justified because they were the means to that perfect society. The fit would survive. Every social and industrial violence,
every outrage caused by competition, was beatified with an aura
of destined good in the philosophy of Social Darwinism. This
put the humanitarianism and idealism of the nineteenth century
under a frightful strain. The blessed prospect of the perfect
society springing from child labor called for specially tinted
lenses.

For many, a central figure in the social struggle came to be the
"superman." In his ruthless quest for power this giant among

men would help along the selection of the fittest by crushing the weak and helpless. The superman so appealed to Spencerian thinking that surely he would have been invented by someone else if the German philosopher Nietzsche had not done so. In fact the term "superman" by itself had the power to inflame the imaginations of many who had never read *Thus Spake Zarathustra*, and the rugged individualist supermen that emerged in popular literature — often ferocious blond Vikings — bore small resemblance to the type of genius Nietzsche described.

At the same time the role of unbridled individualism in the evolution of society was being challenged by the philosophy of socialism. In *The Communist Manifesto* Karl Marx had called upon the workingmen of the world — the supposedly weak and help-less victims of natural selection — to unite and overthrow their exploiters and oppressors, the industrialist ruling classes. According to the followers of Marx, not the superman individualist but the socialist community of workers must be the instrument of evolutionary progress.

It was this complex of ideas, contradictions and all, that captured the strong but untutored mind of young Jack London and permeated his writing. If we look briefly at his early trials in a world of extremes in wealth and poverty, in opportunity and helplessness, we may be led to understand how he came to fight — in his private life and in his work — up and down the line between Social Darwinism and social justice, between individualism and socialism. He had the physical and intellectual powers to make him identify with the superman sweeping lesser beings out of his way in the upward climb to the perfect society; at the same time he had both the experience of privation and the capacity for sympathy to make him take up the cause of all the hapless waifs crushed under a ruthless industrial juggernaut. He was inspired by the American dream of success even while he was living among the most oppressed of outcasts.

London was the offspring of a strange union between Flora Wellman and "Professor" W. H. Chaney. Flora came of sturdy

Welsh stock, but she had been stricken by typhus in her girlhood, and afterwards she was unstable if not unbalanced.
Chaney was an itinerant intellectual who made all knowledge his
province and apparently remembered everything he had ever
read. He always denied the paternity of Jack London, but the
evidence of physical appearance and intellectual quality seems to
be undeniable. Irving Stone, biographer of London who made
considerable study of Chaney's writings, reports that they reveal
"a clear, forceful, and pleasing literary style, an authentic erudi-
tion, courage to speak his mind, a sympathy for the mass of
humanity, and a desire to teach them to better themselves. His
point of view is modern and progressive." Chaney believed that
a proper use of astrology would enable mankind finally to improve the human condition.

Flora was an ardent spiritualist, and séances were offered
along with lectures on astrology and spiritualism while she and
Chaney were living together, from June 1874 to June 1875. Flora
wanted marriage and a child, but Chaney was too distressed by
her violent temper to consider a permanent union; when she
declared that she was pregnant by him and he denied responsibility, she either genuinely attempted to commit suicide or pre-
tended to do so. In any event, Chaney was denounced and ostra-
cized, even by his own family. Flora gave birth to a son on
January 12, 1876, in San Francisco. Eight months later she married John London and named her child for him, John Griffith
London.

John London went into one business after another in California. Although he was a man of character and determination, he
was repeatedly ruined, sometimes by the scoundrelism of a
partner or, more typically, by the irresponsible plans of Flora.
Young Jack lived from hand to mouth, getting a spotty primary
education and working at one job after another to help his indi-
gent family, which finally settled in Oakland. When he was thirteen he bought a small boat and learned to sail on San Francisco
Bay. A year or so later, out of school, he got a larger boat and
became an expert sailor. But just when freedom seemed within

his grasp, John London was injured and Jack became the main-stay of the family. He supported this crushing load by becoming an oyster pirate — one of a gang of small boat owners who raided the oyster beds in the dark of night and sold what they stole to markets and saloons in San Francisco. On his first raid he made as much money as he had been earning in three months of "legitimate" toil.

Jack had a young mistress on his oyster boat, the *Razzle Dazzle*. He also began at the age of fifteen to drink very heavily and nearly killed himself in the process. At the same time he was devouring books taken from the Oakland library. From oyster pirate he became a member of the State Fish Patrol, whose duty it was to arrest illegal fishermen. At seventeen he shipped on a sealing vessel, the *Sophie Sutherland*. After seven months on the Pacific he returned to California and worked about a year at common labor for miserable wages (the Panic of 1893 had caused widespread unemployment, depressing wages). London then joined the march on Washington of Kelly's Industrial Army, which planned to join forces with Coxey's Army in the East to demand government aid for the jobless. His affiliation with the Army was rather loose, for he acted as a self-appointed advance guard, arriving in town ahead of the Army and living in solid comfort for a day or so while the residents debated how to wel-come (or rebuff) the main force when it appeared. The march on Washington failed, and London became a hobo. He served time in prison for vagrancy and saw the seamiest side of Ameri-can life before making his way back to California.

Determined to prepare himself for better than common labor, he entered Oakland High School when he was nineteen. He published in the school magazine, made interesting friends, and through the Henry Clay Debating Society was put in touch with a widening circle of stimulating people. He had become an avowed socialist, however, and when he was thrown in jail for speaking in a park without a license he found that many of his more prosperous new acquaintances drew back. The newspa-pers reported on him as if he were a combination of devil and maniac. In 1896, after a summer of merciless cramming (nineteen hours a day, according to him), he passed the entrance examinations and entered the University of California. There he was popular in a small circle of students and seemed happy, but life never left London in peace. After a single semester he had to leave and go back to work to support his parents, John London's health having failed. But first he had a heroic go (fifteen hours a day) at writing, turning out stories, poetry, essays, and tracts and sending them east with his last pennies. The manuscripts all came back. Jack went to work. After some months of exhausting physical labor he borrowed a considerable sum of money from his stepsister Eliza and embarked for the Klondike in March 1897.

London came home a year later without an ounce of gold but with head and notebook full of plans for stories. It turned out to be the most valuable period of his life. He wrote like a man possessed, gaunt, hungry, twitching. This time he found success. In May, June, and July 1899 his stories and articles appeared in the *Overland Monthly, Orange Judd Farmer, Black Cat, Buffalo Express, Home Magazine, American Journal of Education,* and *The Owl.* In December the *Atlantic Monthly* accepted a long story for the princely sum of $120, and Houghton, Mifflin shortly afterwards contracted to publish a volume of short stories. At the same time London was avidly reading and taking notes on the best writers in the new sciences of nature, man, and society. His dedication to the enlightenment of man and the cause of socialism was terribly earnest and people felt his strength and his sincerity; he made many friends and impressed whomever he met. He and his mother (John London had died) moved into a large house in Oakland that became a center of social, intellectual, and roistering activities; old friends from the sea and the road rubbed elbows with writers, philosophers, anarchists, and literary highbrows.

Three critical events took place in the spring and the summer of 1900. His stories appeared in book form as *The Son of the Wolf* and won extraordinary acclaim. Editor-publisher S. S. McClure asked to become his literary sponsor and took a steady flow of his stories for good prices; McClure also agreed to advance the young author $125 a month while he wrote his first novel. And London gave up the girl he had been courting, Mabel Applegarth, whose mother dominated her and promised to dominate the marriage, and married instead Bessie Maddern. This turned out to be a leap from the frying pan into the fire, for London's mother, the neurotic Flora, now proceeded to make home a hell as she battled with Bess for control of the premises. Moving Flora into a separate house added to London's expenses without solving the problem, for she promptly laid siege to the main house, carried the campaign to the neighbors, and went back to her old business schemes — making new debts for her son.

McClure's "salary" was stopped after October 1901 because the editor did not find London's output holding up to the quality he had expected. But London's reputation was growing. Macmillan accepted a volume of stories about the Indians of Alaska, *Children of the Frost* (1902). He turned out two juveniles, *The Cruise of the Dazzler* (1902) and *Tales of the Fish Patrol* (1905). Lippincott published his first novel, *A Daughter of the Snows* (1902). He worked with one of his few platonic women friends, Anna Strunsky, on a volume called *The Kempton-Wace Letters* (1903) in which he took the scientific-intellectual point of view on various topics and she the romantic-aesthetic position. He set out for South Africa in 1902 to report the Boer War for the American Press Association. When he arrived in London en route to find a cable canceling the assignment, he bought himself shabby old clothes and plunged into London's East End where humanity languished in one of its lowest depths. From his observations he wrote in the three months he was there *The People of the Abyss*, a powerful image of misery. "Year by year rural England pours in a flood of vigorous young life that perishes by the third generation. At all times four hundred and fifty thousand human creatures are dying miserably at the bottom of the social pit called London." When he landed in New York, George Brett, head of the Macmillan Company, promptly accepted the manuscript and agreed to pay London $150 a month for two years while he wrote the novels that he was now confident about.

This was only the beginning. Home in California, he was inspired to write a dog story. What he began as a short story grew and grew until it became *The Call of the Wild*. Macmillan gave him $2000 for all rights to the book in lieu of royalties — much more than London had ever made from a book or expected to make in the near future. By 1900 standards it was more than a generous income for a year. To London, who scarcely three years before had been pleading in vain for five dollars which the *Overland Monthly* had promised him for "To the Man on Trail," it was a fortune. He was happy to accept the offer. Macmillan made a fantastic profit on the arrangement: well over two million copies of the English edition alone have been sold. Even so, it was for the best. According to Irving Stone, "No less than a hundred people a week walked through his front door, enjoyed his hospitality," and occupied his time. It was his salvation to have cash to buy a good sloop on which he could disappear for weeks at a time to write in peace. London also received a substantial sum for *The Call of the Wild* from the *Saturday Evening Post*, which serialized it.

The pattern of prodigious success and prodigious spending was now set. *The Call of the Wild* (1903) was immediately declared a classic. Serialization of *The Sea-Wolf* (1904) brought $4000 from *Century* magazine, and the book sold forty thousand copies in advance of publication. Three weeks after publication it topped the best-seller list. These books plus *The People of the Abyss* (1903) and *The War of the Classes* (1905) were on everybody's lips, Also topics of widespread interest were London's ardent preaching of socialism, his divorce from Bessie in 1905, and his marriage to Charmian Kittredge two days later. He bought a large ranch in California and planned to cruise around the world for seven years, on a ketch to be called the *Snark*, while the ranch's crops were developing. He burned his way through *Before Adam* (1907), going back to the dawn of humanity, and *The Iron Heel* (1907), jumping prophetically forward seven hundred years to a Marxist analysis of the triumph of fascism. Meanwhile he had decided to build the forty-five-foot *Snark* himself, a decision that proved the costliest of his life up to this point. He poured between $30,000 and $50,000 into a boat that was not as good as one he could have bought for $5000. He was cheated and victimized; and yet one cannot escape the impression that he created many of his own troubles. Sailing time was repeatedly put off but finally he limped out of San Francisco Bay in a boat that had been crushed, foundered in mud, almost sunk — and was still far from finished — limped off in worse debt than ever before. The chaotic voyage lasted over two years, taking London to Hawaii, the Marquesas, Tahiti, and Australia, and among other troubles it came very close to ruining his health. Yet during the course of it he wrote a long novel, *Martin Eden* (1909), also *Adventure* (1911), and many stories. Returning to San Francisco in July 1909, his business affairs in a desperate state and his literary reputation at low ebb, he plunged into another nineteen-hour-a-day orgy of work to rehabilitate himself. He came back so strongly that by 1911 he was again earning hugely and enjoying renewed critical acclaim. And again he plunged into new buying and building.

London's land holdings increased in a few years to fifteen hundred acres; he employed more than a hundred people, with a payroll of $3000 a month. While a stone dream palace was a-building, he had a great house called Beauty Ranch reconditioned and set up as a mecca for the guests from all over the world who daily poured into the Glen Ellen station, took the wagon that met every train, and enjoyed the Master's hospitality while they contributed to his knowledge of human nature. He impressed visitors of every level as one of the most brilliant minds they had ever encountered. At the same time he was steadily writing a thousand words a day, with contracts for everything he could turn out. Earning $75,000 a year, he was never less than $25,000 in debt and often $50,000: he was panhandled by acquaintances, milked by people he had never met, cheated by friends who were handling his affairs or his money, and robbed by his employees.

A climax came in 1913 when his magnificent dream castle, called Wolf House, built over four years at a cost of perhaps $100,000, was destroyed by fire shortly before the Londons were to move into it. Someone had apparently done it deliberately — and it was uninsured. During the same year London published *The Night-Born, The Abysmal Brute, John Barleycorn, The Valley of the Moon,* and *The Scarlet Plague* (in serial form), completed *The Mutiny of the Elsinore* (1914), and began *The Star Rover* (1915). But his faith in man was shaken, his drinking increased with his debts, drought ruined his crops, disease plagued his stock, and his own health was failing.

During his last three years he became more businessman and less artist. He said to a young interviewer, "I dream of beautiful horses and fine soil. I dream of the beautiful things I own . . . And I write for no other purpose than to add to the beauty that now belongs to me. I write a book for no other reason than to add three or four hundred acres to my magnificent estate." He was more renowned now for husbandry than for his writing; he laid plans to revitalize California stock breeding and agriculture by scientific methods. He did not care about his debts because he was sure that he was creating a self-sufficient empire at Glen Ellen where he could defy the world. Irving Stone says that he was "a modest megalomaniac, like most native Californians"! His latest biographer, Richard O'Connor, says, "He was gypped, hoodwinked, overcharged and outbargained wherever he went, but the illusion of fiscal capability would not die. Like Mark Twain, and along much the same lines, he was tempted to beat the businessmen at their own game and make himself independent of any income from writing."

But the writing still paid. In April 1914, when the United States was landing troops at Vera Cruz, he was offered $1100 a week by *Collier's* to report events in Mexico. There the pacifist-socialist revealed a changing face. He admired the American army and navy, affirmed that war was fundamental to the human condition, and took the side of American oil interests against the Mexican freedom fighters whom he saw as simply bandits and robbers. He was roused by World War I to declare that Germany was a mad nation that should be destroyed at any cost. Disillusioned with socialism, he now resigned from the party because it blamed the war on international capitalism rather than on Germany.

Increasingly London became a man yearning for the past. His greatest literary resource was, after all, the Klondike. As it receded from the public mind, London found himself falling behind Harold Bell Wright as an entertainer and Theodore Dreiser as avant-garde. He found Charmian increasingly possessive, jealous, childish. But worst of all he was very sick: constant headaches, agonizing uremia and nephritis, rheumatism, dysentery, and excess weight — all apparently due to his heavy drinking and voracious eating. He died from an overdose of narcotics. It was not a premeditated suicide, for he had gone to bed after making plans for the morrow, but apparently an attack of uremia brought more pain than he could bear, and he took the fatal dose in order to escape. At forty he had written fifty books and piled up a burden of debt and illness that he could carry no further.

London's Klondike stories brought strong praise; he was called the successor to Poe, the equal of Kipling, a new voice rising above the prissy sentiment of the genteel tradition. The best of his stories have extraordinary power, which is generated by bold ideas, vigor and concreteness of language, and that combination of mystery and suspense that is the mark of the born storyteller. London jumps into the middle of his situation; he keeps the reader on tenterhooks by withholding facts in a way that makes him participate in the action.

One of London's earliest stories, "The White Silence," written in 1898, published in February 1899 in the *Overland Monthly*, is typical of the best. It introduces the Malemute Kid and his pal, Mason, caught two hundred miles from town in weather sixty-five degrees below zero with starving dogs and inadequate food for themselves. With them is Ruth, Mason's devoted Indian wife, carrying his child, sustained by the hope of seeing the white man's great cities. They experience the White Silence: "All movement ceases, the sky clears, the heavens are as brass; the slightest whisper seems sacrilege, and man becomes timid, affrighted at the sound of his own voice. Sole speck of life journeying across the ghostly wastes of a dead world, he trembles at his audacity, realizes that his is a maggot's life, nothing more." Mason is fatally injured by a falling tree. If they wait for him to die, they will all die. He insists that they go on. After a day of grim waiting, Malemute Kid sends the girl on ahead, shoots the dying man, and lashes the dogs into a wild gallop as he flees across the snow.

"To Build a Fire" (1908) describes in minutest detail a man in the same cold "The White Silence" describes, trying to build a fire to warm himself before he freezes to death. He does get a fire going, but underneath a spruce tree, and the snow falls off the tree and puts it out. Lighting it the second time is the ordeal; his toes are frozen, his fingers too numb to feel the match, and he does not quite make it. The cold rapidly closes in on him. Dreams and hallucinations flutter through his consciousness as the end comes near. The suspense builds to an intense pitch.

"Bâtard" (1902) is a rich concoction of raw elements. Bâtard is the son of a gray timber wolf and a "snarling, bickering, obscene, husky" bitch with "a genius for trickery and evil." Black Leclère buys this dog because he hates him and wants to torment him. But Bâtard had "his mother's tenacious grip on life. Nothing could kill him. He flourished under misfortune, grew fat with famine, and out of his terrible struggle for life developed a preternatural intelligence. His were the stealth and cunning of the husky, his mother, and the fierceness and valor of the wolf, his father." Dog and master are bound by a savage hatred.

In their first major encounter, the dog leaps at Leclère's throat while he sleeps; the master disdains weapons, and in the ensuing fight they almost kill each other: "It was a primordial setting and

a primordial scene, such as might have been in the savage youth
of the world. An open space in a dark forest, a ring of grinning
wolf-dogs, and in the centre two beasts, locked in combat, snap-
ping and snarling, raging madly about, panting, sobbing, curs-
ing, straining, wild with passion, in a fury of murder, ripping
and tearing and clawing in elemental brutishness." Still the dog
does not run away, and the master does not kill him, for they are
linked by their hatred. But the master torments him incredibly
— and with a reason: Bâtard invokes a subconscious death impulse in Leclère: "Often the man felt that he had bucked against
the very essence of life — the unconquerable essence that swept
the hawk down out of the sky like a feathered thunderbolt, that
drove the great gray goose across the zones, that hurled the
spawning salmon through two thousand miles of boiling Yukon
flood."

The climax is a masterpiece of fiendish savagery. And appalling as it is, it is also convincing. The hate lives in London's
intense language; even if that language is somewhat extravagant
— as it certainly is — it convinces. It shows what it was that
enthralled his audience by outdoing readers' wildest dreams of
adventure. Perhaps the single word to describe it is energy: the
writing renders a fierce commitment to life. It was the quality
that made London's personal magnetism, and it vibrated in his
prose.

The three volumes of his Yukon stories that appeared in 1900–
2 — *The Son of the Wolf, The God of His Fathers,* and *Children
of the Frost* — established his reputation. At the same time he was
turning to the novel form, in which his first try produced a
tangle of ideas that merits discussion. As he complained later, *A
Daughter of the Snows* (1902) contains enough material for several
novels. It has a lavish assortment of ideas. To begin with, London asserts determinism: people's actions are the result of forces
working upon them. A man may run, "each new pressure prod-
ding him as he goes, until he dies, and his final form will be that
predestined of the many pressures." He celebrates primor-
dialism, which is another name for atavism; it is the notion that

man's adaptability depends upon his possession of primitive qualities that existed before men became highly specialized and therefore incapable of adapting to new challenges. There is also a subordination of morals to survival. The superwoman heroine of the novel, Frona Welse, glories in physical strength, obeys her own instincts, and makes them the measure of what is good: "Why should she not love the body, and without shame?" Presently, however, these physical survival values are endowed with spiritual qualities: the choice of strength is a choice of good; weakness is evil; for it is the strong who will redeem mankind.

Now a set of ideas is one thing, but dramatizing them in a plotted action is quite another. The action here involves two suitors for the hand of Frona Welse. One is Gregory St. Vincent, who has already won her heart when Vance Corliss arrives in the frozen North, straight from the effeminacies of civilization, yet already responding atavistically to the challenge of the frontier. In order to create suspense, Frona must be blinded to the cowardice and treachery of St. Vincent, and Corliss must stand by heroically silent while she manifests her goodness by her loyalty (noble because misguided) to St. Vincent. Thus the action rests upon standard Victorian pieties. The moral order triumphs when St. Vincent is providentially exposed for the base creature he is, and Frona is free to pledge her heart and hand to Corliss. In the choices that, finally, determine characterization, Frona and Corliss are chaste, loyal, morally courageous, whereas St. Vincent is ruthless, selfish, and dominated by his impulses. These qualities should make him a perfect natural man, but in fact they make him the villain.

London was at the height of his powers in 1902 when he began writing the dog story which he thought of as balancing his account of the vicious husky given in "Bâtard." London finished *The Call of the Wild* in just over a month, his prose flowing pure and sharp with the story line, free from excessive expositions of intellectual theory.

Buck, a pleasant big dog, half Scotch shepherd, half St. Bernard, was stolen from his comfortable home in California and sold. Taken to the Yukon and put into brutal service in a dog team, he quickly learned the law of club and fang, learned that to survive in these arctic wilds he would have to be stronger and more cunning than other dogs on the team. His first big step was stealing a morsel of bacon from the other dogs. In this act his comfortable old morality was rejected as "a vain thing and a handicap in the ruthless struggle for existence," where respect for others might be suicidal. Soon he began to feel some savage atavism stirring his depths, and with the aurora borealis flaming overhead he joined in the old mournful song of the huskies, "old as the breed itself — one of the first songs of the younger world in a day when songs were sad." He fought with the leader of the team and took his place.

After several journeys, Buck was sold to another owner who was going to kill him when he was rescued and cared for by John Thornton. A great love grew between Buck and Thornton, and Buck more than once saved Thornton's life in camp and on the trail. Thornton almost brought Buck back to his old self, and perhaps he would have in time. But Thornton was murdered by Indians while Buck was chasing a moose. When Buck returned to find his dead master and the slayers, he raged through the camp like a thunderbolt, killing several Indians and wounding others. Then he fled into the wilderness, eventually becoming one of a wolf pack.

The story ends with a sentence that shows London at his best, a sentence that must have flowed in triumph from a writer who had come to the end of his purest book: "When the long winter nights come on and the wolves follow their meat into the lower valleys, he may be seen running at the head of the pack through the pale moonlight or glimmering borealis, leaping gigantic above his fellows, his great throat a-bellow as he sings a song of the younger world, which is the song of the pack."

At first glance *The Call of the Wild* seems to be entirely outside any traditional society and therefore free from its tensions, but in fact the narrative reveals various sorts of relations to the patterns of such a society. The values of love and fair play are central to the story; these are traditional and even heroic values. Buck begins happy and satisfied in a setting of comfort and love. Standard justice is betrayed when he is stolen and sold into bondage, but he rises to the challenge by drawing upon qualities of courage and hardihood. These are presented as atavistic, but they are also "moral" qualities that have always been respected in Western literature. And they are given new dignity when Buck responds to the love of John Thornton: the subordination of strength and courage to kindness and love is profoundly rooted in chivalry — which comes from the deep heart of Europe. Vengeance on the "inhuman" Indians who kill Thornton is chivalric too; it reaches back to the Crusades and beyond. So strong are these appeals, indeed, that one may feel a certain regret when Buck finally abandons human society.

Civilized man — especially American man — lives constantly with the call of the wild, but the call is quite different from the thing itself. The call represents the yearning toward freedom and purity that is an aspect of any human involvement; but one retreats in order to return with new strength. Robert Frost, climbing his birches to get away from it all, is very explicit:

> I'd like to get away from earth awhile
> And then come back to it and begin over.
> May no fate willfully misunderstand me
> And half grant what I wish and snatch me away
> Not to return. Earth's the right place for love . . .

If we substitute "society" for "earth" we have the same problem stated more literally. Buck represents the human qualities that are always somewhat sullied in the actual world; he represents revolt and escape; and he enacts his qualities in the story. Running at last, full-throated through the pale moonlight, exulting in his freedom and strength, he "sings a song of the younger world," which is the song of the American dream of innocence and Adamic purity, when man was fresh-minted and society had not bowed him down under its load of falsity. In this light, *The Call of the Wild* shines almost as a lyric rather than a novel. In any event, London here achieved an ideal fusion of form and subject. Since perfect escape is inhuman, it is not so extraordinary that his hero should be a dog.

Three years later London wrote *White Fang* (1906), a companion piece to *The Call of the Wild*. If in the first book he had shown a domestic dog reverting to wolf, the later one told how a wolf was domesticated. White Fang is three-fourths wolf and bred in the wild like a wolf. First he makes the "old covenant" between the wolf and man, which goes back to primitive times, by which the wolf adopts the man-god for protection and food while in turn he obeys and protects his master. White Fang's first covenant, with a harsh Indian, is based on instinct, fear, and respect but there is no love or affection. This covenant is broken during a great famine, restored when the wolf comes back, but broken forever when the master sells him for a bottle of liquor to a man who pits him against a bulldog, for money, and is willing to see him killed. In his second covenant, to his rescuer, White Fang gives himself wholly in love. He ends in just the sort of luxurious comfort that Buck enjoyed at the beginning of his story. *White Fang* is twice as long and perhaps not as bare, tense, and gripping as *The Call of the Wild*; but it is a powerful book.

In these two stories we can see the disguised and projected expression of London's contradictory theories of individualism and socialism. Buck is the individualist who defies society and finally rejects it completely. White Fang is tamed by love and turns from a savage wolf into a loving and home-keeping dog. This is the theory, but the impact of *White Fang* is still in violence, war, and survival by prowess. Most of the book concerns White Fang's struggles with savage nature, Indians, dogs, and white men, struggles that are as harsh as those of Buck in the first story. White Fang as clearly as Buck enacts London's own myth of a man unloved by his mother, unknown to his father, reared in poverty and deprivation, yet growing stronger and craftier because of innate powers that assert themselves and enable him to survive under extreme adversity.

The conclusion is prepared for by a vivid account of the experiences that molded White Fang's heredity while he was becoming fit to survive in the jungle of life: "Hated by his kind and by mankind, indomitable, perpetually warred upon and himself waging perpetual war, his development was rapid and one-sided. . . . The code he learned was to obey the strong and to oppress the weak. . . . He became quicker of movement than the other dogs, swifter of foot, craftier, deadlier, more lithe, more lean with iron-like muscle and sinew, more enduring, more cruel, more ferocious, and more intelligent. He had to become all these things, else he would not have held his own nor survived the hostile environment in which he found himself."

It is a wolf book, in short, and if at the end the wolf is tamed by love he is still a wolf. This merely reinforces one's conviction that London's heart was in individualism rather than socialism. His lip service to the latter is a protest against his early poverty; but he does not dwell on the presumed benefits of a socialist society. He writes instead of the evils of capitalism, the brutality of the industrial world, and the need for violent revolution to destroy them. The peace in his writing is the opulent peace of the great individualist who has beaten the system single-handed and can now afford to relax and live like a lord on his baronial domain. This is the peace of White Fang after he has conquered the world of club and fang by his prowess as a fighter. Near the end of the book White Fang kills a desperate murderer bent on destroying his master's father, thus showing the great power that is his, the power that he relaxes into love and ease but still keeps ready in case there is need for it in the treacherous world.

If White Fang ends where Buck was until he was stolen and sold into bondage, the lesson is that he must be stronger and smarter than Buck if he is to maintain his comfortable retirement in baronial splendor. This was London's dream of Wolf House — built of solid stone to outlast the ages while its master enjoyed the rewards of success. London loved to be called Wolf, signed his letters "Wolf," and had his bookmarks engraved with a picture of a wolf-dog's head. He wrote of animals as if they were people — and of people as if they were animals, recognizing no essential difference between human and animal societies.

White Fang begins with two men traveling through the arctic with dog team and sled, followed by a pack of famished wolves who pick off the dogs, one by one at night, get one of the men, and almost get the other. The point of view then shifts to the wolves and stays with them. Far from being a defect, the shift shows that the struggle for survival prevails in the same terms on all levels of life, with the same need for craft, strength, and courage. It is interesting to note, in this context, that Jack London wrote *The Call of the Wild* immediately after returning from his visit to London's East End, where he had seen society in the harshest terms of dog-eat-dog. Having established himself — largely with that book — he moved toward separating himself from society, buying more land than he could afford in order to have his own self-sufficient domain. In the beginnings of this withdrawal he wrote *White Fang*, symbolically projecting the lonely wolf into his own specially chosen world of love and security.

In *The Sea-Wolf* (1904) London ventured his second bout with a superior human being, this time a superman rather than a superwoman. The story begins with Humphrey Van Weyden, a rather delicate aesthete who has not been exposed to the harsh realities, swept off a ferry crossing San Francisco Bay and presently rescued by Captain Wolf Larsen of the sealing schooner *Ghost*. Humphrey, forced to work as cabin boy, is on hand to study Wolf Larsen. He is terribly strong, totally amoral, contemptuous of civilization's slave morality. He is also something of an intellectual, close to genius, who has read the philosophers and become an avowed materialist. Humphrey finds his powers in atavism: "he is the perfect type of the primitive man, born a thousand years or generations too late and an anachronism in this culminating century of civilization. . . . He was a magnificent atavism, a man so purely primitive that he was of the type that came into the world before the development of the moral nature." Wolf is a fascinating character. He may turn from reciting poetry or expounding philosophy to kick a troublesome sailor in the stomach; he sneers at God and morals;

and yet the sense of waste of his great powers compels the reader's sympathy, as it does Humphrey's. A third of the book is taken up with this exposition.

The plot begins when the *Ghost* picks up a handful of survivors from a wreck. Among them is a beautiful, delicate, genteel poetess, Maud Brewster. Humphrey, with high idealism, falls in love with her; Wolf lusts after her with heartless egotism. Humphrey can no longer be a spectator to Wolf's self-assertion. He escapes with the poetess in a small boat and through stormy seas fetches an island seal rookery in far northern waters. The lovers establish themselves chastely in adjoining cottages and prepare to lay in supplies of seal meat against the long winter. And now the dismantled *Ghost* floats into their little harbor bearing only Wolf Larsen, who has been abandoned by his crew. Humphrey could kill him, but he is inhibited by his morality and by the force of Wolf's personality. Wolf is having terrible headaches, and presently he goes blind. Humphrey sets about readying the *Ghost* to sail, but at night the blind Wolf gropes over the ship and destroys what Humphrey has done. In this suspenseful situation, while Humphrey is trying to summon the resolution to act, Wolf is stricken by paralysis — and presently dies.

The Sea-Wolf seems to turn into a different book with the appearance of Maud; the reason may be that it corresponded with a turning point in London's life. When he was halfway through writing the book, in 1903, he deserted Bess for Charmian Kittredge. Charmian, gushy, flirtatious, an intellectual chatterbox with a fine seat on a horse and an energetic social gaiety, set her traps for London and snared him. The relationship was kept secret for a long period during which the lovers exchanged volumes of fluttery, shrill, passionate letters. Charmian's style invaded Jack's style, and it was never quite the same again. Charmian is the model for Maud, "a delicate, ethereal creature, swaying and willowy, light and graceful of movement. It never seemed . . . that she walked, or, at least, walked after the ordinary manner of mortals. Hers was an extreme lithesomeness, and she moved with a certain indefinable airiness, approaching one as down might float or as a bird on noiseless wings." At about the same time, Charmian was writing to London, "Oh, you are wonderful — most wonderful of all. I saw your face grow younger under my touch. What is the matter with the world, and where do I belong. I think nowhere, if a man's heart is nowhere." And he wrote to her: "My arms are about you. I kiss you on the lips, the free frank lips I know and love. Had you been coy and fluttering, giving the lie to what you had already appeared to be by manifesting the slightest prudery or false fastidiousness, I really think I should have been utterly disgusted. 'Dear man, dear love!' I lie awake repeating those phrases over and over."

London has been roundly criticized for his treatment of Wolf Larsen. Lewis Mumford says that instead of a higher type of human being, he created "a preposterous bully . . . little more than the infantile dream of the messenger boy or the barroom tough or the nice, respectable clerk whose muscles will never quite stand up under the strain. He was the social platitude of the old West, translated into a literary epigram." London later insisted that "the hurried superman of action" was doomed because he "is antisocial in his tendencies, and in these days of our complex society and sociology he cannot be successful in his hostile aloofness. . . . he acts like an irritant in the social body." This seems to be hindsight. Wolf Larsen had to be disposed of because of the new turn the book had taken, toward romantic love.

London later told the story of such a creature more consistently. *Burning Daylight* (1910) is about a comparable (if somewhat less intellectual) frontier superbrute. At one point he rushes into the office of the corporation that is cheating him and forces the squirming capitalists at gunpoint to do him justice. Here the hero represents a natural force asserting itself against the corruption and hypocrisy of the modern world; he gains sympathy and approval. Wolf too is presented as despising and defying the petty viciousness of a business-ridden society and the slave morality that sustains it; but once Maud Brewster took over the novel, London did not know what to do with him. The

conflict with his crew or even with his soul (in the manner of a
Captain Ahab) had to be abandoned. His reappearance at the
seal island, stricken with blindness and paralysis, does not
dramatize the forces presented earlier with so much intensity
The original Wolf could have become involved in an exciting
and significant action.

Startling subjects, a bold narrative line, and the play of new
ideas constitute London's appeal. As the years went by, his personal tie with his reader became an important element as well
He recognized the need for interesting material. He was always
reading, meeting new people, and taking notes by the boxful
He was a tireless observer of events, situations, and matters of
intellectual novelty. His famous Wednesday evening parties,
attended by a parade of bums, grifters, cranks, and intellectuals,
were not merely an indulgence, for these people were a source
of characters and ideas. He even bought plots from the young
Sinclair Lewis to bolster flagging invention. In his search for the
unusual, the attention-catching, however, he increasingly moved
too far from the representative concerns of men into the realm
of fantasy. Without describing his works to tedium we may
profitably follow this trend through a few of his stories, all written before 1906 (and all collected in a book of that year, *Moon-
Face*).

An unsettling story, which joggles the bases of the social struc
ture, is "The Minions of Midas" (1901). A multimillionaire is
blackmailed for twenty million dollars by "members of [the] intellectual proletariat" who remind him that his wealth rests on
power and declare that they will kill a designated person every
week until he pays the sum demanded. He does not pay, "And
week by week, as certain as the rising of the sun, came the
notification and death of some person . . . just as much killed
by us [the millionaire and his secretary] as though we had done it
with our own hands." The millionaire holds out, disbursing "at
the rate of one hundred thousand per week for secret service.'
As the murders continue, he increases it to a quarter of a million.
He offers rewards totaling ten million dollars, but the murders

continue. Then the symbolism is spelled out with a most ingenious ambiguity: "As I said before," the narrator explains, "a word from him and the slaughter would have ceased. But he refused to give that word. He insisted that the integrity of society was assailed; that he was not sufficiently a coward to desert his post; and that it was manifestly just that a few should be martyred for the ultimate welfare of the many." The narrator means by "a few" the people being murdered, but the reader is forced to think of people sacrificed to make capitalism flourish — whether in sweatshop, industrial strife, or wars. The millionaire kills himself in anguish. And now the Minions of Midas speak more explicitly in another letter. They declare, "We are the inevitable. We are the culmination of industrial and social wrong. We turn upon the society that has created us. We are the successful failures of the age, the scourges of a degraded civilization. . . . We meet force with force. Only the strong shall endure." Capitalism has crushed wage slaves, shot strikers; now it is a free-for-all of power against power. So bold a stroke through the foundations of society must have been disturbing in 1901, although subsequent history has made it comparatively feeble.

Straight out of Edgar Allan Poe comes "Moon-Face" (1902), told by a man consumed with hatred for his jolly neighbor. The narrator kills his neighbor's dog, burns his barn, forecloses his mortgage, and finally commits the perfect crime. It is "William Wilson" and "The Cask of Amontillado" compressed into ten lively pages. Out of Mark Twain and the other humorists comes "The Leopard Man's Story" (1903) of how the knife thrower in a circus gets revenge on the lion tamer for looking at his wife. He drops some snuff on the lion tamer's hair, and when at the culmination of his act the latter puts his head in the lion's mouth, the lion sneezes and bites off his head with a *crunch*.

The infatuation with language so characteristic of the period, which seems to assume that anything is funny if it is told in three times as many words as necessary, overflows in "Local Color" (1903) in the account by a philosophical hobo of how he demonstrated that it would cost a town less to entertain a tramp in its best hotel than to arrest, convict, and incarcerate him for the same period. The hobo got thirty dollars for the story from a newspaper editor, put in some "local color" at the request of the editor who was pushing a campaign against the incumbent magistrate — and got sixty days in jail when haled before said magistrate after drinking up his thirty dollars in a brawl at the hoboes' haven. The picture of the magistrate had been too vivid.

Out of Poe, again, and the humorists comes "The Shadow and the Flash" (1903), a story about two brilliant rivals who become distinguished scientists. They compete desperately, whether for honors or women, until finally they take up the challenge of invisibility. One contends that there can be a black so black that it will be invisible because it reflects no light at all; the other seeks a chemical that will make him perfectly transparent. Both succeed, but the first when coated with his black paint has a shadow, and the second when made transparent by an injection emits a flash whenever the sun hits him from a certain angle. They come together in a final fury and kill each other in an invisible battle.

When the situations are thus bizarre, the story leads to a conflict and choice likely to be equally bizarre; and the characterization which is the product of that choice will be fantastic. The jealous geniuses of "The Shadow and the Flash" cannot be taken seriously as people. And the same is true where the character is so enveloped in mystery that we can't know what makes him tick. For example, in "Planchette" (1906) a man endowed with godlike beauty and charm refuses after four years to disclose the mystery that prevents him from marrying the girl he deeply loves, who loves him as intensely. Two horses try to kill him. Then at a planchette (Ouija board) session, the spirit of the girl's father, who was a cavalry officer, promises to kill him. A day or so later another horse, famous for its steadiness, suddenly leaps over a cliff, carrying the man to his death. There is no explanation in this hair-raising tale, just suspense and mystery and a rich sensual throb that is sustained between the girl and the man up to a moment before his death. The assumption that the spirit of the father had some special influence over horses is not explanation enough.

Several qualities of *The Cruise of the Snark* (articles 1906–9, book 1911) strike the reader immediately. There is, first, the evidence that London has a public to whom he speaks directly and intimately. Like Mark Twain he assumes that the smallest detail of his life will be of interest. He talks about Charmian and Roscoe Eames (Charmian's uncle and nominal navigator on the *Snark*) by their first names as if the reader shared his connections with them. He builds suspense and emotional involvement for the reader over the question of how he (London) felt about every item in the calendar of delay and fraud that marked the building of the boat. A whole chapter tells how the months crept by while he lost bet after bet on his sailing date, spent $30,000, and was frustrated at every turn. The suspense grows from his original description of the wonderful Nova Scotia deck planks, the watertight compartments, the special engine, the power windlass, and all the custom-forged fittings to his successive discoveries that the planks were not full length, the compartments leaked, the engine was not secured properly (it broke loose from its bed and was carried to Hawaii as ballast), and the windlass and fittings were inferior (the windlass broke on first trial and the fittings snapped like matches). He maintains an air of happy trust and exuberance, leaving the reader to grind his teeth over the outrages London is suffering.

One feels here the pressures on a man trying to live three or four lives at once. Love, business, sailing, and debt consume London's time and vitality while forcing him to grind out his thousand words a day even if he has nothing to say. Thus a very little fact is stretched out over page after page with humorous repetition. We are told that the *Snark* won't heave to in a high wind; then this monstrous defect is rehearsed as every sail in the locker is tried. A whole chapter quotes letters from people all over the world who volunteered for the cruise. How London mastered the mysterious art of navigation in a couple of afternoons is told, then retold.

To sustain creation from almost nothing implies a powerful talent, and the more one reads the more one is struck by London's control of the language. He can evoke sharp images,

explain complex procedures, describe intricate mechanisms and
processes with economy and clarity. In Hawaii he does not
merely admire the Kanakas surfing; he goes into the theory of
wave motion and explains it in detail: "The face of that wave
may be only six feet, yet you can slide down it a quarter of a mile
or half a mile, and not reach the bottom. For, see, since a wave is
only a communicated agitation or impetus, and since the water
that composes a wave is changing every instant, new water is
rising into the wave as fast as the wave travels. You slide down
this new water, and yet remain in your old position on the wave,
sliding down the still newer water that is rising and forming the
wave. You slide precisely as fast as the wave travels. . . . If you
still cherish the notion, while sliding, that the water is moving
with you, thrust your arms into it and attempt to paddle; you will
find that you have to be remarkably quick to get a stroke, for that
water is dropping astern just as fast as you are rushing ahead."
This passage is an epitome of London's appeal: he involves the
reader in an intellectual adventure that is just difficult enough
to keep him alert with the effort to understand. The rush of
thought is of a piece with the rush of discovery and adventure;
here it surges along with the foaming racing sea. London not
only draws the reader into the intellectual theory but also makes
him participate in the adventurer's first incompetent attempts to
master the skill. An intimacy is established thus and maintained
through the book, as London enacts the reader's romantic
dreams and timid impulses.

London's heart goes out to the lepers of Molokai, and he
explodes the myth of their horror and despair by showing how
active and happy they are in their colony. The description of the
sixty-day passage, without sight of smoke or sail, from Hawaii to
the Marquesas rivals *Kon-Tiki*. At Nuka-hiva he follows Melville's
footsteps into the Valley of Typee, to find those magnificent
people almost exterminated by white men's diseases. The closing
paragraph of this chapter, although it has one or two false notes,
ends with a cadence that links it to the best of American prose:
"The feast ended, we watched the moon rise over Typee. The

air was like balm, faintly scented with the breath of flowers. It was a magic night, deathly still, without the slightest breeze to stir the foliage; and one caught one's breath and felt the pang that is almost hurt, so exquisite was the beauty of it. Faint and far could be heard the thin thunder of the surf upon the beach. There were no beds; and we drowsed and slept wherever we thought the floor softest. Near by, a woman panted and moaned in her sleep, and all about us the dying islanders coughed in the night."

As the party moves into the Solomons, they are overwhelmed with fever and various sores and infections; and so while the material grows richer, the ability of the author to handle it weakens. Hair-raising adventures are lost under the welter of medical detail. One wonders how the Londons survived this trip that was "all for fun." Jack in fact finally had to abandon the cruise and wound up with a long stay in an Australian hospital.

London drew heavily upon the romantic myth of himself for interest in his books. From the very first story of the Yukon, he was living violence, adventure, and triumph vicariously for the common reader. What is frankly central to the appeal of *The Cruise of the Snark* lurks in varying degrees very close to the surface in other books that his readers took as autobiography.

For London the living and writing became almost one, but it may be said that the writing really came first in the sense that it defined and directed the living. Just as the anguish of Hamlet's

> If thou dids't ever hold me in thy heart,
> Absent thee from felicity a while
> And in this harsh world draw thy breath in pain
> To tell my story

is unimaginable without the language in which it comes to us, so London's agonies had to be expressed if they were to achieve fullness and intensity. Hamlet of course lives only in the poetry. There he only is. But the same is almost true of a Jack London. He exists in his books as he writes, as he expresses, as he discovers the meanings and intensities for which he could not even yearn without language. He grows in the books and lives his evolving role between them, as the man in the flesh enacts the man in the books. London's biographers comment in surprise on the fact that he could be almost dead with thirst on the becalmed *Snark* and stagger down to the cabin to write a story about a sailor dying of thirst. But he had to write the experience before he really knew it.

The interest in *Martin Eden* (1909) is richest if we read the book to see what sort of sense London could make of the intellectual and psychological materials that he knew best in himself. The long "novel" begins with an uncouth sailor entering the luxurious home of a cultured friend (whom he has, characteristically, saved from a gang of toughs). His wide shoulders and lurching walk make a space large enough for six people seem too narrow; he breaks out into a sweat of anxiety. An amused glance from the friend "burned into him like a dagger-thrust," for "under that muscled body of his he was a mass of quivering sensibilities." The exposition proceeds to show a mind of dazzling intensity that jumps from the present event to evoke brilliant images of past experience. While he talks painfully to the friend's ethereal sister (Ruth Morse), scenes of brawls, whores, engine rooms, prisons, and wild seas surge and tumble before his mind's eye. The excitement grows in a new dimension as the frail girl responds — and is shocked by her response — to his superb body while she is horrified by his grammar.

Martin Eden is famished for knowledge, power, life — and the story plunges straight into his quest for them. He goes on to great successes, to disillusion, to suicide. But the struggles surging through the mind of the author break the confines of the single story he had to write and so confuse the characterization of the hero. London was indignant with his notices and said "Not one blessed reviewer has discovered that this book is an attack on individualism, that Martin Eden died because he was so utter an individualist that he was unaware of the needs of others, and that, therefore, when his illusions vanished, there was nothing for him for which to live." This sentence may describe London better than his hero, for while creating his self-destructive individualist London was also creating and exploring the mystery of his own famished spirit that could never rest while it could never be satisfied, because it did not understand (and could not understand) that its trouble was rooted in his fatherless, homeless, famished childhood. And London edits his own life in ways that tell more than he could have realized. The anemic Mabel Applegarth is transformed into a Ruth Morse who is beautiful and proud and harries Martin Eden because he is not respectably employed. Jack broke with Mabel because she could not get free from her dominant mother. Money was not the problem. Ruth breaks her engagement when Martin is reported in the press as having made a flaming socialist speech (falsely, for it was a Nietzschean attack on socialism). Bessie Maddern does not appear in the book. And Ruth evolves somewhat. Late in the story she offers to become Martin's mistress so that she can convince him of her sincerity and persuade him to marry her. This is a disguised Charmian London, who did indeed seduce Jack and then lured him away from Bessie by holding herself at a distance until he got his divorce. Charmian was five years older than Jack; Ruth is three years older than Martin.

Martin Eden turns into a daydream of prowess, wish-fulfillment, and revenge. London's own problems are transmuted into glories of beauty, strength, and intelligence pitted against supernal outrages. His face "was once as white as the underside of his arm; nor did he dream that in the world there were few pale spirits of women who could boast fairer or smoother skins than he — fairer than where he had escaped the ravages of the sun." As, fired by love, he begins to educate himself, "She detected unguessed finenesses in him . . . and was often puzzled by the strange interpretations he gave to mooted passages [in Browning's poetry]. It was beyond her to realize that, out of his experience of men and women and life, his interpretations were far more frequently correct than hers. . . . He was tortured by the exquisite beauty of the world . . . He was drunken with unguessed power," which is not only creative but also physical, for "The old familiar blaze of health rushed out from him and struck her like a blow. It seemed to enter into her body and course through her veins in a liquid glow, and to set her quivering with its imparted strength." Inspired by her, "he spent the day in the white-hot fever of re-creating the beauty and romance that burned in him." Hints of megalomania abound, as when "he rented a typewriter, and spent a day mastering the machine" — rather in the manner that the young Mozart is said at the age of six to have picked up a violin and performed a part in his father's string quartet.

The romance with Ruth, floating on his inchoate but enraptured vision of the beauty of the world, bumps against her cultured disdain for excess — which is, however, not able to suppress her physical response to his electrifying power. "Mentally she was in a panic to shoot the bolts and drop the bars into place, while wanton instincts urged her to throw wide her portals and bid the deliciously strange visitor to enter in." She would like to kill the male in him and yet have it too, but under her genteel control and guided into profitable and respectable channels. Consciously, however, she recoils from physical contact with a man who has lived through the imagined and unspeakable evils of a sailor's world. Finally her mother-dominated spirit gives in to her burgeoning womanhood and she discovers a passionate (but of course chaste) love for Martin, even though she remains spiritually absorbed, self-centered, uncommunicating, hoping he will give up his mad writing and get a steady job.

Martin toils on, knowing that he is Ruth's intellectual superior, as he also knows that inspiration alone is not enough and that his genius must be supported by knowledge. Now "His was deliberate creative genius, and, before he began a story or poem, the thing itself was already alive in his brain, with the end in sight, and the means of realizing that end in his conscious possession." His studies led to a synthetic essay. "It was brilliant, deep, philosophical, and deliciously touched with laughter. . . . The writing of it was the culminating act of a long mental process, the drawing together of scattered threads of thought, and the final generalizing upon all the data with which his mind was burdened." Such ability and application should have been recognized, but the weeks of heroic toil went on and on, while the rejection slips accumulated and the money dwindled until Martin had nothing but potatoes to eat. He was out of his head with starvation and fever when the big letter came (not from the *Black Cat* as in London's life, but from the *White Mouse*) offering him $40 for a story.

The action of this novel drags along as Martin's intellectual explorations are spelled out, for these are used to represent the period of his apprenticeship, in place of London's own Klondike adventures, months on the road and in prison, assault on high school and university, and days at sea. The effect is to make the period of his self-education more concentrated and intense than the corresponding years of London's life, but also much more limited in activities. The debaters, socialists, and professors in Eden's life are met at Ruth Morse's home, and he is more than a match for them all, even for the most brilliant professor in the university, whose intellect he diagnoses as deficient in biological insights. "Professor Caldwell sat for a full minute, silent and fingering his watch chain. 'Do you know,' he said at last, 'I've had that same criticism passed on me once before — by a very great man, a scientist and evolutionist, Joseph Le Conte. But he is dead, and I thought to remain undetected; and now you come along and expose me.'" The rest of the upper class Martin considers parasites, but he is aligned with them because he is an avowed individualist, not, as London thought he himself was, a socialist.

He does not stay on their side, however, because he rapidly sees what shams and leeches they are. In ruthless discussions with pompous bankers and judges at the Morses' dinner table, he confutes them with facts and abuses them with eloquence. He makes one brilliant insight here into the future of American politics. "'You persuade yourself,'" he tells the judge, "'that you believe in the competitive system and the survival of the strong, and at the same time you endorse with might and main all sorts of measures to shear the strength from the strong. . . . It's on record, your position on interstate commerce regulation, on regulation of the railway trust and Standard Oil, on the conservation of the forests, on a thousand and one restrictive measures that are nothing else than socialistic.'" These predictions, milder than the prophecy of world fascism in *The Iron Heel*, are much nearer the truth — although they are not essentially different.

Eden meets an incomparably brilliant nihilist named Brissenden, who argues that the critics, the publishers, and especially the magazines are despicable haters and destroyers of literature. Brissenden writes the greatest poem of the century ("It was a mad orgy of imagination, wassailing in the skull of a dying man who half sobbed under his breath and was quick with the wild flutter of fading heart-beats"), which he refuses to sully by publication. He begs Martin to give up his quest for wealth via the contemptible magazines: "'Love beauty for its own sake . . . and leave the magazines alone. Back to your ships and your sea — that's my advice to you, Martin Eden. What do you want in these sick and rotten cities of men? You are cutting your throat every day you waste in them trying to prostitute beauty to the needs of magazinedom. If you got [fame] it would be poison to you. You are too simple, too elemental, and too rational, by my faith, to prosper on such pap. . . . It is not in what you succeed in doing that you get your joy, but in the doing of it. . . . Beauty hurts you. It is an everlasting pain in you, a wound that does not heal, a knife of flame. Why should you palter with magazines?'" Brissenden expresses what Martin believes with increasing conviction, but this is very far from the real Jack London, who always wrote for the market and bragged of doing so. Martin Eden, too, studies the magazines to discover the formula of success; his later despair over the public's failure to appreciate the utter passionate beauty of his work is as phony as a three-dollar bill. London's wish-fulfillment makes Martin's motivation inconsistent, his characterization a failure.

Brissenden takes Martin to an enclave in the slums where a group of intellectuals who have renounced the bitch-goddess success and all that goes with "respectability" engage in far-ranging discussions that embrace all knowledge. The words describing the brilliance of these men are as excessive as the actual discussion is sophomoric: "He swiftly saw, no matter upon what they talked, that each man applied the correlation of knowledge and had also a deep-seated and unified conception of society and the Cosmos . . . Never had Martin, at the Morses', heard so amazing a range of topics discussed. . . . Martin was struck by the inside knowledge they possessed. They knew what was never printed in the newspapers — the wires and strings and the hidden hands that made the puppets dance." The debate ranges Locke, Berkeley, Hume, Kant, Spencer, and Haeckel against each other through two pages of highfalutin oversimplification. It provides the perfect footnote to the statement that London was an uneducated man of genius.

At a socialist meeting, Martin brilliantly expounds the Nietzschean attack on socialist slave morality which protects the weak and prevents evolutionary development. He is reported in the papers as a socialist; Ruth breaks their engagement; he is denounced by his neighbors, his family, and the tradesmen who have given him credit. Brissenden commits suicide, leaving Martin alone and really at the end of his rope. He is in a daze of exhaustion, despair, disappointed love, and, most of all, utter disillusion with the stupidity of critics and intellectuals.

Then a long-overdue check comes, and Martin uses it to send out all his manuscripts for a final try at the market. Success! They are accepted one after another and the money comes in faster than Martin can spend it. A book of philosophy (forsooth!) causes a sensation, sells sixty thousand copies; the publisher sends a blank contract for anything he has either planned or written and responds with a check for $5000 when he writes a title on the blank line. His first and second books now top the best-seller list, week after week, "thus proving himself to be that rare genius, a critic and a creator in one." Still numb, he forgives his enemies, buys a milk farm for his kind Portuguese landlady, allows himself to be interviewed by the reporter who wrote him up as a socialist, and accumulates a fortune without writing another line.

As Martin turns the other cheek to one indignity after another (he finances the two brothers-in-law who forbade him their homes), the effect is of a childish, sulky daydream of revenge. He is an angry infant breaking his toys to spite the grownups. He broods incessantly over the fact that the work was all performed when he was a lonely outcast; now the stinking world wallows at his feet while he smiles in tight-lipped disdain. Ruth's attempt to seduce him is an ultimate abasement that lets him pour out all his disgust for "bourgeois vulgarity." But the question he keeps asking with such tormented intensity — "And what is puzzling me is why they want me now. Surely they don't want me for myself, for myself is the same old self they did not want" — is a question to which he has known the answer all his life: they want him for his fame and his money. Anybody knows that. It's so obvious that it's not worth saying; it makes the ending painfully false; the suicide becomes an act of sulky spite, of childish pique.

Martin Eden has been considered London's best work, but I believe it is among his worst. It lacks aesthetic distance; it lacks the sense of control that comes when a writer has *made* a book. Its author is nakedly, naively, embarrassingly present in its situations. The best of London is to be found in the short stories, *The Call of the Wild*, and *White Fang*.

Burning Daylight (1910) is cut from the same cloth. London plays the Viking hero bearding the pigs of capitalists and making them eat crow; he is heroic as socialist and as individualist. *John Barleycorn* (1913) is an incantation, a solemn ritual of exorcism. London writes in the first person to explain the perils of drink and to tell how he conquered it. The book is wish-fulfillment, for London was far gone in alcoholism when he wrote it and was to be a physical ruin in a year or two more. The psychology of alcoholism is profoundly — if unconsciously — revealed in this book. *The Valley of the Moon* (1913) concentrates on the struggle of a young couple through the social jungle and on to where they leave society and become scientific farmers in their private valley. This book is full of Anglo-Saxon racism, a misbegotten offspring of Darwin and the notion that only a pure breed could be strong. *The Little Lady of the Big House* (1916) is all about Jack and Charmian and Wolf House. Into their Eden comes a friend from Yale who unintentionally falls in love with the heroine. She then finds herself in love with both men. The hero insists that she make a choice freely, and the story descends into bathos; yet one cannot avoid the impression that the sentimental death of the heroine represents Jack's growing impatience with his jealous, frilly, demanding, and irresponsible wife.

London contributed greatly to one myth of the American writer, which he passed from Mark Twain on to F. Scott Fitzgerald and Ernest Hemingway. All these writers (and the line extends thinly back to Poe) tried to live several lives at once and in the attempt sacrificed their lives, their art, or their peace to the excess they attempted. London was like Mark Twain in his grandiose and disastrous business schemes. He was like Fitzgerald in alcoholism and in his involvement with a woman who took so much of his life that she invaded his art. He was like Hemingway in his boyishness, his two-fisted courage, his public display of dangerous living, and even his great capacity for friendship. Like the others, he seemed always to be in a desperate struggle with his writing, so that the extra activities might be regarded as symptoms rather than causes of their frustration.

The classic book about this problem is Van Wyck Brooks's *The Ordeal of Mark Twain*. Brooks maintains that Twain, with an incomparable genius, was frustrated by Puritanism, by frontier distrust of excellence which forced him to be a funny man, and finally by his own sellout to the Gilded Age, which disastrously compromised his art. Brooks says that Twain would have had to become a great satirist if he was to fulfill himself and defeat the Gilded Age. London, in a similar state, did become a satirist. He spent his life discovering and castigating abuses of every sort, from capitalism in all its corrupt manifestations, through organized religion, and on even to bullfighting. And he was confused and frustrated in the same way that Mark Twain was.

It may be suggested that the root of this problem is not what Brooks claims, but is rather the absence in America of an established society that could be taken seriously by the artist because in its manners, customs, and values he found problems about which he could write a rich and steady flow of serious novels of manners. Or perhaps one should say either the absence of such a society or the absence of a *tradition* of taking it seriously. Once a writer like London or Twain has uttered his wild assault on the stupidity of society in general, he is out of material. He must go to the Klondike, or back to the Middle Ages, or into boys' stories, or through the green hills of Africa with rod, gun, and pen, or down into the South Seas; or contrive hoaxes like *Tom Sawyer Abroad*; or bring the devil himself down to discuss what man is; or make fun of Europe; or create a popular myth of himself to exploit. With exotic subjects and intellectual protest he will have the greatest difficulty making plots that move seriously through the center of society, and therefore he will not generally be able to create characters that are representative. They will instead be burlesques, outlaws, brutes, Indians, children, or adventurers.

To make the point by way of contrast, one may look at the career of J. P. Marquand. He did find American society, with all its defects, worth his sustained and serious attention. He was able to write one long book after another dealing with various problems of that society, problems of war, business, love, and so on, that moved right through the heart of American life. Marquand has generally been considered a writer just below the first rank, but the point here is that he was always interesting, always serious, and never in the least danger of running out of materials. It is significant, in passing, that Marquand began with satires — *The Late George Apley* and *H. M. Pulham, Esq.* — but abandoned this tone apparently because its burlesque note faded quickly.

Jack London never wrote a novel of manners, never took the patterns of American society seriously, never found typical problems in it with which he could wholeheartedly engage himself. His stories of the Klondike are valid because the Gold Rush was an actual experience of Americans in an actual part of the continent; the Darwinian struggle for survival was at that time a foremost preoccupation in American thought. His socialist writings are often moving because they take us into areas of misery and deprivation with which modern man is deeply concerned; but this stream soon runs into the sands, compelling the author to invent new fantasies of violence or prophecy. These elements place London in the naturalistic movement, which embraces scientific determinism, Darwinism, the Spencerian philosophy of evolution, and Marxism, all of which in some way reflect the anti-supernaturalism and anti-traditionalism of a presumably scientific approach to human affairs. These all theoretically (although never in practice) renounce the free will and ethical responsibility that underlay the classic well-made novel of manners — and thus contribute to the restless search for form that has characterized the American novel since 1900.

London's special genius appears in his command of detail and pace. He knows how to produce realism and suspense by giving the minutest factual items of a situation — and how on the other hand to jump over large areas of fact and make the reader supply the information or the meaning. He can bring the most seasoned sophisticate to the edge of his chair and have him fidgeting with anxiety as a story builds toward its climax. A good introduction to London is the three-volume *Bodley Head Jack London*. Reading this collection of his best in novels and stories, one must acknowledge that that best is very good indeed.

SHERWOOD ANDERSON

Life, not death, is the great adventure." So reads the inscription engraved on Sherwood Anderson's tombstone in southwestern Virginia in accordance with a request he made not long before his death at sixty-four in 1941. At first glance, the buoyancy of the epitaph seems strangely at variance with the facts of his career. For a few triumphant years after the publication of *Winesburg, Ohio* (1919), Anderson was acclaimed a major figure of modern literature. He was regarded with Theodore Dreiser as a liberator of American letters from the debilitating effects of the genteel tradition. Then, in the mid-1920s, repudiated by critics, abandoned by his early discoverers, parodied by his protégés, he slipped from the foreground, even though his writing continued to influence diverse writers such as Ernest Hemingway, Hart Crane, Erskine Caldwell, Katherine Anne Porter, Henry Miller, William Faulkner, Nathanael West, and James T. Farrell.

Anderson thought humbly of himself at the end as merely a minor artist who had contributed only a minor classic — *Winesburg, Ohio* — to American culture. Still, it was his dedication as an artist that enabled him to sustain his faith in the adventure of life — and fully examined, his career truly justifies his

168

epitaph. It was with grace and justice that Faulkner, responding to an inquiry from a *Paris Review* interviewer in 1956, declared of Anderson's stature: "He was the father of my generation of American writers and the tradition of American writing which our successors will carry on. He has never received his proper evaluation."

The major theme of Anderson's writing is the tragedy of death in life: modern man, lacking personal identity and with his senses anesthetized, has become a spiritless husk unfitted for love of man and community. This perennial theme is common enough in our time, though it was relatively dormant in the late 1910s when Anderson first enunciated it. It became his leitmotiv when, in 1912, at the age of thirty-six, he suffered a nervous breakdown and rejected his past. Thereafter he viewed this event as a symbolic rebirth which had purified him of false values and freed him from the confines of deadening institutions.

The pattern is classic in Western culture. It has recurred often in American life since Puritan times, with special frequency in the nineteenth century after the rise of transcendentalism. But in the 1920s it was somewhat anachronistic for a man to present himself dramatically, not only as artist but also as human being, in the messianic role of someone who had achieved a second birth and now had come forth to utter prophetic truths. Nor did Anderson's lower-class origins in Ohio, his vaunted and obvious lack of education, his emphasis upon the American and the common, his bohemian dress and manners, his concern with lust and love, and his charismatic religious overtones make him more palatable either to the intellectual or to the average man.

The reasons for suspicion are understandable. It followed upon an extension of Emersonian-Whitmanian thought by some transcendentalist disciples who, abandoning whatever altruistic motives had animated them, degenerated into cultists and opportunists. Emerson and Whitman have been, and perhaps should be, censured for the ease with which their romantic idealism has nurtured and cloaked a phantasmagoria of gross materialism and spiritual masquerade. Admittedly, however,

neither Emerson nor Whitman, despite the extremist possibilities inherent in their paradoxical universality, put them into
the realm of action. But the disciples who fused Emersonian-
Whitmanian extremes in their behavior and ideas, frequently
larding their roles with quotation from and allusion to the masters, set up a counterreaction which suspected humbuggery even
where it did not exist. One of these archetypal disciples, unfortunately for Anderson, was Elbert Hubbard, still vividly remembered in the 1920s though no longer alive.

Hubbard had publicized his idealistic escape from business in
the late nineteenth century in order to pursue a life of pure art,
plain living, and high thinking, then proceeded to bespatter
American culture with a deceptive, essentially commercial literature, arts and crafts, communalism, and quasi-religious ideology
until he sank with the *Lusitania* in 1915. Many had been deceived
by the Emersonian-Whitmanian cover of Hubbard, with the result that Anderson — who, like Hubbard, stemmed from the
Midwest, sported an arty costume, and had also worked in business and advertising — was regarded with some wariness even
while his fiction was praised.

In private life, letters, and autobiographical publications, Anderson tenaciously mixed art and life until he became a fictional
character for himself and his times. Many supposedly objective
details in *A Story Teller's Story* (1924), *Tar* (1926), and the posthumous *Memoirs* (1942) were products of "fancy," a term he used
interchangeably with "imagination." He preferred these imaginative constructions to "facts" which he believed concealed
"the essence of things." The angry corrections of relatives and
friends did not alter his belief that a man's vision of himself and
his world contained more meaningful truth than did a birth
certificate or an identification card. There was no real ground
for embarrassment. In the opening pages of his autobiographical works, readers were forewarned at once about Anderson's
method. There is something playful and ingenuous in such typical fictions as his Italian grandmother and his southern father;
they happen to be profoundly true in revealing the surprise and

shock of a passionate "Ohio Pagan" who couldn't otherwise explain the incongruity of having been spawned in an American Midwest dominated by what he regarded as the chilly values of its "Puritan" New England settlers.

Sherwood Anderson was born on September 13, 1876, in Camden, Ohio. He was the third child of Irwin M. Anderson, who made and sold leather harness, and Emma Smith Anderson. The Anderson family had moved about from town to town in Ohio before Sherwood's birth. A few years after that event, Irwin Anderson's small business failed and the Anderson family resumed its travels. Not until 1884 was a permanent home established, this time in Clyde, a small farm town.

The strain of economic difficulties and wandering seems to have affected the father, who began to drink heavily and was so often unemployed that the family's needs frequently were satisfied only by the children's earnings and the strenuous efforts of their mother. Irwin Anderson as father and fictional character was to be an obsessive and ambivalently treated concern of Sherwood's thought and art. He and the other children would feel that Emma Anderson's death in 1895 might have been caused by her husband's neglect and frivolity. But Irwin was nevertheless lovable, in many respects admirable. His misfortunes had not soured his temper, and he joyfully gave rein to his aptitudes for music, theater, and literature. If a parade or vaudeville performance had to be arranged, Irwin Anderson was the man for the job; he acted; he blew the cornet in a local band; he entranced his friends and children with skillfully told tales. Such a role could excite admiration and respect; there were penalties too — family hardships and the probability that town and family alike would consider one a quixotic clown and fool. It was not until Sherwood Anderson was in his mid-forties that he highly valued what he had earlier feared, namely, his similarity to his father.

Young Sherwood's willingness to take on odd jobs earned him money and the nickname of "Jobby." He worked as a farmhand in the surrounding country; in Clyde as grocery delivery boy, laborer in a newly established bicycle factory, and newsboy, and in various menial capacities in a livery stable and a racehorse stable, where he mingled happily with drivers, jockeys, grooms, and trainers. Though an average student, his various jobs and interests made it difficult for him to attend school regularly; he finally quit high school before graduation.

Anderson's life in Clyde ended when he left in 1896 for Chicago, where his brother Karl had gone earlier. For the next two years, Anderson was a manual laborer in a cold-storage warehouse. With the outbreak of the Spanish-American War, he volunteered for army service in Cuba. His regiment arrived there in January 1899, almost four months after hostilities had ceased. Though he never underwent the combat experience which other American novelists such as Hemingway, John Dos Passos, Thomas Boyd, and Faulkner were to incorporate into their fiction, Anderson had an opportunity to become aware of the problems faced by the individual in a mass society requiring conformity to a single mode of conduct. That Anderson knew how to adjust himself may be gauged from his attainment of a corporal's rank. It was probably this slight success which encouraged a belief — embodied most fully in an early novel, *Marching Men* (1917) — that man as individual was ineffectual until, absorbed into a faceless mass led by a charismatic leader, he contributed his will and body to an invincible social entity.

At loose ends in 1900 after his army service, Sherwood again followed his brother, this time to Springfield, Ohio, where the latter was employed as an artist by the Crowell Publishing Company, which issued mass-circulation magazines. Aware of his need for more education, Anderson in September enrolled at Wittenberg Academy, a preparatory school, where he earned eleven grades of A and three of B for his proficiency in Latin, German, geometry, English, and physics. He was twenty-four years old at the time, but he did not feel it demeaning to pay for his food and lodging by working as a "shore boy" in the boarding-house where he, Karl, and various editors, artists, advertising men, and teachers resided.

These men and women were the most culturally advanced Anderson had met as yet. Their interests in art and literature, as well as business, uncovered new, if limited, worlds of action and thought for him. But as it happens it was in the field of business that the Springfield group ultimately did most for him. Through the intercession of the advertising manager of Crowell, Anderson was appointed to the Chicago advertising office of the firm as a copywriter. He was among the first and not the last of modern American writers whose imagination and expression have been affected by such experience.

Anderson initially took to advertising with gusto and a belief in the efficacy of the products he touted and the means used to sell them. Businessmen whom he met in his later role as advertising salesman liked him because of his "charm, interest, and sympathy," his physical attractiveness and lively spirit. His mental alertness and sensitivity to the language of the average mind made him an irresistible copywriter. One of his associates related that Anderson "bragged to the office girls that he could get them good husbands by mail-order letters."

The most revealing expression of his attitudes is to be found in the inspirational articles and sketches he contributed to *Agricultural Advertising*, his firm's house organ, during 1903 and 1904. Written in a clumsy, banal style, these pieces on the whole echo the platitudes of popular American business philosophy, uncritically expounding the virtues of industry, acquisition, aggressive competition, optimism, success, and service, while chiding those who prated reform morality and ignored the ethical values and practices of the businessman. Though Anderson in later years would denounce success and extol failure, he never became an enthusiast of radical social change except sporadically during the 1930s. He regarded most social activists and revolutionists as opportunists who concealed their search for power under showers of misleading "talk." During the 1930s, when many of those who earlier had championed his work were involved in leftist activities, his unwillingness to commit himself fully to radical programs led to sharp criticism or neglect of his last writings.

Whatever confidence and success advertising brought Anderson, and it also enabled him in 1904 to marry Cornelia Lane, the daughter of a wealthy Ohio wholesaler of footwear, the afflatus of sales promotion did not continue to satisfy him. His rising sense of frustration was fanned by the genteel achievements of his wife, who had been graduated from Western Reserve University, possessed the traditional knowledge of literature and the arts which he lacked, and had even studied in Europe. In a conversation of the mid-1900s with a Chicago advertising associate before departing on a business trip, Anderson said that he had decided to choose between becoming "a millionaire or an artist." He explained that, "if only a man will put the making of money above all other things in life," wealth could be attained. The role of an artist was more difficult, "but if it is in a fellow, he can do it. I don't know what I shall do — paint, sculp, maybe write. But I think I will come back determined on an artistic career."

The transition from copy writing to literature as art, which Anderson was to make, seemed easy and natural to him because in both language is manipulated to give an illusion of meaningful reality. His view was implicit in an advertising man's comment on a verbally gifted railroad man in one of Anderson's *Agricultural Advertising* sketches: "He knows how to use words and that's why I think he'd make an advertising man. How to use words, and say, Mr. Cowman, that's what advertising is, just using words; just picking them out like that fellow picked out his swear words and then dropping them down in just the right place so they seem to mean something. I don't want you to be making fun of that brakeman. . . . He's a word man, that brakeman is, and words are the greatest things ever invented."

Anderson's reverent attitude toward language was a wholesome sign of his promise as a writer. In the 1900s, it was useful to him because of his limited vocabulary and his unfamiliarity with the range of rhetorical devices to be found in literature. But his emphasis upon "words" as self-sufficient entities, and his lack of concern with their meaning, foreshadowed his later obsessive preoccupation with them. As he struggled unsuccessfully with the expression of ideas and emotional nuances in his first two novels, he came to believe that his failure resulted from the faulty character of his words rather than from the absence of that profound imaginative experience which willy-nilly finds vivid expression even in a limited language. "There is a story. — I cannot tell it. — I have no words," he would write in 1921.

This was to an extent only an element of the guileless and natural literary personality Anderson fashioned as a self-portrait. It came properly indeed from one whose advertising experience had shown him that words could be used without responsible interest in their human meaning and who was determined not to repeat his errors. On the one hand, therefore, Anderson's love and fear of the word stimulated great stylistic purity; on the other hand, this ambivalence also led on occasion to a "basic mistrust of language itself" and to the artistically destructive belief that "reality remains ultimately inexpressible" to which Anderson alluded in the epigraph of *A New Testament* (1927): "They talked and their lips said audible words but the voices of their inner selves went on uninterrupted."

Anderson continued to nourish hopes of an artistic career while adjusting himself to the responsibilities of a bourgeois husband who had fathered three children. Leaving Chicago in 1906, he returned to northern Ohio. During the next six years, he managed a mail-order business in Cleveland and later two paint manufacturing firms. In dress, country club membership, church attendance, and all other externals, Anderson conformed to the standards of respectable convention. But first secretly, in the night-time privacy of an attic at home, and later openly, in his office and elsewhere, Anderson began to write with such industry and devotion that friends and business acquaintances could not help becoming aware of his double existence. He centered more and more energy on his writing as an estrangement from his wife deepened in intensity and as financial difficulties made it likely that his business was going to fail.

On November 27, 1912, Anderson left his office in Elyria, Ohio, suddenly and was not heard from again until he turned up in Cleveland on December 1, disheveled and in a state of shock. In the Cleveland hospital to which he was taken, examining physicians diagnosed his condition as a mental collapse. Although he recovered quickly, the event was a turning point. He severed connections with his manufacturing business and, in order to support himself and his family, returned to his old Chicago advertising job in February 1913, bringing with him the manuscripts of *Windy McPherson's Son, Marching Men,* and other works.

Anderson's version of his departure from Elyria, presented in an article entitled "When I Left Business for Literature" (*Century,* August 1924) and incorporated in *A Story Teller's Story,* became a classic anecdote in the 1920s and 1930s. For Anderson and some younger writers, it symbolized the heroism of rebellion against the materialistic values of a business-dominated culture. Predictably, however, not all of his version was accurate. As he viewed the event in 1924 and later in the *Memoirs,* he ignored his psychic breakdown and slighted his precarious financial state, thus giving the impression that his flight had resulted from a wholly conscious decision to repudiate wealth and embrace art. To this extent, his story was misleading. But he also stated the essential truth and it was unimpeachable: after much struggle, he had committed himself to a disinterested life of art and thereafter had flaunted his disbelief in the moral integrity and social value of the advertising copy he continued to write so well until 1922.

Anderson's first two novels are apprentice efforts. He was never proud of these books, even when they were published. Later, in the *Memoirs,* he called them imitative and "immature." It is regrettable that Anderson permitted them to be published without extensive reworking, for in 1915, before their appearance, he was already writing the first brilliant tales of *Winesburg, Ohio* and undoubtedly was aware of the weaknesses of the novels. At this time, as later in his career, Anderson made the mistake of publishing work which did not reflect his full talent and thus gave rise to mistaken impressions of his progress and promise.

Although Anderson later said that he had tricked the reader with a happy ending, *Windy McPherson's Son* (1916) has a tragic or at least quasi-tragic ending. Sam McPherson's search for meaning in life concludes in a chaos of emptiness and negation. The dominant tone is one of darkness and frustration, steadily increasing in intensity. Young Sam — eager to acquire wealth — flees to Chicago from his Iowa village and becomes a robber baron. He is diverted from his unsatisfying material quest after meeting a perfect woman who convinces him that he will achieve fulfillment by creating perfect children with her. This eugenic goal is abandoned after she proves incapable of giving birth. Sam returns to business and finance, attaining vast power but no more satisfaction than before. He rules faceless men and cannot discover his own face. The social reform faddishly taken up by his frustrated wife does not attract him. In all action, idealistic or selfish, theories are discarded and the urge for power nakedly revealed as motive force. Sam flees Chicago in desperation.

Dressed in the costume of a Whitmanian rough, Sam McPherson wanders about as vagabond and workman "to seek Truth, to seek God" among the common people. He finds labor confused and its leaders power-hungry. Love is missing. Dissipation and vice have destroyed the moral character of the people. Sam cannot find God in man or society, thus repeating a boyhood experience when he had read the Bible and discovered that "Christ's simple message" of love and community had been rejected by the Iowa villagers. Wearied by "thinking" and searching, Sam loses faith in hope.

The resurgent theme of fertility rouses Sam briefly. He brings three neglected children home to his lonely wife, who has found solace, ironically, in the writing of Emersonian "articles about life and conduct." Upon Sam's return, she derides them as "pettiness." Both hope that, with the aid of the children, they may be able to realize their earlier unifying aim of nurturing perfect beings for the future. But the concluding paragraph of the novel is far from hopeful. The last lines are unmistakably despairing: "A shudder ran through his body and he had the impulse to run away into the darkness, to begin again, seeking, seeking. Instead he turned and going through the door, walked across the lighted room to sit again with Sue at his own table and to try to force himself back into the ranks of life." Nothing in the novel promises that Sam will be able to remain in the light.

Anderson's later weakness as a novelist is evident in his inability to make Sam McPherson see, feel, and evaluate his experience with concrete details and expanding complexity. Sam yearns to break loose from the sterilizing confines of existence, but his spirit is subdued by a numbing sameness that renders him unfit for observation and participation. Had Anderson created suspense by involving Sam in a more detailed inner drama of conflicting emotion and idea or in a more detailed outer drama of disturbing social interaction, the tragic conclusion would have embodied a persuasive force. As it is, Sam's impotent isolation ultimately tends to become more pathetic than deeply tragic.

The limited dimension of Sam is paralleled in most of the other characters, who remain undeveloped sentimental stereotypes. Some of these recur with haunting regularity in Anderson's later work: the kind, maternal schoolteacher who talks about books and art; the loved and hated braggart father; the exhausted, sacrificial mother who dies too soon; the wife who doesn't understand her husband or give herself to love; the promiscuous woman who cheapens physical passion.

The strengths of *Windy McPherson's Son* reside primarily in the first eight chapters dealing with Sam's village life before his quest for money and power in Chicago. This section of the book might almost be a discarded draft of *Winesburg, Ohio*. Many sentences are packed with the hum of feeling and have a Biblical cadence; "tears" express a specific emotional reaction and are not just plashed for dubious sentimental effect; imagery and diction generally are free from cliché and stereotype. Three characters anticipate the figures of *Winesburg, Ohio* in their expressiveness, the depth of their passion and insight, and the incongruity between their powers and their limited achievement.

John Telfer is an articulate and vivid man whose failure as painter has led him to a richer role: artist of living. His talk of Whitman, love, purpose, and ideals almost sways Sam from devotion to money; it is Telfer who emphasizes the difference between corn as a symbol of materialism and corn as a symbol of the *élan vital*: "I see the long corn rows with the men and the horses half hidden, hot and breathless, and I think of a vast river of life. I catch a breath of the flame that was in the mind of the man who said, 'The land is flowing with milk and honey.'" But Telfer cannot affect Sam's future any more than Sam's emotionally profound father, Windy McPherson, or the "savage and primitive" Mike McCarthy. The latter delights in fertilizing village wives whose miserly husbands have forsworn "carnal love," and the children it produces, in favor of saving money. Like Telfer, both have virtues worth emulating. Yet each is ultimately defeated, Windy by his hollow pretensions and Mike by the uncontrollable passion which leads to his murdering a resentful cuckold.

Anderson's second published novel, *Marching Men* (1917), although structurally flawed, is noteworthy for its greater stylistic fluency and more subtle fusion of ideas and dramatic action. This is not surprising, for Anderson was by no means a literary *naïf* in the mid-1910s as he and others have suggested. In Chicago after 1912 he had come to know such literary figures as Floyd Dell, Carl Sandburg, Margaret Anderson, and Ben Hecht; Anderson also contributed to the *Little Review*, along with *Poetry* the most important American "little magazine" of the 1910s. There are references to Poe, Browning, Carlyle, Keats, Balzac, Whitman, and Mark Twain in *Windy McPherson's Son*, as well as allusions to unspecified French, Russian, and other European writers; in a 1923 letter, Anderson asserted that he had read Turgenev about 1911 and Tolstoi and Dostoevski afterward. Shakespeare and Dante are mentioned in *Marching Men*. Ac-

cording to Anderson's *Memoirs*, he was already familiar with the
novels of Bennett, Wells, Hardy, and Moore. His brother Karl
had introduced him to Gertrude Stein's experimental *Tender
Buttons* (1914) soon after its appearance; he had read her *Three
Lives* (1909) earlier.

Marching Men is a social novel. In it Anderson examined the
destructive impact of industrialism in a Pennsylvania coal-
mining town upon a sensitive boy and traced the harmful effect
of his warped personality upon society. Ironically nicknamed
"Beaut" because of his gawkiness and physical ugliness, Norman
McGregor's lyrical response to nature and his affectionate spirit
are brutally crushed. Beaut McGregor grows to hate man and
society. In Chicago he finds opportunity, as lawyer and charismatic leader, to obtain revenge for his youthful sufferings. View-
ing urban, industrial man as a dehumanized shell, he accelerates
the dehumanization by organizing the masses into battalions
which, subjected to strict discipline, march in military fashion.
His intelligence and emotional mystique bring him the devotion
of many men who are glad to surrender the last remnants of
individuality. McGregor thus becomes the master of a terrifying
collective force whose power can be exerted against society. The
collective mass, rejecting the false premises of a democracy that
is disorderly, will create a new order, a new mind. "When you
have marched until you are one giant body then will happen a
miracle," McGregor tells his followers. "A brain will grow in the
giant you have made."

Had Anderson been able to stop the novel at that point, he
would have written a meaningful indictment of American life
and a warning of its self-destructiveness. Supporting the indictment are many valid social criticisms, some in the form of
Anderson's authorial comments and others in passages of description and narration. His ideas on the shoddy ugliness of
goods, homes, cities, and living patterns, on the inequitable
character of law, on the avid quest for sensation, and on other
problems of the day were pertinent for the early twentieth century and are still relevant in many respects. Anderson was echo-

ing earlier protests by Hawthorne, Melville, Thoreau, and Whitman; he was in tune with such perceptive contemporaries as Thorstein Veblen, Frank Lloyd Wright, and William James.

But though Anderson could objectively summon up the root causes for McGregor's Nietzschean nihilism, clearly portrayed as a negative philosophy, he paradoxically shared McGregor's faith in blind action. The novel struggles unsuccessfully to maintain equilibrium between Anderson's constructive critical temper and his unabashed impulse for collective physical violence and social destruction. As if to mark his inability to resolve the novel's chaotic lack of focus, Anderson dropped McGregor from the narrative before its close. The final chapter completes the book's disintegration. A foreshadowing of *Many Marriages* (1923), the conclusion whips up a mélange of sex and philosophy in portraying the success of a Chicago industrialist's effort to persuade his daughter that he is more desirable than McGregor, whom she has loved but to whom she has been afraid to give herself.

The idea and form of *Marching Men* were confused. But Anderson's style had progressed beyond the clumsy rawness of most of his earlier novel, had moved closer to the prose poetry of *Winesburg, Ohio*. His growing mastery of imaginative detail is visible in young McGregor's shocked perception that the coaltown minister is laughing callously at a cruel story about the boy: "The Reverend Minot Weeks also laughed. He thrust four fingers of each hand into the pockets of his trousers, letting the extended thumbs lie along the swelling waist line. From the front the thumbs looked like two tiny boats on the horizon of a troubled sea. They bobbed and jumped about on the rolling shaking paunch, appearing and disappearing as laughter shook him."

The urban scene evokes cold, sharp disgust:

The people of Chicago go home from their work at evening — drifting they go in droves, hurrying along. It is a startling thing to look closely at them. The people have bad mouths. Their mouths are slack and the jaws do not hang right. The mouths are like the shoes they wear. The shoes have become run down at the corners from too much pounding on the hard pavements and the mouths have become crooked from too much weariness of soul. . . . It is evening and the people of Chicago go home from work. Clatter, clatter, clatter, go the heels on the hard pavements, jaws wag, the wind blows and dirt drifts and sifts through the masses of the people. Every one has dirty ears. The stench in the street cars is horrible. The antiquated bridges over the rivers are packed with people. The suburban trains going away south and west are cheaply constructed and dangerous. A people calling itself great and living in a city also called great go to their houses a mere disorderly mass of humans cheaply equipped. Everything is cheap. When the people get home to their houses they sit on cheap chairs before cheap tables and eat cheap food. They have given their lives for cheap things.

In opposition to that nightmare horror, Anderson chanted the promise of nature in prophetic Biblical cadences:

And back of Chicago lie the long corn fields that are not disorderly. There is hope in the corn. Spring comes and the corn is green. It shoots up out of the black land and stands up in orderly rows. The corn grows and thinks of nothing but growth. Fruition comes to the corn and it is cut down and disappears. Barns are filled to bursting with the yellow fruit of the corn. And Chicago has forgotten the lesson of the corn. All men have forgotten. It has never been told to the young men who come out of the corn fields to live in the city.

The invigorating effect of Gertrude Stein's experimentation with language in *Tender Buttons* is evident in *Marching Men*. Her theory is virtually summed up by Anderson in the novel: "It is a terrible thing to speculate on how man has been defeated by his ability to say words. The brown bear in the forest has no such power and the lack of it has enabled him to retain a kind of nobility of bearing sadly lacking in us. On and on through life we go, socialists, dreamers, makers of laws, sellers of goods and believers in suffrage for women and we continuously say words, worn-out words, crooked words, words without power or pregnancy in them."

For Anderson, Miss Stein always remained a "writer's writer," a literary pioneer, not a writer for the general reader. He recognized that her abandonment of conventional syntax, punctuation, and spelling was therapeutic for the American writer because it made the latter conscious of the deadness of conventional language and rhythm, of a literature based on literary custom rather than on objects, associations, functions, and speech freshly articulated. In 1914 such a revivification of style was needed. Gertrude Stein was a pioneer in the undertaking, soon to be joined by Anderson, Pound, Eliot, Joyce, the Dadaists, Cummings, Hemingway, and Faulkner. The poetic repetition and variation of words and phrases, the uncluttered images of objects, the varying musical beat and swing of sentences and paragraphs, noticeable in the passages quoted above from *Marching Men*, were stylistic techniques Anderson learned from her and passed along to Hemingway and Faulkner.

In the late fall of 1915, Anderson began to write the tales that make up *Winesburg, Ohio*. The majority were executed before the middle of 1916. A controlling plan apparently guided him, for the tales were composed almost in the sequence they occupy in the book. (An exception must be made for the four-part "Godliness," which Anderson salvaged from an unfinished novel of 1917.) The tales' unusual quality was recognized almost at once by "little magazine" editors in rebellion against the values dominating American letters and culture. Floyd Dell, Anderson's Chicago friend who helped arrange publication of *Windy McPherson's Son* and was an editor of *Masses*, printed three tales in 1916 beginning with "The Book of the Grotesque." Waldo Frank, editor with James Oppenheim and Van Wyck Brooks of *Seven Arts*, published four tales in 1916 and 1917. Two tales appeared in 1916 and 1918 respectively in the *Little Review*. Anderson had gained an audience that was small but appreciative of his lyrical prose.

William Phillips's study of the Winesburg manuscripts shows that Anderson wrote his first drafts with spontaneity and speed, then polished with considerable care. The manuscript of "Hands," the second tale written, bears "almost two hundred instances in which earlier words and phrases are deleted, changed, or added to, to provide the readings of the final published version of the story." The revisions, ninety percent of which were made after the initial writing, added to the size of the draft; they amplified the tale's subtlety by increasing its suggestive elements and symbolic content. The style was molded into greater informality by the addition of colloquial words and repetitive rhythms, and by the deletion of words that were "overworked or awkwardly used."

Much in the tales had prior existence in Clyde, Ohio, and Anderson's earlier life, thus justifying the subtitle: "A Group of Tales of Ohio Small Town Life." But the book, written in retrospect in Chicago, also reflects and illuminates urban American life. Winesburg as a microcosm is ultimately more than a national phenomenon; its proportions are universal, like the whaling ship in Melville's *Moby Dick* and Faulkner's mythical Yoknapatawpha County.

The structure of *Winesburg, Ohio* was suggested by Edgar Lee Masters's *Spoon River Anthology*, an elegiac series of character sketches in poetry. The influence of Turgenev's *A Sportsman's Sketches*, in which a sympathetic but unsentimental narrator permits Russian character types to reveal themselves, is also evident. There are also precedents for the book in nineteenth-century American literature, most notably the collection of local-color tales centered in a single geographical place, the obsessed monomaniacs of Hawthorne's fiction, and the mordant temper of E.W. Howe's *The Story of a Country Town*. The uniqueness of Anderson's book consists of the unusual quality of the precise, ironic voice offering delicate accounts of grotesque human creatures.

A partial key to the elegiac form and tone of the tales is embodied in the book's theory of the grotesque. At some distant time in the past, man had created and believed many satisfying, contradictory truths, "each truth . . . a composite of a great many vague thoughts." Then the healthy wholeness of a multiplicity of truths was lost; man picked out one particular truth, based his life upon it, and became a grotesque, his exclusive truth "a falsehood." The theory, like Hawthorne's statement in *The House of the Seven Gables* that in "an odd and incomprehensible world . . . a man's bewilderment is the measure of his wisdom," epitomizes the philosophy of uncertainty that dominated Anderson's thought and art: the "meaning of life" could not be defined by an absolute truth which limited man's possibilities, for the universe was open rather than closed. "Seeds," a tale first published in 1918, rounds out Anderson's theory by asserting that a confused woman who has mistaken selfish lust for selfless love "is a grotesque, but then all the people in the world are grotesques. We all need to be loved. What would cure her would cure the rest of us also. The disease she had is, you see, universal. We all want to be loved and the world has no plan for creating our lovers."

Everything in *Winesburg, Ohio* sets forth Anderson's vision of the grotesquerie of modern life, though in surrealistic rather than realistic fashion. The characters are deluded and solipsistic; they misunderstand themselves and others; they speak jerkily, explosively, mumblingly, or are inarticulate; their bodies are deformed or subject to muscular twitches, sometimes remain rigid while parts such as hands or feet move about independently. Frustrated, distorted, violent or passive, aggressive or self-destructive, the citizens of Winesburg are the living dead, victims of limited, life-denying truths and guilty for having chosen them.

The grotesques strive to tell their life stories to George Willard, young newspaper reporter. Their recitals are disjointed; their encounters with Willard episodic and inconclusive; his understanding of them incomplete. The tales are static episodes, empty of discovery and change. George Willard is on the whole a passive participant, himself a victim like the others, incapable of distinguishing between love and lust until the conclusion of the book, at which time he leaves Winesburg for a future that is dubious.

Anderson's subtle literary voice enriched the static nightmare of grotesquerie by infusing it with the dynamism of irony. The self-depreciating narrator struggles to be free of the limitations imposed upon him as a Winesburg grotesque. "And yet that is but crudely stated," he confesses humbly and typically in "Hands." "It needs the poet there." But it was as a truly great prose poet that Anderson took up the dormant literary tradition of mock oral narration, briefly revivified by Mark Twain, and transformed it afresh into a vibrant literary medium.

The book's narrator lacks the godlike knowledge and consequent arrogance of an omniscient author. Only to the extent that he artfully presents other grotesques, implying that he has attained an objective distance from them, will he transcend his grotesque configuration and justify his difficult effort to assume the role of artist rather than remaining a Winesburg zombie. The narrator, therefore, abjures sentimentality and pity as much as possible; his tenderness and sympathy are restrained and balanced with an astringent objectivity frequently brutal in contrast to the sufferings of his characters. The narrator's distance from his characters is established by reticence concerning physical details and by the use of a minimal amount of speech and scenic confrontation: the entangling possibilities of physical and dramatic immediacy are thus avoided. However, the narrator cannot help becoming subjectively involved. He observes, feels, digresses, analyzes, and generalizes. Yet he is often wrong, shortsighted, naive. He has become a major character in the tales who, like the symbolic objects liberally strewn about the pages of *Winesburg, Ohio*, must be metamorphosed into full meaning by the imaginatively stirred reader.

At the last, the narrator's stance of simple, artless sincerity revealing all is only a guise for artistic purpose and effect: all is actually given, but only as hint, clue, suggestion, implication, ambivalence, indirection. The covert truths proffered by Anderson never become didactic absolutes imposed by the narrator and remain implicit and open-ended. Each reader of the tales will grasp only as much of their essence as his individual insight is capable of apprehending.

Winesburg, Ohio is the first modern American expression of the wasteland theme later adumbrated in T. S. Eliot's *The Waste Land* (1922), F. Scott Fitzgerald's *The Great Gatsby* (1925), Hemingway's *The Sun Also Rises* (1926), John Steinbeck's *To a God Unknown* (1933), and Nathanael West's *Miss Lonelyhearts* (1933), the latter, like Hemingway's novel, greatly indebted to Anderson's model. Unlike most of the writers who followed, Anderson attempted to fructify his wasteland, which symbolized the world of provinciality, gentility, and business he had rejected spiritually in his flight from Elyria to Chicago in 1913.

Winesburg, Ohio had delineated the arid context of Anderson's first life. Having given it aesthetic form, he believed it imperative to create — again in art — the context of his new life. The aim had been formulated with yearning simplicity by George Willard, like the new Anderson an artistic creation: "In every little thing there must be order, in the place where men work, in their clothes, in their thoughts. I myself must be orderly. I must learn that law. I must get myself into touch with something orderly and big that swings through the night like a star. In my little way I must begin to learn something, to give and swing and work with life, with the law."

The difficulties Anderson faced were great, particularly since he was still working on the Winesburg tales during 1916 and 1917, when he began his quest for new definitions, and the mood of Winesburg pervaded him. There was nothing in Winesburg as he had portrayed it, with the exception of nature, to which he could return; the ties which bound men in community had withered; love had degenerated into conflict, sexual repression, and disappointing lust; familial relations mirrored the larger social emptiness; the traditional reliances of religious orthodoxy and ritual modes of cultural behavior were nonexistent. He had cast aside the illusions of business and the ugliness of the city. In every respect, then, he was free and unattached, young in situation and possibility, ready to make the world live up to its fruitful potentialities and become a habitable place for human beings.

In actuality, of course, the matter was not so simple. Anderson was in his early forties, exuberant but also physically and mentally weary. As he later granted in his *Memoirs*, the Winesburg vision of his Ohio town had been harshly biased and he had too hastily rejected its few worthy attributes. It is apparent from the revelations in the early novels and the letters of this period that he had been psychically maimed by the experiences of his first forty years. Nor, regardless of how much will he exerted, could he easily slough off the worldliness of his mind, or easily assume the role of newborn infant or virginal adolescent after the mature triumph of his repudiation of business and familial ties, after the even greater triumph of having transformed himself into an accomplished artistic creator. The record of Anderson's progress as a new Adam is inevitably a compilation of noble effort, heroic attainment, and pathetic failure. As it must have been for one who, as he wrote in the poetic epigraph of "From Chicago" (*Seven Arts*, May 1917), was a "man child, in America, in the west, in the great valley of the Mississippi . . . a confused child in a confused world."

Henceforth, Anderson's art and life were inseparable. Instead of remaining hidden behind his work like James Joyce, Anderson made the problem of self-understanding and revelation the focus of his best work. He found it as necessary to write about himself as an artist as to work at his art: "While he is still young and pregnant with life it behooves the artist who would stand unashamed among men to make his contribution to the attempt to extend the province of his art. And as his struggle as an artist is and must be inseparably bound up with his struggle as a man, the attempt may fairly be said to fall under the head of an effort to extend the possibilities of human life." So opens "From Chicago," but it concludes humbly on a foreboding note so strong that Anderson self-consciously omitted the section when reprinting the piece in *Sherwood Anderson's Notebook* (1926): "I am looking forward to the coming of the new artist who will give us . . . the beautiful and stirring story of the spirit that failed just as the artist himself shall fail and who, like the Christ, or

hat dramatic night in the garden, must come at last to the facing
>f truth and know that he must always fail, that, even in keeping
alive the memory of his struggle, all men shall fail." This temper-
ng of egoism with limitation helped save Anderson from be-
:oming, except briefly in the 1920s, a tiresome brayer of virtuous
selfhood in the manner of some of his less gifted imitators.

Mid-American Chants (1918), a collection of free-verse poems in
he Whitmanian manner which Anderson began writing early in
1917, illustrates one phase of his attempt to fill his void. The
poems are generally inept. Only a few manage coherently to
unite their fragmentary rhapsodic ejaculations with the kind of
sustained emotional energy, intellectual content, and symbolic
structure present in Whitman's best poems. Anderson wanted to
re-create the religious spirit and mythology of pagan Indian
culture in the Ohio Valley before the culture's destruction by
New England's pioneers. But he was insufficiently familiar with
he details to do more than refer vaguely to the culture. On the
other hand, when he did achieve a fragile identification, he
blurred it with an alien prophetic exhortation and imagery de-
ived from the Old Testament and Carl Sandburg. Not until Hart
Crane wrote "The Dance" (*The Bridge*, 1930) were the primitive
ertility rhythms of sacrifice, harvest, and rebirth celebrated in
modern American poetry with the Dionysian richness Anderson
,ought to express.

Anderson was surprised that the editors of *Seven Arts* — one of
whom, James Oppenheim, even wrote Whitmanesque poetry —
frowned upon the poems later collected in *Mid-American Chants*.
The apocalyptic spirit of the magazine, which found hope for an
American Renaissance in "self-expression without regard to current magazine standards" and eulogized Anderson in the first
issue as an emergent Whitman, had diverted him from the disciplined temper governing the Winesburg stories. It had encouraged him to assume the role of ebullient national bard and to
find in the seeds, roots, stalks, and husks of corn — the major
symbol of the chants — a means of ordering his chaos. However,
he excesses which *Seven Arts* encouraged as one product of its

doctrines were actually abhorrent to men like Frank and Brooks. Their most fervent aim was to awaken an idealistic national art rather than to discard traditional standards of literary taste and accomplishment. Anderson's friendship with these men and his respect for their judgment declined in the heat of argument, though he maintained his intimacy with them for some years thereafter.

"An Apology for Crudity" (*Dial*, November 8, 1917) was a manifesto of his independent literary position which sniped at the formalism of his *Seven Arts* critics and others who ridiculed several poems that had appeared in *Poetry* (September 1917). Significant literature, he asserted, could only come after a writer's immersion in the life of his times. Since "crudity and ugliness" were prime characteristics of American industrial society, modern literature must be affected by it. He rejected, consequently, the "intellectuality" and "subtlety" of Henry James and William Dean Howells as ends in themselves, though he granted that both men were "American masters in prose." He linked himself to the tradition of Walt Whitman, Mark Twain, and Theodore Dreiser, who had not ignored the common.

But Anderson did not espouse realism. Vaguely he set forth the ideal of "subjective writing" as an alternative, the writer serving as an imaginative distiller of persons and experience. Later, in "A Note on Realism" (*New York Evening Post Literary Review*, October 25, 1924), he phrased his conception more concretely: "The life of the imagination will always remain separated from the life of reality. It feeds upon the life of reality, but it is not that life — cannot be. . . . Upon the fact in nature the imagination must constantly feed in order that the imaginative life remain significant. . . . The life of reality is confused, disorderly, almost always without apparent purpose, whereas in the artist's imaginative life there is purpose. There is determination to give the tale, the song, the painting Form — to make it true and real to the theme, not to life. Often the better the job is done the greater the confusion." Essentially, then, form and style were organic discoveries of imaginative creation, not preexistent molds chosen in advance of the literary adventure.

Despite Anderson's impatience with the conventional novel and his recurrent effort to discover a "looser" form, his next major work failed to demonstrate any "experimental" characteristics. *Poor White* (1920) delineated the decline of the "pastoral golden age" in his Midwest during the 1880s and 1890s, the years of his childhood and adolescence. The book is crammed with information, for Anderson tried to anchor it in the facts of cultural, social, and economic history. Furthermore, he enveloped life in the Ohio town of Bidwell — which also appears in other post-Winesburg fiction — with a quiet charm derived from stable community relations, proximity to nature, intellectual curiosity and discussion, old houses, and streets shaded with old overhanging trees. Much of the vision is valid, but Anderson's nostalgia led him to idealize the town and its region until they became as exaggeratedly beautiful as Winesburg earlier had been exaggeratedly ugly. Yet this excessively rosy portrait of Bidwell was also aesthetically sound, for it enabled Anderson to dramatize the emotional and social significance of its degeneration into Winesburg.

The corrupting agent in the agrarian paradise was industrialism, which had elevated materialism and turned men into mechanical monsters. Hugh McVey, a Huckleberry Finn-type from the Mississippi River town of Mudcat Landing, Missouri, symbolically embodies the process. With unsparing realism, young McVey is shown to be a shiftless and lazy "poor white," redeemed, however, by his tendency to daydream and transcend himself pantheistically in sky, earth, and water.

Orphaned, McVey lives with a family which indoctrinates him with the virtues of industry and profit. Gradually he becomes wholly mathematical in mind and mechanical in spirit, channeling his imagination into the invention of labor-saving agricultural machinery. The machines bring him financial success even though, ironically, they turn out to be unworkable and thus symbolically fraudulent. They involve the town in a fever of speculation, disrupting all patterns of behavior, all relations. The novel contains many vivid episodes of the degenerative transformation of characters into tormented grotesques when they

are suddenly deprived of the self-fulfilling creative tasks of old
In all of Bidwell, the only creatures who remain virile and sentient are horses. McVey is also a grotesque, unable to consum-
mate his marriage because of psychic impotence, roused finally
from his dehumanization by the beautiful appearance of some
brightly colored stones he has found. At the end, after a symbolic attack upon McVey by a maddened handicraftsman
Hugh's patient wife — a "new woman" given to thinking rather
than feeling — is roused to maternal womanliness by his reversion to adolescent helplessness. The novel grinds to a confusing
halt as Hugh, stirred by "the disease of thinking," is told by "his
woman" of the forthcoming arrival of "a man child." This news
is greeted mockingly by "a great whistling and screaming" from
Bidwell's factories.

The style of *Poor White* is effectively elegiac and muted as
befits the portrait of an unrecoverable past. It is also generally
free of the grammatical errors and poor punctuation that had
marred *Winesburg, Ohio* slightly and to a greater extent the earlier novels. *Poor White* was the high point of Anderson's novelis-
tic career. However, it represented a mere refinement of the
structure and materials of *Windy McPherson's Son* and *Marching
Men* rather than a significant advance. All three novels are essentially accounts of the distortion of a man in youth, his subsequent
involvement in a maturity of social fraud and emotional impoverishment, his attempt to attain self-fulfillment in escape and
love with an unsatisfactory woman who symbolizes reason and
convention rather than emotion and revolt, and the uncertainty
of the man's future at the conclusion.

Undoubtedly these novels served Anderson as self-analysis.
But the requirements of their objective form kept him from
venturing deeply into a personal probing that would have
brought him profoundly into himself and encouraged analytical
subtlety and particularized detail. The novels come perilously
close to being true-confession literature in which the apparent
openness of the writing hardly conceals the complacent obdu-
racy with which the author reiterates rather than explores the
troubles from which he supposedly has escaped.

Anderson's next novel, *Many Marriages* (1923), exemplifies the impasse to which such writing could lead; with its publication — it was initially printed serially in the *Dial* — came the first strong reaction against Anderson by the newer generation of American writers. Abandoning the chronological time sequence of the early novels, *Many Marriages* focused upon an extended moment of escape. This was given a past by means of flashbacks that vividly re-create the inhibition of feminine passion. But Anderson did little to set forth the positive hopeful quality of his masculine protagonist's passion beyond having him posture nakedly in presumably ritualistic fashion before a statue of the Virgin Mary. This ritual is neither primitive nor Catholic, for Anderson failed to provide any meaning for his key symbol, which he had picked up in *The Education of Henry Adams*. The result was a stasis, the temper of the Winesburg tales, that violated the thematic meaning of *Many Marriages* and revealed a disturbing lack of literary self-consciousness. What might have been a good short story had been turned into a faulty novel.

Anderson published three more novels: *Dark Laughter* (1925), *Beyond Desire* (1932), and *Kit Brandon* (1936). All of them, like his preceding novels, have extraordinary scenes and passages whose high quality has been overlooked. These last novels also show that he endeavored to cope with the problems of extended narrative fiction in different ways; his solutions, however, were generally unsatisfactory, whether it was the attempt to portray the stream of consciousness in *Dark Laughter* or the device of having a central character relate her life story in an extended monologue in *Kit Brandon*.

Anderson's letters and writings from the mid-1910s until shortly before his death reveal that the objective novel, particularly the social novel, had interested him deeply only before the composition of the Winesburg tales. During the late 1910s, before the publication of *Poor White*, he began and abandoned several novels. After 1925, the pattern was repeated. His impulse was for expression in short forms: the poem, prose poem, and lyrical short story. But he felt compelled, particularly since he had begun his career as a novelist, to continue writing novels. As late as 1933, for example, the publishing house of Scribner's invited him to become one of its authors with the stipulation, according to Anderson, that the first of his books "must be either a novel or a continuous narrative."

It was not merely the pressure of publishers, as well as readers and critics, which pushed Anderson toward the novel against his natural inclination to work in shorter forms. Anderson shared the erroneous cultural belief that a novel is qualitatively as well as quantitatively more valuable than a short work. Had he been a younger man in the late 1910s and early 1920s, it is possible that he might have been able to develop the lyrical novel, a delicate form that would have best utilized his talents as it did those of Virginia Woolf, his admirer. But he had insufficient time in which to work slowly and perfect his art in every form. By 1919, at the age of forty-three, he was exhausted with the difficulty of earning his living as an advertising man and writing in his spare time. Not until 1922 did he finally leave the advertising business, convinced by the size of his earnings from books and magazines that he would be able to survive as a professional writer.

As it turned out, he was unprepared to work at the pace required of a professional writer whose contractual obligations force him to produce publishable materials on a regular basis. He wished to experiment, to work as the impulse to create arose, to make discoveries as any other young writer who still has his future ahead of him: Anderson believed that his life had begun in 1916 with the publication of his first book. Yet, as a professional writer in the 1920s, he allowed himself to publish whatever he wrote, regardless of whether or not he was proud of it. Thus he ironically was seduced by the same dream of success that he had repudiated in business.

Nevertheless, the bulk of Anderson's important creation is far greater than many critics and readers appear to have realized. His significant contribution to American literature begins with *Winesburg, Ohio* and includes many pieces of prose and poetry published in books and magazines from 1916 to 1941. To that body of work should be added the successful chapters and sections from generally unsatisfactory books, as well as the luminous autobiographical sketches compiled in the posthumous *Memoirs*.

One reason Anderson's writing did not at once receive full recognition, apart from the disappointment aroused by his novels, is the uneven character of his books. Anderson's eagerness to publish, encouraged by editors and publishers, is partially responsible. For example, the two books which crystallized his fame as a short fiction writer in the early 1920s — *The Triumph of the Egg* (1921) and *Horses and Men* (1923) — are mixtures of quality and dross. In both books he included pages salvaged from discarded novels which were on the whole below the level of his current work. "Unlighted Lamps" and "The Door of the Trap" (*The Triumph of the Egg*) are sections of novels begun before 1913. "A Chicago Hamlet" (*Horses and Men*) is a portion of a 1918 novel; "An Ohio Pagan" and "'Unused'" in the same collection are parts of unpublished novels begun in 1920. A little more than half of *Horses and Men* thus belies the subtitle's description of the contents as "tales." Anderson's last collection of short fiction, *Death in the Woods* (1933), is similarly uneven. It should be noted, however, that the novel fragments frequently contain some of Anderson's most evocative writing. The pantheistic embrace of nature in "An Ohio Pagan," for example, has rarely been equaled in American literature.

Another reason for the relative neglect of Anderson's total accomplishment is the special nature of his talent. He wrote in an age which believed it could master the disorder of existence with patterns of order derived from myths and ideologies of the past or else with descriptions of objects and behavior that possessed the irreducible precision of scientific writing. Because Anderson did not adopt either one of these solutions, his reputation was severely damaged during the 1920s. A reassessment is now underway, for his alleged weaknesses ironically have become strengths which link him with some of the most vigorous currents in contemporary literature. Anderson's vision and method reappear triumphantly in recent American literature in the writing of Carson McCullers, Bernard Malamud, Flannery O'Connor, Tennessee Williams, Edward Albee, Saul Bellow, and John Hawkes. Anderson's pioneering conglomeration of the picaresque, the antiheroic, the grotesque, the passionate, and the rebellious is no longer puzzling nor is it a sign of irresponsible "mindlessness."

One of the most interesting discoveries to be made is that sentimentality is not one of the chief characteristics of Anderson's writing. When dealing with characters whose suffering and confusion he delineated at excessive length, failing to complicate and particularize their uniqueness or to impart visible moral and intellectual significance to their predicaments, he did become pathetic and sentimental. Illustrations of his failure to claim the complex response of a reader are *Many Marriages* and "Out of Nowhere into Nothing."

But Anderson's critical temper conflicted strongly with his tendency toward acceptance and complacency. He could become exceptionally sharp, often brutal, in combating the impulse of quiescence. The lively battle he carried on elicited an amused, ironic attitude toward himself and his world. He often wrote satirically ("The Egg," 1920, and "The Triumph of a Modern, or, Send for the Lawyer," 1923) and often comically ("I'm a Fool," 1922, "There She Is — She Is Taking Her Bath," 1923, and "His Chest of Drawers," 1939). To have separated satire and comedy is misleading, however, for Anderson at his most humorous gives us that rare blend known as the tragicomic. When he achieved it, as in "The Egg," it rested in a delicate suspension of irony that looked back to the narrative voice of *Winesburg, Ohio*. Despite lapses into what Faulkner in 1925 described as an "elephantine kind of humor about himself," Anderson's vision remained deeply, incongruously tragicomic. Despite the dark years through which he passed in the late 1920s, this vision re-emerged in his last decade of life, typically in his insistence in *Plays: Winesburg and Others* (1937) that the dramatized version of "The Triumph of the Egg" must be carefully directed in order to maintain a balance between comedy and tragedy; to play it either for "laughter" or "tears" alone would destroy the play.

Essentially Anderson was a lyric writer. Having accepted middle-class thought uncritically at first, then having rebelled against it, he feared that any other system of thought would be equally delusive, would limit and frustrate him, especially since reason tended to become abstract and to ignore the heart. "Feeling instinctively the uncertainty of life, the difficulty of arriving at truth," he resolved to remain "humble in the face of the great mystery" ("'Unused,'" 1923). He might have been describing his own work when he wrote in *A Story Teller's Story*: "Dim pathways do sometimes open before the eyes of the man who has not killed the possibilities of beauty in himself by being too sure."

Anderson could be irritatingly blunt in stating his position, sneering at "slickness," "smartness," and glibness in all fields including literary criticism; thus he inevitably aroused charges of "mindlessness," "immaturity," and "distrust of ideas." Though he winced under the blows of increasingly harsh criticism, he unhesitatingly rejected ready-made truths of past and present. He turned his gaze inwards, searching for tentative explanations of mystery in the texture of his own emotional and social experience. His writings articulate the development of his perceptions of self in relation to the world, of the difficulties encountered on the way.

Anderson never abandoned the vision of himself as a poet despite the unfavorable reception of *Mid-American Chants*, as late as 1930 writing an extraordinary prose poem in "Machine Song" (*Perhaps Women*, 1931). From 1919 to 1927 he assiduously wrote prose poems which appeared in magazines and *The Triumph of the Egg* and were collected in *A New Testament* (1927). He regarded this work at the outset as "a purely insane, experimental thing . . . an attempt to express, largely by indirection, the purely fanciful side of a man's life, the odds and ends of thought, the little pockets of thoughts and emotions that are so seldom touched." The poems on the whole are inchoate, too vague and incoherent to communicate more than faint hints of subconscious existence. But they were valuable exercises nonetheless. When Anderson turned to prose during this period, he passed beyond the mere undisciplined expression of self and made skillful use of poetic techniques which he never forgot.

As in *Winesburg, Ohio*, the varying perceptions of a poetically conceived narrator animate and unify most of Anderson's best stories, quite a few of which are products of the 1930s. For the sake of convenient reference, I cite only those stories that are accessible in book form, namely, Anderson's three collections of his fiction and the first posthumous collection of his writings: *The Triumph of the Egg*: "I Want to Know Why," "Seeds," "The Other Woman," "The Egg," and "Brothers"; *Horses and Men*: "I'm a Fool," "The Triumph of a Modern, or, Send for the Lawyer," "The Man Who Became a Woman," "Milk Bottles," "The Man's Story"; *Death in the Woods*: "Death in the Woods," "There She Is — She Is Taking Her Bath," "In a Strange Town," "A Sentimental Journey"; *The Sherwood Anderson Reader*: "The Corn-Planting," "A Walk in the Moonlight," "The Yellow Gown," and "His Chest of Drawers." The first-person narrator sometimes merely introduces the monologue of another character, as in "The Other Woman" or "His Chest of Drawers." Only a few of Anderson's stories related from a third-person point of view possess high quality: "Senility" and "The New Englander" (*The Triumph of the Egg*), "Another Wife" and "Brother Death" (*Death in the Woods*), "Daughters" and "Not Sixteen" (*The Sherwood Anderson Reader*).

The uncertain, groping narrator of an Anderson story employs an art of suggestion to articulate his search for pattern and meaning in human existence. His experiences are fragmentary, incoherent, inexplicable. The chronological sequence of time may be interrupted and reversed by memories, inadvertent thoughts, gusts of emotion, and frustrated attempts at comprehension. Objects and people are haphazardly perceived, grotesquely distorted. Absurdly helpless, the narrator may succumb to impotence, give vent to explosive stirrings in his subconscious, flee the envelope of his body in mystical anguish or ecstasy, obsessedly focus upon trivialities such as a bent finger, find momentary relief in the muscular health and grace of animals.

Since the story is an articulation of the narrator's experience, its movement is repetitive and circular; it is not rounded off with a meaningful conclusion, for that would violate the narrator's integrity, his stance of wonder and search. Anderson's rejection of conventional plot and climax was aesthetically appropriate. So was his frequent representation of physical detail as incomplete image and generalized noun, his emphasis upon the musical sound of language before it becomes sense in order that he might portray the transformation of undifferentiated sensation and emotion into intelligible form.

The welter of sensuous and emotional perceptions is integrated — despite the powerful centrifugal impulse — by various unifying elements. The narrator maintains a consistent tone of voice. Whether youth or adult, light or serious, comic or satiric, critical or suppliant, he is also visibly interested and compassionate, anxious to discern the reality behind appearance. Moments in the story — episodes, sensations, repetitions — suddenly blaze up to give intense thematic illuminations. Objects, gestures, and events are encrusted with symbolic meaning. These symbols recur and invest the narrator's perceptions with deepened or new significance. Often these symbols are transformed into archetypal patterns of elemental human experience, such as sacrifice, initiation, and rebirth; Anderson's corn seed, for example, is a fertility symbol, its planting a ceremonial drama of death and resurrection.

Many of Anderson's stories, like his novels, are autobiographical either wholly ("In a Strange Town") or partially ("I Want to Know Why"). Presentation of a story from the first-person point of view encouraged an autobiographical concern. On the other hand, as a writer of autobiography, a form that fascinated him because of his vision of himself as "the American Man . . . a kind of composite essence of it all," he tended to fictionalize the details of his biography. This fusion of fact and fiction produced some of Anderson's finest lyrical prose. For example, "Death in the Woods," regarded as one of Anderson's best stories even by unfavorable critics, appeared as a third-person narrative (Chapter XII) in his autobiographical novel *Tar* (1926). In the same year, it also appeared as a story in the *American Mercury*; the name "Tar" had been replaced by "I" and third-person pronouns and other details revised to clarify the narrator's personal relations and experiences. "A Meeting South," the subtle account of Anderson's intimacy with Faulkner in New Orleans, conceals Faulkner under a pseudonym and was probably read as fiction in the *Dial* (April 1925). It reappeared the next year as an autobiographical sketch in *Sherwood Anderson's Notebook* and finally was identified as a story in *Death in the Woods*. Anderson's autobiographical writings, which compose much of his total work, must be taken into account before any definitive conclusions about his literary significance can be ventured.

A starting point might well be Chapters X and XI of *Tar*, portrayals of horse racing as brilliantly colored and airy as Raoul Dufy's watercolors of French tracks, written in a supple vernacular that captures motion and youth with clear-eyed verve. Another excellent piece is "The Nationalist" (*Puzzled America*, 1935), a satirical dialogue with "the rat king of the South" who wants Congress to abolish the law protecting snowy egrets from shooting by feather-hunters. "'It isn't the money I am thinking about,' he said. There was a grave injustice being done. 'These egrets,' he said again, 'are not American birds. They are foreign birds and they come up here only to eat our American fish.'" Two sketches, "White Spot" (1939) and "Morning Roll Call" (1940), both published posthumously in *The Sherwood Anderson Reader*, are brilliant examples of his ability to express himself during his last years with the vibrancy that had been a basis for his distinction during the early 1920s.

Anderson had intended "White Spot" and "Morning Roll Call" for his last major work, a retrospective account of his "adventures of living" and search for their meaning. Begun in 1933, the project was well advanced, but not yet completed, before Anderson's death in the Panama Canal Zone on March 8, 1941, during the beginning of a South American goodwill tour. When the first edition of *Sherwood Anderson's Memoirs* appeared in 1942, it embodied a well-intentioned if misguided editorial treatment that involved deletion of "White Spot" and "Morning Roll Call,"

addition of magazine pieces published before 1933, and revision
of manuscript lines.

Even so, Anderson's rich touch permeated the book. All of his
earlier concern with self-revelation, perception of others, and
expressive nuance seemed to have borne fruit in charming, lyrical pages that left one in awe at the resiliency of the human spirit
as it copes with being in art. How much more remarkable the
book would have been if Anderson had lived to finish it to his
satisfaction may be grasped in the excellent, scholarly second
edition, published in 1969, which closely realizes Anderson's authorial intentions.

The vivacity and insight of Anderson's memoirs are remarkable in view of the severe decline of his reputation in the
mid-1920s and the lengthy emotional depression that affected
him thereafter. To those critics who did not read his works at-
tentively or at all after 1925, when *Dark Laughter* appeared, and
to those who know Anderson's writing only on the basis of
Winesburg, Ohio and two over-anthologized stories — "I'm a
Fool" and "I Want to Know Why" — the vibrancy of the
memoirs will be truly inexplicable.

Perhaps Anderson should not have expected his work early or
late to be wholly or widely appreciated. From the very beginning
his literary reputation was shaky. Newspaper and magazine reviewers of his early books regularly oscillated between praise and
blame, often mixing both.

Since Anderson was an avant-garde writer, however, a "little
magazine" phenomenon, he was at first more enthusiastically
received by young writers and critics interested in an American
literature that was original, complex, unsentimental, and bold in
dealing with taboo subjects such as sex. Thus young Hart Crane
in 1921 wrote an encomium of Anderson's "paragraphs and
pages from which arises a lyricism, deliberate and light, as a curl
of milk-weed seeds drawn toward the sun. . . . He is without
sentimentality; and he makes no pretense of offering solutions.
He has humanity and simplicity that is quite baffling in depth
and suggestiveness . . ."

But before long even the recognition of the avant-garde was

qualified or withdrawn. It generally began to misjudge and over-look Anderson's method and to conclude mistakenly that he was an elderly, provincial American realist because he wrote about the Midwest and praised Dreiser for his human sympathy and his frankness in the treatment of sex. Anderson's persistent criticisms of Dreiser's style as clumsy and of Sinclair Lewis's style as superficial were ignored. The epitome of ultimate avant-garde response to Anderson is best seen in the pages of the *Dial*, which published him frequently, printed laudatory statements, and early in 1922 bestowed upon him the first *Dial* award for distinguished service to American letters, then in the next few years directly and allusively in reviews and other forms of comment gradually formulated a negative attitude toward him.

Anderson's rejection by the avant-garde deepened an earlier sense of estrangement from vital currents of modern literature that had begun when his first prominent supporters — Frank, Brooks, Paul Rosenfeld — kept finding fault with his theories and writings. In such works as *A Story Teller's Story* (1924), *The Modern Writer* (1925), and *Sherwood Anderson's Notebook* (1926), he hopefully sought to define and justify his credo. He was not helped in this task by his antipathy to "talk" about literature and ideas or by his aversion to systematic exposition. Much of what he said had the nub of good sense but it was insufficiently clarified, overcast with a playfulness inappropriate for the occasion, and gave the impression of being narcissistic self-praise of an aesthetic phenomenon superior to traditional morality and critical judgment. Self-consciously ironic and derisive references to the "modern" began to appear in his fiction and articles. An attempt to demonstrate superior "modernity" in *Dark Laughter* was a fiasco: its style, supposedly an emulation of that in James Joyce's *Ulysses*, revealed a misunderstanding of the stream-of-consciousness technique; its rendition of expatriate American experience in Europe was ludicrously uninformed and unperceptive.

The strongest blows against Anderson's prestige and well-being came from young writers whom he had befriended.

Hemingway, in whom Anderson had discovered "extraordinary talent" in 1921 and whose *In Our Time* (1925) had been published as a result of Anderson's efforts, parodied Anderson in *The Torrents of Spring* (1926). Faulkner, whose *Soldiers' Pay* (1926) had also been published following Anderson's efforts, less publicly but just as sharply ridiculed Anderson in the foreword to *Sherwood Anderson & Other Famous Creoles* (1926), a book published in a limited edition in New Orleans.

For the rest of his life, from the mid-1920s on, Anderson engaged in a quest for rediscovery of the talent which seemed to have atrophied. F. Scott Fitzgerald had written: "To this day reviewers solemnly speak of him [Anderson] as an inarticulate, fumbling man, bursting with ideas — when, on the contrary, he is the possessor of a brilliant and almost inimitable prose style, and scarcely any ideas at all." Anderson perceived, with utter rightness, that there is no style without form, no form without content, that ideas are no more important than the evocative enunciation of experience. He had traveled much during his early years as an advertising man and now he resumed his travels. His second marriage had ended in divorce in 1924, two years after he left the advertising business; his third marriage broke down in 1929. Restlessly he went about the country, observing men and women, listening, attempting to regain the equilibrium of mind, emotion, and voice that had earlier produced his particular artistic vision. The idea that a permanent home might provide stability attracted him. In 1926 he built a house in the mountains of southwestern Virginia; for several years beginning in 1927 he edited two newspapers in the nearby town of Marion, Virginia. Meanwhile he continued to write stories and articles, to struggle desperately with new novels. He was often stricken with black, destructive moods, on one occasion even threw the manuscript of an unpublished novel out of a hotel window, but persisted in his search for orientation. In 1930 he fell in love with his future fourth wife; their marriage was successful. Slowly he regained his self-confidence, his talent, and his sense of humor. These are embodied in writings which swell the enduring corpus of his work beyond that already produced by 1926, writings in which he returned to the common people and locales he had earlier portrayed with similar irony, pity, and understanding.

The ultimate test of a writer's permanence is the power of his words to kindle generations other than his own. If that be granted, then Sherwood Anderson's stature as a major American writer seems firmly established for decades to come. The "proper evaluation" Faulkner demanded in 1956 has been in progress ever since, with special impetus and fine critical intelligence devoted in the 1960s and 1970s to elucidating Anderson's achievement. His works have been widely reprinted in the United States and abroad; new editions and collections have appeared with impressive regularity. Characteristically humble, Anderson had said in 1921 "that after all the only thing the present generation of men in America could expect to do is to make with their bodies and spirits a kind of fertilizing element in our soil." The issue of grandeur and fame was a matter he left to others, nor did he rack himself with prediction. It remains for us to acknowledge that the American culture whose substance he enriched has grown to value his legacy.

JOHN STEINBECK

Some among the distinguished array of American novelists who volunteered as witnesses to what life was like in the half century after World War I now seem rather far removed from us. The writers who developed themes that were highly personal to their own experience stand apart. Ernest Hemingway, though he exercised enormous influence on the taste, and even the thinking, of the young in his time, has become an aloof presence only the more withdrawn from us because his gifts were so original and striking. His obsession was with crises of courage dramatized, in his best novels, against a background of foreign wars. He seems to be less a product of our tradition than a titan of ego and energy existing in a world all his own. William Faulkner saw his corner of the American world through a Gothic mist of shock and surprise and the high talents used to evoke this strange realm seem to belong to another age and to a place not quite our own.

Other of the novelists of this time have remained close to us because of their preoccupation with the continuing problems of American life, because of their ability to depict a physical, social, and psychological environment that quickens in us a sense of immediacy and recognition. Two such were F. Scott Fitzgerald and John Steinbeck. Between them they divided up the American world of their era. Fitzgerald took as his share the domain inhabited by the rich, the sheltered, the frequenters of cafés, bootleggers' parties, and psychiatrists' consulting rooms. He found pity and terror among these people and had both moving and ominous things to say about his discoveries. Steinbeck, for his inheritance, took the orchards and growing fields of California, the wasteland of the Depression, the refugee camps of rebels and the slums of poverty. He helped himself also to a scientific laboratory and certain places into which men retire to meditate. He, too, found pity and terror among his fellow human beings but, like Fitzgerald, he also found beauty, charm, and wit. Though the two men would never have thought of themselves as collaborators, they shared the responsibility of presenting in fiction all the conflicts that have confused our time and yet confirmed its aspirations.

Steinbeck speaks to us with special immediacy because in a curious way he anticipated attitudes toward the human experience which have particularly engaged the intelligences of the young in recent years. Many of Steinbeck's characters seem to have been the forebears of the rebels who have gathered in centers of protest from Greenwich Village to the Haight-Ashbury district of San Francisco. What can the dissidents of *Tortilla Flat, Cannery Row,* and *Sweet Thursday* be called but dropouts from society who have the same reasons for rejecting old patterns of belief as do members of the hippie generation? On the negative side the credo of today's young revolutionaries seems, like that of Steinbeck, to have been influenced by a pervasive disillusionment with the gospel of success, by contempt for what seems to them to be cynical commercialism, and by resentment of arbitrary authority. On the positive side, as their banners insist, they wish to be guided — again as were the group-conscious residents of Cannery Row — by a preference for love over the destructive impulses of human nature. Steinbeck accepted as early as the 1930s the obligation to take a stand in his writing against tendencies in the American way of life to which the campus rebels of the present have been making vigorous objection.

More than this, however, Steinbeck never forgot the crucial character of the confrontation between man and his destiny. In the least sober of his books, *Sweet Thursday*, he slipped in a statement which succinctly sets forth his own fundamental belief: "Men seem to be born with a debt they can never pay no matter how hard they try. It piles up ahead of them. Man owes something to man. If he ignores the debt it poisons him, and if he tries to make payments the debt only increases, and the quality of his gift is the measure of the man." The novels, plays, and short stories of this conscientious artist represent successive efforts to pay his debt to man. Wide in the range of their interests, diverse in mood, passionately concerned in their sympathies, they all celebrate the worth of man. For that integrity Steinbeck demands justice and respect; to that integrity he lends the support of his own conviction that all men everywhere are and must be inextricably identified with their kind. Much more clearly than in the instance of any other American writer of his time Steinbeck's consistent effort to establish the dignity of human life offers the measure of the man.

He was born (on February 27, 1902) into an environment that served well to develop his inclinations and to satisfy his needs. The Salinas Valley of California provided a physical setting in which majesty and menace were mixed. Its alternate promises of fertility and threats of drought woke wonder in a sensitive, plastic nature and stirred an alert intelligence. He developed a passion for all the sounds, scents, and tastes of things, animate and inanimate. These crowded in upon him making him conscious, as he once expressed it, of "how the afternoon felt." The sentient boy, recognizable in transfiguration as Jody in *The Red Pony*, was father to the sentient man. And it was in his youth that Steinbeck seized on the belief, which remained with him always, that he shared with all living things the same essence and the same destiny, that there is a oneness of man with men and man with nature.

Spontaneously investigative and responsive from the first, the young Steinbeck found himself in a family setting that he could enjoy. Its assets included many books from among which the boy chose what he needed to serve the purposes of his self-education: Malory, Milton, Shakespeare, Dante, Goethe, Dostoevski, and Thucydides. That he digested instruction well is evident in the enduring influence that many of these guides had on his own work. The oneness of human experience was real to Steinbeck in relation to time as well as to space. What he read seemed to be not about events and passions of far away and long ago but rather, as he observed, "about things that happened to me."

His family, neither rich nor poor, made up a comfortable community the members of which helped each other when they could but encouraged any show of initiative and independence. The father, always unobtrusively sympathetic to the younger Steinbeck's desire to become a writer, once paid, out of a small salary as an official of city government, a minute allowance which kept his son in the bare necessities of life while he worked at his manuscripts. The mother as a girl had been a school-teacher and, though she did not want her son to become a writer and would have preferred to see him established in a profession of acknowledged prestige, she set him on the long search for enlightenment through books.

Olive Hamilton Steinbeck appears briefly on the autobiographical periphery of the novel *East of Eden*, a creature of intense feeling, "as intuitive as a cat," but incapable of disciplined thought. Her theology, Steinbeck wrote, "was a curious mixture of Irish fairies and an Old Testament Jehovah." This naive effort to integrate unlike deities in a Pantheon all her own dazzled the imagination of her son and Steinbeck's fiction was to receive great drafts of refreshment from mythology. He did not hesitate to give to a character of his own creation traits which he had first perceived in figures as unlike as Christ, Faust, and the lord of Camelot. From one or another of the great fables, read in his youth, he borrowed here an intimation, there an insight. These stories were for him myths "which have their roots in reality." In his tireless investigation of their roots, he refined and enriched what he had absorbed under his mother's unsophisticated instruction — and placed it in logical perspective. She had tried to obliterate any reality that threatened her whims either by refusing to believe in it or by raging blindly against it. Steinbeck's own reconciliation with reality became in the end complete. "Things are as they are," he wrote, "because they must be."

Though his logic was cool his temper was not. All his work steams with indignation at injustice, with contempt for false piety, with scorn for the cunning and self-righteousness of an economic system that encourages exploitation, greed, and brutality. What saved him from the helpless vexation against frustrating reality that characterized his mother was in part his humor, which exercised a sanative and corrective influence on all his judgments, and in part his belief in oneness, in "a kind of wholeness to sense and emotion": "Good and bad, ugly and cruel all [are] welded into one."

Throughout the six years of Steinbeck's intermittent attendance at Stanford University (where he did not in the end bother to earn a degree) he worked at odd jobs usually involving physical labor — rancher, hod carrier, deck hand. He found these occupations congenial because they brought him into intimate association with the great company of workers among whom he chose his friends long before he used them as models for characters in stories. These were men whose courage he admired, whose rejection of cant and hypocrisy he applauded, and whose "high survival quotient" became for him the essential proof of a human being's success.

The man was ready for his work at twenty-seven when he published his first novel, *Cup of Gold* (1929). During the next quarter of a century he produced copiously: eleven novels (*To a God Unknown*, 1932; *Tortilla Flat*, 1935; *In Dubious Battle*, 1936; *The Red Pony*, 1937; *The Grapes of Wrath*, 1939; *Of Mice and Men*, 1940; *The Moon Is Down*, 1942; *Cannery Row*, 1945; *The Wayward Bus*, 1947; *The Pearl*, 1947; *East of Eden*, 1952), as well as two collections of short stories (*The Pastures of Heaven*, 1932; *The Long Valley*, 1938), dramatizations of two of his novels (*Of Mice and Men*, 1940; *The Moon Is Down*, 1942) and a play in story form (*Burning Bright*, 1950), a documentary (*The Forgotten Village*, 1941), two volumes of reportage (*Bombs Away*, 1942, and *A Russian Journal*, 1948), and a journal of travel and scientific research (*Sea of Cortez*, 1951). His performance from the start was accomplished and professional: his books were carefully designed according to artistic principles of his own. The results were often moving, always disturbing, and in several instances strikingly impressive.

There were still two novels to come (*Sweet Thursday*, 1954; *The Winter of Our Discontent*, 1961), and a variety of other publications. But the later phases of Steinbeck's work were largely disappointing to thoughtful critics. That they were disappointing to the writer himself is made clear by a confession which, with a total lack of histrionism, he introduced into *Travels with Charley* (1962). This account of a trip made across the United States with his pet dog is as much an experiment in self-discovery as it is an effort to rediscover America. It contains a scene in which the lonely traveler listens to a fire-and-brimstone sermon preached by an old-fashioned fundamentalist in a Vermont pulpit. Steinbeck reports that he took this indictment of human frailty to himself: "I hadn't been thinking very well of myself for some years." It was at this precise moment that the Nobel Prize for literature was belatedly and almost apologetically awarded him. The vehement protest that the selection roused from many commentators must have made the laurels weigh on his head like a crown of thorns.

Steinbeck did no more significant work. Because he had not lost his taste for the art of communication he took to writing journalistic pieces like *America and Americans* (1966). This study of the native scene is steadily appealing and often shrewdly, though generously, critical. But a tone of autumnal melancholy broods over its pages.

His private life cannot have been without conflict, for he was married three times and divorced twice. However, certain shy liftings of the veil upon his privacy which occur in *Travels with Charley* indicate that his last marriage was happy and that the way of life it brought him — complete with cabin boat on Long Island, town house in New York, and loyal friends — was congenial.

His outlook changed in many ways. A return to Salinas showed him that, as Thomas Wolfe had also found, "you can't go home again." The boys in the back room of his favorite bar were no longer the brothers in spirit that they once had been. And in one significant way Steinbeck was surprisingly out of sympathy with the young whose protests he had so articulately anticipated: he sided with the hawks on the issue of war in Vietnam. Despite these ironies of psychological change, the end of his life did not forget or reject its beginnings. Steinbeck's last intimate communication to his following, contained in a chapter of *Travels with Charley*, expresses, with a ringing echo of the old anger, the "weary nausea" he experienced as he watched a "demoniac" crowd in New Orleans baiting a frightened black child as she entered a previously all white school. In the midst of momentary despair, his pity and pride were invested as deeply as ever in the fate of the miserable and the dispossessed.

John Steinbeck died on December 20, 1968, in New York City.

While he lived Steinbeck was regarded by many of his critics as a kind of perennial apprentice. He experimented with many forms and, as he once boasted a little boyishly, none of his books was like any other. He seemed always to be beginning anew and this suggested to some that he lacked a sense of direction. Doctrinaire critics tended to dismiss any claim that might be made for him as an artist of rank and even the most sympathetic of his contemporary appraisers temporized with a cautious attitude of "waiting to see." Now that the record is complete a dispassionate inspection of his work and an assessment of his accomplishment are in order. It says something significant about the importance of Steinbeck's work that the testimony must be examined on several different levels of interest. The same can be said of

comparatively few American writers up to the very recent
phantasmagorical/psychedelic experimentation with forms of
fiction. Earlier storytellers conformed to familiar methods, producing, like Edith Wharton, the novel of manners; like Sinclair
Lewis, the novel of social satire; or more or less like the master
Henry James, the novel of subtle inquiry into states of mind
induced by exquisite crises of loyalty. Below such enduring
figures as these stood the great mass of fictioneers who ground
out replicas of the well-made novel all having similarly stupefy-
ing patterns of predictable climaxes.

In contrast, Steinbeck from the moment when he made his
debut with *Cup of Gold* was ever an audacious creator of new
worlds. Exploring as broadly as possible the secrets of the species
man, he presented himself simultaneously as storyteller, fabulist,
critic of social institutions, innovative stylist, and appraiser of
experience in philosophical terms. In all these roles Steinbeck
struggled to give the upper hand to the original over the banal,
to fresh intuition over accepted doctrine or dogma, to generous
values over shabby ones, and to personal observation over the
clichés of image, emotion, or conviction. The degree of success
that he attained must be examined separately for each of the
roles he played.

That Steinbeck was a storyteller of persuasive power is clear.
Always the quintessential dramatist, he demanded of a reader
that he identify himself with a particular moment of crisis. Then,
by selecting the most revelatory bits of evidence, he wooed his
audience subtly but insistently into acceptance of whatever he
wished the meaning of an incident, an event, or a passion to be.

The story called "The Chrysanthemums" (from *The Long
Valley*) presents the problem of the artist in conflict with philis-
tinism. It does so in a way that makes a familiar, but often drear-
ily detailed, complaint seem immediate and moving because the
storyteller has offered a small, unexpected, fully dramatized instance. A woman whose painstaking creativity has been invested
in growing flowers is persuaded to give some of her precious

sprouts to a man who, while he pretends to warm sympathy with her work, is in fact only exploiting her dedication to gain a petty advantage for himself. When she finds that he has thrown away her sprouts as worthless she suffers the shock of an encounter with insensate brutality. Imbedded in the narrative, which is tense despite its seeming casualness and powerful despite the modesty of its material, is the further implication that to be touched by meanness, even accidentally, is to be a little tainted by it. A struggle to maintain her integrity ends in failure for the once sturdy woman when she finds that vengeful hatred has transformed her into a feebly weeping victim.

André Gide was an admirer of Steinbeck's stories, likening some of them to the best of Chekhov. What these talents have in common is an economy of means which yields a wealth of implication. Steinbeck's attack on what he wished to unmask and to destroy was far more aggressive than that of Chekhov but equally effective. He knew how to touch the sensitive area.

Many stories in *The Long Valley* present subtly convoluted patterns of suffering, the bitterness of which becomes evident gradually as the spirals mount. The storytelling method seems casual and detached; it admits to making no judgments. But in the end a severe indictment has been drawn up against one aspect or another of man's inhumanity to man — mindless cruelty, insensitivity, hypocrisy. In "The White Quail" a man's nerves have been frayed to the point of momentary madness by his wife's frigid exquisiteness. He evens the score by shooting the rare bird that she has loved with a kind of flaccid self-appreciation, likening herself to it. Rejection, rage, revenge, crime, guilt — the design for misery which Steinbeck took 500 pages to develop in *East of Eden* here is compressed into fewer than twenty.

It is one thing to be able to improvise telling incidents and quite another to build a solid narrative out of such materials. In *The Grapes of Wrath* Steinbeck demonstrated that he was indeed master of this technique. His expertness of craftsmanship was not, however, evident to some critics when the novel first ap-

peared. One even said that *The Grapes of Wrath* was as formless as a
novel could manage to be. To such critics this seemed to be a
haphazardly charted odyssey unworthy of its classical model in
that it lacked a hero, like Homer's, whose various adventures
were held together by his compelling drive to escape danger and
find his way home. Yet this is, in fact, precisely the pattern that
The Grapes of Wrath does possess. Instead of one central figure
there is the family of the Joads, dispossessed tenant farmers of
Oklahoma who take to the highway in a collapsing truck. These
people are in flight from danger even as Odysseus was; they, too,
are trying to find their way home, to a new home which will give
them a secure way of life and enable them to achieve dignity.
The encounters they have along the way — across the desert,
toward the orchards and growing fields of California — are not
merely random adventures but the meaningful events of a vigorous struggle for survival.

Viewed from the perspective of the present day, three decades
after its first appearance, *The Grapes of Wrath* seems not merely a
"proletarian novel," to be dismissed for its vulgar, fleeting time-
liness, but an admirably modeled work of art having impressive
size and just proportion, movement, balance, symmetry, and
power. Each incident representing the struggle of the Joads
against time and fate is precipitated onto the stage with the
persuasiveness of immediate crisis: the loss of a machine part
essential to the operation of the truck; the perilous crossing of
the desert in a decrepit vehicle; the betrayal of the workers by
landowners who lower wages below subsistence level simply because there is a surplus of fruit pickers; the cynical parody of the
rule of law and order in which men wearing badges as deputy
sheriffs turn their guns on men who want nothing but the right
to support their families; the herding of itinerant workers into
squalid camps; the cunning defense by the group of laborers
against gross injustice, against the threat of extinction of their
kind. Each event in this crucial series is precisely, dramatically
defined; each is articulated into the next; the mass of happenings is formed into a climax; the climaxes gain in power until the
significance of the group adventure is impressively clear.

The essential point made by this study of the plight of man under the conditions of the Great Depression is that, no matter how bitter the assault on its existence may be, the group will defend itself unyieldingly. It obeys what Steinbeck called in the *Sea of Cortez* "the one commandment for living things: Survive!"

This is what he is able, with the aid of a rich variety of demonstrations, to persuade us is true of the Joads and of the group that forms around them. The families seem to disintegrate; the old members die of hunger and exhaustion; those who expose themselves to special danger as leaders are beaten and one is killed; some of the young people defect through moral weakness or in the service of self-interest. But even as the old group falls apart, a new one is seen to be forming. Tom Joad will become the leader of a new and better trained army fighting for the survival of his kind.

A literary device used by Steinbeck to amplify the meaning of his story may have been what made the book appear formless to certain eyes. Not infrequently he interrupts the flow of narrative to introduce chapters of comment and generalization. One is reminded by them of the way in which the chorus of a Greek play intervenes in the action. These passages contain parables dealing with the problem of survival and with the intricacies of the economic system in which the Joads find themselves inarticulately enmeshed. Abstract though these discussions are, and theoretical, they preserve the tone of drama and parallel the concerns of the story itself.

One of these sections describes, with an air of tension that might be appropriate to the detailing of a performance of a high-wire circus act, the dogged behavior of a turtle crossing a road, evading the purgatorial horrors of highway traffic and finally achieving its goal in the dust of a sheltered place. This minute spectacle dramatized in essence the meaning of the struggle in which the Joads are engaged.

In another of these excursions into allegory Steinbeck dramatized the unending debate between man and a powerful institution which he himself has created but whose vast, impersonal power now threatens to destroy him. The bank which owns the land on which people like the Joads live must put it to more profitable use than tenant farming. The inadequate worker must be put off and his house bulldozed to the ground. "The bank," says the oracle of this ingenious side drama, is "something more than men . . . It's the monster. Men made it, but they can't control it." Thus, without indulging in the moralizing rhetoric of the more usual proletarian novel Steinbeck establishes his point. Man, as victim of his own technological skill, must learn patiently to unweave the noose around his neck.

The Grapes of Wrath enriches the tradition of American writing and serves an interest which *Moby Dick* once held as its unique possession. The novels are alike in that each tells a powerful story of conflict dramatizing the wild compulsions of human behavior and also the curious and unexpected generosities of the human heart. Each offers philosophic insight into man's deep preoccupation with the secrets of his own nature. Melville's book, rejected when it first appeared, by critics and readers alike, found its place at long last among the most original and important contributions to native literature. *The Grapes of Wrath* should have less difficulty in maintaining its place on the same shelf.

The Grapes of Wrath does not stand alone as evidence of Steinbeck's storytelling skill. The earlier novel *In Dubious Battle* (still surprisingly neglected) is virtually a model for a certain kind of craftsmanship. Hard, tight-packed as a bullet in its form, its propulsive power matches its theme. *In Dubious Battle* is like *The Grapes of Wrath* in no way except that both books are concerned with workers in a California valley who test fate by defying the power of a growers' association. If *In Dubious Battle* had been intended as a strikers' handbook it could hardly have been more explicit about the tactics of conflict, more scrupulously factual in its concentration on the events of one crisis in full ferment. The novel's unity of time and its strict enclosure within the limits of a particular place give it a classical sharpness of design. Within that pattern the style is as native as the scene is peculiarly American. The language is blunt, colloquial, emphatic, the mood resolute and impersonal.

As the novel opens, the wage scale in the apple orchards of Torgas Valley has been dropped in direct proportion to an increase in the number of available pickers. A Communist organizer, Mac, precipitates himself into the situation, assuming a proprietary right to any battlefield of frustration and discontent. Influenced by his delicate manipulation, the workers walk off the job. Mac sees little hope for this particular strike but foments its violence with dedicated zeal and with great skill in the strategy of disruption. In the interest of his party's war on capitalism he maneuvers this skirmish toward its foredoomed tragedy.

When this book was first published Steinbeck was accused of harboring Communist sympathies. Because his strikers are presented as men suffering from unbearable wrongs it was possible for a heedless or prejudiced reader to assume that the novel constituted an endorsement of any movement that promised to correct these wrongs. But the author of *In Dubious Battle* remains as coolly detached as his characters are hotly involved. He puts his own attitude into the mouth of a young doctor who has come voluntarily to this battleground simply to patch up broken heads. Doc is challenged by Mac to clarify his position. "If it rains good and hard tonight the men'll be sneaking out on us. They just won't take it, I tell you. It's a funny thing, Doc. You don't believe in the cause, and you'll probably be the last man to stick. I don't get it at all." And Doc responds: "I don't get myself. . . . I don't believe in the cause, but I believe in men. . . . I have some skill in helping men, and when I see some who need help, I just do it."

Steinbeck's realistic concept of society ("Things are as they are because they must be") had no room in it for any but a clinical interest in a system like that of communism. Its theories seemed to him not merely arbitrary but degrading. One of the most revealing scenes of *In Dubious Battle* exposes a professional revolutionary, the young apprentice, Jim, indulging in an almost orgiastic love of violence for its own sake. Steinbeck's distaste for such doctrinaire dedication is evident. Uncommitted to any cause but the affirmation of the dignity of man, he offered *In Dubious Battle* as a study of the way in which the compulsive behavior of a group may threaten its own survival. It threatens, he seems to insist, and yet cannot finally defeat. Like Doc, Steinbeck did not believe in causes but in men. His novel comments on the problem of man's conflict with his environment, suggesting with a kind of somber optimism that though a battle may end in stalemate the war itself is not lost. Steinbeck followed his classic model to the end, presenting a climax in which a tremendous bout of "pity and terror" purges and purifies the emotions, satisfying the principle of catharsis. But the method casts no shadow of pretension or of artifice on the contemporaneity of the material. The men of *In Dubious Battle* are engaged in a struggle, not with austere and demanding gods, but with the equally harsh, quite as imperiously controlled, conditions of their social environment. The violent ending manages to suggest the possibility of a new beginning. If the ways of the ancient gods were ambiguous yet somehow benign, so the no less oppressive ways of society may eventually become generous and supportive.

East of Eden presents Steinbeck in a contrasting facet of his role as storytelling craftsman. The longest of his novels, it manages to be intimate and personal in tone, establishing itself as a kind of genial father-confessor among his books. The contrast with *In Dubious Battle* is complete; one is as diffuse in interest as the other is compact; the later is as full of conversational perambulations as the earlier is severely shorn of such devices. A diary Steinbeck kept for the benefit of his editor during the composition of *East of Eden*, and published posthumously, throws curiously little light on his creative method. But it is clear that in this effort he drew his inspiration from the symphonic form of which he was a devoted student. Into the novel he weaves three themes. Each is given its major and minor variations which play upon each other with harmonic intricacy, producing crescendos of cumulative power. The motifs reveal their interrelationships with ever increasing lucidity so that in the end the work is discovered to be a hymn to earth and to man as protector, expander, and fulfiller of its destiny.

The first motif may be identified by the word "westering." The compulsive movement of men and women across a sea and a continent, to establish a new society in a setting foreign to its origins but sympathetic to its needs, is dramatized in the chronicles of two families, the Hamiltons out of Ireland and the Trasks out of Connecticut. They come together in the Salinas Valley, there to enact the scenes that are vital to Steinbeck's story of a new creation, this time the creation by man of his own world. This is, however, no usual family record of getting and spending, begetting and dying. The events are numerous, spectacular, often violent. They involve all the inevitable crises of conflict ranging from personal feud to war itself. But these concerns of individuals are offered as evidence that a far more significant story is in the process of unfolding. Steinbeck defines westering as the impulse of the group to transform itself into "one great crawling beast" compelled by the secrets of its nature to move through perils, survive disaster, and "get there." This is, in effect, an account in allegorical terms of the great yearning of man ever and again to reenact the drama of Genesis.

The second motif searches out the personal compulsions which in each individual underlie the urgent thrust of the will to survive. In each generation of the family of Adam Trask the conflict of Cain and Abel is paralleled. This, Steinbeck suggests, is "the symbol story of the human soul" and he undertakes to explore the maze of hostilities through which each man must make his way in the inevitable struggle for dominance of brother over brother. The same fateful pattern of ambivalence is evident in the relationship of father and son. As Steinbeck's spokesman observes: "The greatest terror a child can have is that he is not loved, and rejection is the hell he fears. I think everyone in the world to a large or small extent has felt rejection. And with rejection comes anger, and with anger some kind of crime in revenge for the rejection, and with the crime guilt." Steinbeck's two versions of the passion of Everyman, dramatized in Adam Trask's struggle first with a violent brother and then with a difficult, demanding, sensitive son, play contrapuntally on each other until the significance of each phase is fully revealed. The "story of mankind" has been restaged, losing none of its complexity, in the homely setting of the Trask household. The purpose of the author in doing so is, again in the words of his spokesman, to show how many "pains and insanities" could be "rooted out if the causes were known."

The third motif is also a familiar one but it is given a new variation. What Steinbeck contributes to the discussion of humanity's Problem One — the conflict between good and evil — is his own concept of the doctrine of free will. Again he refers to the Biblical story recalling that the Lord, in the severity of his love, says to Cain: "If thou doest well, shalt thou not be accepted? and if thou doest not well, sin lieth at the door. And unto thee shall be his desire, and thou shalt rule over him." Steinbeck became convinced that the King James version of the Bible erred in its translation of the significant word in this passage, the Hebrew verb *timshel*. His redefinition makes it a word not of command but of counsel: thou mayest, rather than thou shalt, rule over sin.

When the book first appeared a brisk controversy arose over Steinbeck's interpretation of the meaning of *timshel* and over his spelling of the word as well. Scholars challenged both and then a second group of scholars challenged the first. Steinbeck, beset and defended, held his ground with characteristic self-assurance. In the absence of divine guidance in the matter he may be allowed to accept responsibility for his philosophy and for his orthography as well.

For him the difference between thou shalt and thou mayest works a peaceful revolution in the world of morality. Man ceases to be the slave of unintelligible forces over which he has no control; he becomes master of his destiny when he is given "the glory of the choice" between good and evil. It was Steinbeck's philosophy to the end of his life — as his Nobel address revealed — that three wills are operative in man's experience: the will of the group, the will of the individual, and the moral will which must in the end prevail over the lesser two.

East of Eden is parable, poem, and tale of action all in one. Its panorama is vast, yet its passions are intimate. Its adventures are concerned as much with spiritual values as with physical enterprise. Its people are truly representative of the problem of American society, yet they are individualized in exhaustive detail, foibles and strengths inextricably intermingled. An imaginative reach so encompassing characterizes few works of fiction of which *War and Peace* is one. In the scope of his ambition Steinbeck allied himself with the monumental figures of world literature.

For contrast to this amplitude of design one may turn to an entirely different example of Steinbeck's technical skill. *Of Mice and Men* is so essentially dramatic in its structure that to adapt it to the requirements of the theater it was necessary only to compress its descriptive passages into stage directions and allow the remaining dialogue to take command. Here in the simplest possible terms Steinbeck offers a statement of his belief in the importance of a voluntary acceptance of responsibility. It reminds us again that "man owes something to man."

The central character, George, is a typical Steinbeck figure, a man of the humble workaday world who, as migrant worker, has shown a high survival quotient both in physical resourcefulness and in independence of mind. But his freedom is grotesquely limited by the fact that he has assumed guardianship over a creature of monumental ineptitude, a retarded child in a man's huge body. Lennie's great hands, not being under the control of an adult conscience, cannot resist the temptation to touch and caress any soft thing they encounter. A mouse will do but a girl is better. Inevitably he brings trouble down upon the ill-matched pair wherever they try to settle as workers.

On a ranch where George finds employment for both the fateful routine is enacted again. The provocative, amoral wife of the ranch boss's son attracts Lennie's limited but disastrous interest. What Lennie's weakness urges him to touch his strength compels him to kill. To run away from the fear of punishment is the only wisdom available to the totally inadequate creature and he obeys it. The search that follows must, if it is successful, end in a ritual murder of revenge. George is obliged to find his pitiful friend before the posse can do so and shoot him as an act of kindness.

The novel's climactic scene has been anticipated by one having exactly the same import. The stench of an old dog, owned by one inmate of the ranch barracks, has become intolerable to the other men. He is destroyed in all decency — even with respect for his blameless integrity as ranch animal — by one bullet aimed at the back of his head. The point of the parable is explicitly made: no life is unworthy of reverence, not that of an ailing dog, not that of an idiot. Life must be sacred even to a man who is obliged to destroy in order to save.

The small book of related sketches called *The Red Pony* has been overpraised as Steinbeck's best artistic achievement. One may well agree that this portrait of a sensitive boy is indeed distinguished without finding the work as a whole satisfactory. Seldom has the identification of a fledgling artist with the natural scene that surrounds him been presented with a lyricism so innocently appealing. But the structure is topheavy. The one decisive act in this study of an approach to maturity occurs in the first episode, leaving the others to taper off in successive stages of anticlimax. When the boy, Jody, beats in frantic rage at the buzzards hovering over the body of his beloved dead pony, managing to kill one, he declares his sentiments and his loyalties with dramatic eloquence. In the other experiences of the story he is revealed with steadily less ingratiating poignancy. An interesting comment on Steinbeck's preoccupation with problems of technique is to be found in the fact that when he prepared his own scenario for a film version of *The Red Pony* he corrected his mistake by putting the climax where it belongs — at the end.

It is the vocation of the storyteller to communicate to readers a sense of life lived outside the confines of their own skins and beyond the limitations of their own intelligences. To respond to such an evocation is to become momentarily a new man, quickened in flesh, mind, and spirit to new awareness and alerted also to the powerful influence of a certain setting upon all the sensibilities. A world unlike one's own is all at once made intimately familiar.

A writer may be a genius without possessing this special gift of persuasion. Edith Wharton once — quite innocently as she insists in her memoirs — made the confidence of Henry James falter by asking: Why do your characters seem never to have any other place to go when they leave the printed page? James's abashed acknowledgment that he did not realize this was so made tacit confession to certain limitations in his art.

Another highly gifted novelist, John O'Hara, in his stories of conflict over crises in manners, ambitions, and loyalties made do with a similarly restricted realm of creativity. His characters exist tantalizingly, pugnaciously within the space of each well-contrived scene in which they play their parts. But absence from the next scene suggests only that they are being hastily repaired for the ardors of another passage in a love duel or for the rigors of a still more intense struggle for domination in the immediate situation.

The total environment of Steinbeck's world is quite different. Its physical manifestations — the menace of a desert, the peril of flood in a valley — are introduced not as mere stage effects; their impacts fall as awesomely on the reader as they do on the Joad family in *The Grapes of Wrath*. In *East of Eden* the unwritten scenes of Aaron Trask's yearning for identification with his father tug at the imagination with implications of an unappeased desire that grows even during the author's silences. It is the novelist's method to cut into the midst of a scene that seems to have been in progress before the factual report begins and to go on after it closes. The loyalties and hostilities of the hobo jungles that give the setting to *In Dubious Battle* constitute a way of life that seems to draw energy from forces far beyond the arbitrary control of a mere contriver of happenings. The variety, urgency — even the quirkiness — of the mental adventures of many of Steinbeck's characters suggest a richness of experience the like of which is to be found only in the work of the important Russian writers. Indeed it might be said of his novels, as Virginia

Woolf said of Dostoevski's, that they are "composed of the stuff of the soul."

Because his creations seem to leap over the barriers of lines on a printed page into an existence of their own, Steinbeck must be credited with distinguished success not merely as storyteller but as reflector of the quality of contemporary American life.

Steinbeck's gift as fabulist contributed heavily to making his work unique among American writers of his time. His borrowings from literature's wealth of folklore and his evident desire to show a kinship between many of his chief characters and the towering figures of myth are evident in *The Grapes of Wrath* and *East of Eden*. But it is in a comparatively obscure early novel, *To a God Unknown*, that his concern with man's heritage from the past is most apparent. This is a book of striking interest, strewn tantalizingly with samples of what he himself described as "the harvest of symbols in our minds [which] seem to have been implanted in the soft, rich soil of our pre-humanity."

The novel may be read on its surface as another story of westering. Joseph Wayne finds the Vermont farm on which he has lived with his father and brothers too small to satisfy his land hunger and, with the blessing of his parent, leaves home. "After a time of wandering," he comes at last to a promising valley of California. He feels close to the land, nourishes its needs, sends for his brothers to join him, becomes the acknowledged patriarch of his clan, marries, loses his wife, faces disaster from drought, and literally gives his life to the soil he loves.

But Steinbeck means to imply much more in this allegory of man's unity with nature. Joseph Wayne is not merely a priest of natural religion; he is one of its demigods, feeling himself to *be* the land, to embody its urgencies, its trials, its failures, and its fulfillment. When at the end he dies by his own hand he regards the sacrifice as having ritualistic significance. Relief from drought immediately follows the use of a knife on the veins of his wrist and he thinks in triumph: "I am the land . . . and I am the rain. The grass will grow out of me in a little while."

Steinbeck did not edge timidly into this large-scale parable of man as "symbol of the earth's soul." He welcomed its challenges boldly. His Joseph Wayne insists upon believing that his dead father has come to live in a tree that stands beside his door; he puts his child into the tree's branches to receive its benediction; he accepts the death of the tree as warning of disaster to come. With these alliances to the occult he passes out of the realm of everyday reality into the realm of mysticism where he reveals his kinship to a cult of primitive deities. A novel must offer many demonstrations of its theme and Steinbeck with his virtuosity of invention finds no difficulty in dazzling a reader with references, back and forth through time, to precedents of wonder. His Joseph is related in the genealogy of letters to Joseph of the Bible who also brought his brothers into a new world, established his authority over the people of a country not his own, and created a society for the protection of all. But Joseph Wayne's ancestry may be traced back farther still to forebears in the primitive world. He is entirely at home among neighbors who engage in rites to propitiate the gods and who, when their incantations seemed to be answered in signs of benediction, erupt lustily into orgies. Even the blood sacrifices of animals in which another neighbor engages, with exquisite skill accompanied by sensations of joy, neither surprise nor appall him.

What must be accepted in order to receive the intended impression of this long prose poem to nature is that Joseph is a creature of earth belonging not to a particular moment in time but, like any figure in mythology, to all time. Or, as the spokesman for Steinbeck's mysticism says: ". . . he is all men. The strength, the resistance, the long and stumbling thinking of all men, and all the joy and suffering, too . . ." There is in him something of the majesty, the harshness, and the detachment of a natural element. What adds greatly to the surprise and high excitement of this conceit is that Steinbeck has been able to give to so extraordinary a being a local habitation and an American name.

A phrase which Steinbeck has used to describe this kind of

exercise is "the working of atavistic magic." Surrender of disbelief may not be easy in the face of so unexpected a demand, but
the reward of making the effort is a kind of pleasure that is also
rare and unexpected. A haunting music flows from every page
and the novel's many incantations are alive with what one of the
Hindu scriptures calls "right rapture." There is evidence in *To a
God Unknown* that, in devising a myth of his own out of a blend of
old and new, familiar and remote, Steinbeck was under the
influence of Eastern literature. The book's title is derived from a
Hindu poem in which these lines occur:

> He is the giver of breath, and strength is his gift.
> The high Gods revere his commandments.
> His shadow is life, his shadow is death;
> Who is He to whom we shall offer our sacrifice?

This impulse to refresh imagination at whatever font world literature may offer was not unlike that of Emerson who, in his
hymn to Brahma, celebrated the same esoteric faith that Steinbeck bespeaks in *To a God Unknown*. "Shadow and sunlight are the
same . . . one to me are shame and fame."

It is the task of the novelist to capture the universal in the
particular, revealing the elusive in intriguing incident. Working
in *To a God Unknown* with materials of a peculiarly volatile kind,
Steinbeck managed to reduce his favorite theme of unity to the
explicit terms of dramatic parable.

A better known example of his skill at mythmaking gives a
droll turn to the enterprise. *Tortilla Flat* encloses a group of
ironic anecdotes within the framework of a romance which
claims kinship with the medieval spirit represented by the
legend of King Arthur and his Knights of the Round Table. The
preface offers this clue to the author's intention: "This story
deals with the adventuring of [Danny and] Danny's friends, with
the good they did, with their thoughts and their endeavors.
. . . It is well that this cycle be put down on paper so that in a
future time scholars, hearing the legends, may not say as they
say of Arthur and of Roland and of Robin Hood — 'There was no
Danny nor any group of Danny's friends . . . Danny is a

nature god and his friends primitive symbols of the wind, the sky, the sun.' This history is designed now and ever to keep the sneers from the lips of sour scholars." Obviously Steinbeck's fluent tongue is, for the moment, lodged snugly in his cheek. This is a grandiose joke. Out of his boyhood love of Malory he has fashioned, still in boyish temper, a good-natured parody of the chivalric tradition. Danny, King Arthur's comic counterpart, is a California paisano, recently returned from World War I. He takes into his house a group of strays ardently devoted to indolence who range through the neighborhood of Monterey seeking liquor, women, and whatever fight may help to while away the afternoon. Their "endeavors" are all exuberant parodies of the questing of Arthur's knights.

The loosely linked incidents are mildly bawdy and Steinbeck's treatment of each is ironically indulgent. It is his gleefully maintained pretense that every drunken bout is a grand ceremonial of comradeship and every buffoonish encounter between the sexes a fine display of chivalric spirit. The success of *Tortilla Flat* rests solidly on Steinbeck's complete savoir-faire in maintaining his own air of gravity. A comic miniature of heroic romance, the book keeps its proportions, its emphases, and its implications all in scale, corresponding neatly to those of the myth of the Round Table. Even when Danny dies, in a fall from a cliff after a drunken party, it is solemnly suggested that he has not been lost to humanity; rather, he has been "translated" to be forever, again like Arthur, "the once and future king."

The idea of the imperishability of the leader haunted Steinbeck's mind. The scenario that he wrote for the film *Viva Zapata* ends with the death of the man who has been the genius of a Mexican revolution. Zapata, shot down by the soldiers of a corrupt government, lies dead in the marketplace. But his followers refuse to believe that he is lost to them. He has, they assure each other, "gone to the mountains" from which he will return when his strength has been restored. The suggestion is that all men, in all times, in all cultures must cling to a belief in the "atavistic magic" essential to survival. Again: "Myths have their roots in reality."

What this parallel treatment of the Arthurian legend implies is that the first prerequisite for knighthood is generosity. And no matter how grotesque the vagaries of Danny and his friends, they are in lively possession of qualities that Steinbeck genuinely admires: virility, honesty, and comradeliness. They are able to make accommodation to circumstance and by that adaptability they manage to survive. Danny's house becomes the symbol of man's environment; the resourceful ways of its inhabitants offer suggestions which are by no means wholly frivolous about how that environment can be made livable.

Steinbeck's one failure in the realm of mythmaking is the play in story form called *Burning Bright*. Here he attempted to re-create Everyman or, perhaps more nearly, the universal father. The central situation is that of a man who, though he does not know of his disability, cannot have a child of his own because he is sterile. In an effort to restore his self-esteem his wife enters into an otherwise meaningless relationship with another man so that she may become a mother. This so closely duplicates a crisis of Eugene O'Neill's *Strange Interlude* that Steinbeck must have believed it to be as legitimate to borrow from one's contemporaries as to borrow from the classics. To the appropriated material he adds something that is entirely his own: the idea that a mature intelligence must accept the oneness of humanity. At the close of the play the protagonist, having learned the truth about the child's paternity, is still able to say: "I love my son." This endorsement carries with it the implication that in a good society every man should consider himself to be the father to every son.

The difficulty with the experiment is simply that it does not come off. As in no other of Steinbeck's works the language is uninterruptedly high-flown and artificial. Even the structure seems labored and clumsy: to emphasize the universality of his characters Steinbeck gives them the same names throughout but in each act presents them in a different social setting, first in a circus, then on a farm, and finally against the background of the sea. Even so, Steinbeck's Everyman dwindles into Every-stereotype. The interest of *Burning Bright* collapses under the burden of its moral purpose which burns only too ardently.

Entirely successful, within the more modest limits of its intent, is the parable called *The Pearl*. In the *Sea of Cortez* Steinbeck tells of hearing a story about a Mexican Indian pearl diver who found such a fine jewel that he knew "he need never work again." Possession of this rare object so poisoned the existence of the fisherman, however, that he cursed it and threw it back into the sea.

Steinbeck's comment on the story, made in *Sea of Cortez*, was that he did not believe it: "it is far too reasonable to be true." But this uncharacteristic literal-mindedness presently gave way to a realization that the legend cried out for elaboration and interpretation. Showing a fine respect for the special quality of the material, he produced a touching story of good in desperate struggle with evil. An infant becomes his symbol of innocence betrayed. The baby, born to a pearl fisherman, Kino, and his wife, Juana, is bitten by a scorpion and the local doctor refuses treatment because he knows the family to be poor. The situation is reversed when it becomes known that Kino has found "the Pearl of the World." Everyone becomes eager to exploit his ignorance. The doctor tries to play on a father's fears for the child, hoping to get the pearl in payment for useless services. The dealer in pearls belittles the jewel thinking to get it for little. Thieves set upon Kino in the dark trying to rob him and beat him viciously in the attempt. His house is burned in the course of another invasion. Crises mount until Kino realizes that he must try to escape from a world that has turned into an implacable enemy. But there is no escape from the evil that has been loosed into this community. Kino is tracked into the mountains where he has taken wife and child to hide. Bullets from the gun of the trackers hit and kill the child. The irony is complete; the pearl which should have been the means of helping to fulfill Kino's ambitions for his son actually has been an agent of disaster, producing only suffering, despair, and finally death. Back it goes into the sea, flung by Kino's hand.

The unfolding of incident presents Kino always as the angry, frightened, but resolute man, determined to keep what he has earned. This establishes the human element with satisfying dramatic emphasis while the allegorical element envelops the child in a miasmic cloud of evil. A pattern of symbols draws the delicate complexity of the parable into a tight design. The sea — Kino's environment — gives and takes away like a superbly indifferent minister of destiny. The pearl itself represents the wonder, the mystery, the maddening, fateful beauty of the world, all in one luminous sphere.

As well as in any other of his stories, major or minor, Steinbeck matches manner to matter in *The Pearl*. The style has a subdued, foreboding lyricism which communicates easily with a reader's sympathies and never wavers toward elegiac excess. Because his people are inarticulate Steinbeck must tell their story in the language of the heart and he is able to keep its idiom warm, believable, and touching. This is perhaps the best of his achievements in the role he liked best, that of fabulist.

Steinbeck, the analyst and critic of society, had in his time to refute many charges of bias against democracy and "the American way of life." Consideration of his work on this level of its interest may well begin with a listing of the kinds of influence he did not aspire to exert. He was never a radical thinker, pamphleteer, agitator, Communist, or fellow traveler.

If evidence is needed that he entertained neither overt nor disguised sympathies with the Soviet system this may be readily found in his *Russian Journal*. The book is not one of his impressive accomplishments. It contains no striking insights and is content to offer merely a rambling account of casual encounters with bureaucrats, fellow writers, students, shopkeepers, official guides, Ukrainian farmers, stage performers, and mighty drinkers of vodka. The tone is relaxed to the point of being flaccid but what it conveys inescapably is a distaste for nearly everything that a repressive government does to its likable victims. Men are good, their institutions dangerous, he seems to be repeating again and again with a kind of unsurprised sorrow. In *The Grapes of Wrath* he had stated explicitly and by implication his dissatisfaction with the status quo in American society. But his comments on his experience in Russia leave no doubt that he had far greater hope for the regenerative power of democratic processes of government than for the arbitrary authority of any totalitarian system.

As one who believed in a writer's duty to try to keep humanity's morale high, Steinbeck believed also in the duty to expose attacks on its well-being. His two most searching examinations of the social scene, *The Grapes of Wrath* and *In Dubious Battle*, reveal clearly his ideas of what had gone wrong with the principles of democracy during the 1930s. He had seen men uprooted, degraded, and finally destroyed by the ruthlessly mechanistic operation of the economic system. He became deeply convinced that the rule of law and order is perverted into tyranny whenever democracy yields supinely to the demands of oligarchy. As propagandist he wished to do no more than to indicate how society, by encouraging morbid growths of special privilege for the rights of property over the rights of men, endangers its own survival. When it allows human beings to starve democracy squanders its greatest asset, creative energy.

Steinbeck had no precise scheme of reform to expound, no nostrum to offer. As an artist he could only observe and record the struggle of man against himself, hoping, by a vivid presentation of a problem in human affairs, to awaken minds to its crucial character. Without assuming the responsibilities of a reformer he wished to influence the temper of the time simply by urging acceptance of sane attitudes in matters of economic opportunity and attitudes favoring equality in the administration of justice.

His first book showed the direction his work was to take. *Cup of Gold* undertakes to demolish the inflated notions about the splendor of derring-do which have always tended to glorify the conqueror. This free treatment of the life story of the British pirate Sir Henry Morgan is offered as the epitome of all tales of ruthless enterprise. Out of the welter of its savage happenings rises the conviction that the most fearful of all false beatitudes might read: Blessed be the arriviste for he shall inherit the earth.

What such antiheroes really inherit, Steinbeck insists, are the rewards of all emotionally retarded creatures: memories of mindless cruelty and visions of a world pointlessly laid waste.

The imaginary Henry Morgan of the novel appears first as a stolid, determined boy of fifteen who leaves his home in Wales to go — as Steinbeck puts it with sly irony — "a-buccaneering" in the flamboyant style of the seventeenth century. He ships to sea, is sold into slavery in Barbados, becomes actual master of his languid, ineffectual owner, enriches himself at the latter's expense, becomes "Admiral" of a fleet of pirate vessels, and accepts commissions for bloody enterprise in international conflicts at sea. His crowning victory in Steinbeck's version of the story comes to him when he captures, sacks, and utterly destroys a rich city of Panama, the "Cup of Gold." With characteristic presence of mind and absence of morality, he manages to leave his followers marooned in the wasteland he has made and sails off with all the booty.

Below the surface of this ravening tale lies a pattern of symbols used to emphasize its meaning as parable. The wisdom of the ages is concentrated in the mind of Merlin, revived out of Arthurian romance to appear as young Henry Morgan's mentor. The symbol figure of Faust is reborn in Morgan himself. The grandiosity of his ambitions matches that of Goethe's heroic sinner though he becomes Faust's antithesis in his utter lack of concern for humanity. Echoes of Goethe's tone keep recurring. In the final scene Morgan on his deathbed is confronted, as was Faust, by the accusing shades of his wasted opportunities, his cruelties, and his crimes.

The clues to Steinbeck's basic intent in presenting so blasted an image of dehumanization are many. It is Merlin who anticipates the moral even before the tale has been told. Morgan, the seer says, will always catch his fireflies — that is, realize his wayward ambitions — if he keeps the heart of a child. What Steinbeck means to suggest is that savagery and blood letting — in general, heedless indifference to human rights — are the perverted pleasures of the immature. By implication he reaffirms the belief, expressed by Shaw in *Back to Methuselah*, that the race can save itself from its own destructive impulses only if it manages at last to grow up.

The man of aggressive, unapologetically acquisitive enterprise continued to be the target of Steinbeck's ironic temper throughout his career. In twentieth-century lore, and particularly on American soil, the buccaneer in the 1920s and 1930s often dwindled to the proportions of the excessively energetic businessman, the "go-getter" of the period's slang. Steinbeck never rested from the self-imposed task of shrinking this figure further still with his ridicule. The group of novels — *Cannery Row, The Wayward Bus*, and *Sweet Thursday* — which appear at first glance to be merely light entertainments actually have the purpose of challenging the values of a society that seeks to make a merit of one of its worst defects. A willingness to prey on others in the interest of self-aggrandizement is, in Steinbeck's code, the bleakest of sins.

The figures of *Cannery Row* and of its companion piece, *Sweet Thursday*, are idlers and drunkards, escapists from all the stern realities that control the lives of devotees of the gospel of success. The only rewards they want are those of the moment and their hedonistic activities as well as their buffoonish practical jokes conspicuously flout accepted ideas of proper behavior. But if they do no good, in the sense that dominates the thinking of conventional men and women, they do no harm either, which, Steinbeck says by implication, is more than can be said of many an enterprise of the righteous. The antiheroes of *Cannery Row* are at least concerned with the happiness of one another. Like their brothers of *Tortilla Flat* they direct their "endeavors" toward the well-being of the group.

Steinbeck's jovial endorsement of this conduct is not to be taken as evidence of capriciousness. When he stands the accepted virtues and acknowledged vices on their heads — making conformity seem stuffily absurd if not altogether vicious and nonconformity somehow estimable in and of itself — he wishes to remind us that, after centuries of combining puritanical sanctimoniousness with Yankee cunning in our philosophy of getting on, we need to reexamine all our presuppositions about morality in the light of generosity and sanity.

Literary quality varies widely from scene to scene in each of these novels. *Cannery Row* contains anecdotes as amusing and as lethal as the best of his short stories offer; it indulges also in parodies of sentiment that seem more waggish than adroit. *Sweet Thursday* constantly threatens to collapse into a completely conventional boy-meets-girl romance, arbitrarily forced into a rowdy setting.

Best of the light entertainments is *The Wayward Bus*, which Henry Seidel Canby likened to *The Canterbury Tales*. Here the reader follows the events of a journey and learns the life stories of the accidentally assembled men and women who make it. Under one kind of stress or another each reveals the animating impulse of his nature. A boy, called Pimples in callous recognition of his affliction, touchingly acknowledges his yearning for dignity and acceptance. A smug woman cannot restrain herself from opening the door on the untidy alcove of fantasy in which she lives. A petty man of affairs exposes the wasteland of his mean ambitions and feeble desires. A dying martinet compulsively uncovers the abject fear that has lurked in the background of his effort to be a tyrant. A prostitute testifies by her behavior to the fact that to be amoral in matters of sex is not necessarily to be lacking in sensibility or personal integrity.

It is not difficult to understand why Steinbeck chose sometimes to present in the form of raucous comedy his deeply felt protest against the false values of a property-minded, profit-obsessed world. The clown is permitted to make severe judgments which, had they been spoken in all earnestness by a declared reformer, would have brought the accusation of lese majesty down on his head. Steinbeck, when he championed the cause of the Okies in *The Grapes of Wrath*, had been subjected to just such vituperation. Though he was ever ready to fight for his opinions and his various literary presentations of them, it satisfied his ironic temper now and again to mask sympathies in ribald hilarity. What he is saying in *Cannery Row* quite clearly and unapologetically is that a society that permits, even encourages, high crimes against humanity and then makes a great show of niggling priggishness in the face of venial sin is a fatuous society.

It was appropriate that Steinbeck ended his career as he began it with a novel of social protest. *The Winter of Our Discontent* presents a crisis in the life of a man of sensibility, intelligence, and humor who undertakes willfully to live by the code of a modern buccaneer. The only reward that comes to him out of this adventure in open-eyed obliquity is a self-disgust so grim as to make him suicidal.

The novel is disarming in many ways. It introduces a new Steinbeck, entirely at home in a New England setting but even more critical of its mores than he had previously been of the blunted conscience of his native place. The central figure is a complex product of an old society and his sophisticated graces make him the complete antithesis of the typical pseudoprimitive of *Cannery Row*. The pervasive wit welling up out of the many soliloquies of the protagonist, instead of being of the locker-room variety characteristic of the lively farces, is mental and intricately involuted.

The intention of *The Winter of Our Discontent*, like that of *Cannery Row*, is to show how false the values of society may be. In the earlier book the theme of protest is treated lightheartedly, with an air of frivolous irresponsibility; in the later the tone becomes progressively more severe until in the end it seems almost grim.

Ethan Hawley, the central figure of Steinbeck's last novel, is out of sorts with his world in many ways. In part his discontent springs from the fact that though he bears a fine family name the society of which he is a member has provided him with no money to support the flimsy benefits of his prestige. His own ill-fortune has reduced him to the status of manager-clerk in a modest grocery store. His wife and children want more than they seem to be getting from their lives. He decides, on his family's account, to transform himself into a ruthless activist.

The examples before him of a world that rewards cunning no matter how low its compromises with conscience may be seen to justify an attempt to enrich himself without concern for the suffering his manipulations may cause others.

Ethan's scheme is intricate and has several facets. With characteristic resourcefulness in the invention of incident, Steinbeck explores every aspect of the story's lurid interest. Crime and cruelty are involved, acts of shocking, degrading kinds. Ethan even betrays to his death a friend whom he professes to love. Steinbeck, one must believe, chose these instances not because he believed them to be sensationally extreme but rather because they seemed to him to be altogether too usual in the workaday world of enterprise. Loathing the mischief he has done, Ethan is almost persuaded to pay for it with his own life. The decision is reversed when he realizes that he still owes a duty to life. Only if he survives can his sensitive daughter be expected to do so.

Many symbolic presences reveal themselves intriguingly in the background of the novel. Its title suggests that Steinbeck was thinking of Shakespeare's Richard III who, like Ethan, is "subtle, false and treacherous," frivolously making evil his good. The dates of the book's events are significant. One cluster of events center around preparations for Easter. If Steinbeck's implication is that society is forever reenacting the drama of the Passion, Ethan is appropriately cast as its Judas. The rest of the happenings occur on the Fourth of July. Ethan's betrayal of his own principles is glaringly highlighted by memories of the day on which American democracy made its bold affirmation of the rights of man. The problem which Steinbeck faced in *The Winter of Our Discontent* was to make Ethan's tragedy seem somehow worthy to stand in the shadow of events so portentous. He did not wholly succeed. Likable though the novel is, it betrays — even as Ethan does — its own intent. The gravity of the situation is covered by a froth of frivolity. The tone of the storytelling is too light to bear the weight of its implications.

But the final comment on Steinbeck's work as critic of society must be that no other writer of our time has found so many ways of reminding us that man should be the beneficiary of his institutions, not their victim. His best work dramatizes the plight of man — now tragically, now humorously, with the aid of challenge, irony, homely eloquence, and subtle insight — as he indomitably struggles to make his environment a protective garment, not a haircloth shirt.

A curious view of Steinbeck, expressed by some of his early critics, presented him as a kind of naive natural genius who, having limited resources of technique and an even more severely limited vocabulary, blundered occasionally into displays of impressive, if brutal, power. Closer examination of his way with words should help to dispel that illusion. He was, in fact, a stylist of originality and grace. Just as he set up the structure of each of his best books in accordance with a well-planned architectural design, so he brought together the elements of his sentences with an artist's disciplined awareness of his own values. He expressed his attitudes, his sympathies, and his ideas in figurative language that remains fresh because his metaphors were entirely his own.

This was not true at the beginning. Steinbeck had his mentors. Some were good; it is not difficult to discern in *Cup of Gold* and *To a God Unknown* reverberations of the stately music of the King James version of the Bible. But the recommendation of others can have been only that they enjoyed, at the moment, wide popularity. One finds, again in *Cup of Gold*, imitations of the verbal tricks of James Branch Cabell and echoes of the self-conscious melodiousness of Donn Byrne. As he became more secure in awareness of his own identity, however, Steinbeck found his own voice.

It is in *The Grapes of Wrath* that the tone of the experienced artist declares itself with quiet confidence. The language of the narrative chapters is that of the people involved — simple, urgent in the expression of primal needs and desires, fresh and colorful within the limitations of the Joads' experience, powerful and poetic in implication. The chapters of comment presented temptations to a writer of Steinbeck's facility. Here and there a momentary lapse threatens the modesty of the style and the organ tones of omniscience swell out fortissimo. But for the most part these passages are kept in harmonic sympathy with the rest of the work. Steinbeck's lucid, generally unpretentious style enables him to present *The Grapes of Wrath* as a grave and respectful celebration of the dignity of man, a homely yet eloquent eulogy of the anonymous great who were his heroes.

Examples of his verbal skill reveal the secret of his method which was to make the simplest words and phrases flash into significance with seeming spontaneity. The quality of patience in one of his characters is established by use of the graphic simile "as enduring as a sea-washed stone." When he describes a woman as being "humorless as a chicken" one immediately sees the skitterings and hears the feeble, repetitive complaints of a creature ridiculously, yet pathetically, at war with a frustrating environment. The same genius for making pictures of mental attitudes reveals itself in the suggestion that the mind of another character — a Chinese shopkeeper who has forever to protect himself against the connivers of Cannery Row — "picked its way as delicately as a cat through cactus." One of Steinbeck's many eager digesters of experience defines himself unforgettably when he says, "I eat stories like grapes." As easily recognizable as an elderly female relative of one's own is the woman who has "a collection of small round convictions." The idiot in the story "Johnny Bear" has only one interest in life which is to cadge drinks at a bar; he keeps reiterating the sounds "Whis-key . . . Whis-key," as Steinbeck says, "like a bird call." By such small touches Steinbeck quickens his men and women into life.

He is equally successful with metaphor in creating landscape. Every season when the drenching rains came at last to his valley, the land, Steinbeck is inspired to say, "would shout with grass." A solitary visitor to a pool frequented by frogs remembers that "the air was full of their song and it was a kind of roaring silence." The modest poetry of surprise leaps out of such phrases as it does even more strikingly in descriptions of wild weather.

An observer is warned of an approaching storm when he sees "a black cloud eating up the sky." In another such moment "a bristling, officious wind raked the valley." The device of making pictures of doleful situations is used to underscore tragedy: "Poverty sat cross-legged on the farm." Mood is established, the nature of a man defined, drama propelled by verbal devices so skillfully suited to their purpose as to be almost unnoticeable in themselves. Yet unobtrusive as these inspirations are they haunt the memory of the reader ever after.

The faults and limitations of Steinbeck's style have to do with matters of taste. Here, indeed, he did sometimes falter. It must be pointed out, however, that certain charges of grossness brought against books like *Cannery Row* would suggest themselves only to readers of parochial sensibility. The candor of the light entertainments belongs as surely to their themes as the bluntnesses of Rabelais, Sterne, and Swift belong to their satiric material. To have turned away in timidity from the obligatory scenes of grotesquerie would have amounted to artistic irresponsibility. Yet it is true that Steinbeck was capable of strewing a page or two with ribaldries that are conspicuously inappropriate to character and mood. *The Winter of Our Discontent* puts into the mouth of a cultivated man, Ethan, bits of verbal outrageousness that would have shocked the outspoken residents of Cannery Row.

The charge that Steinbeck's style is heavily laced with sentimentality should be examined closely on suspicion of bias. Some readers of *The Grapes of Wrath* brought it against him disingenuously, hoping to discredit his social attitudes by demeaning his way of expressing them. Disinterested analysts of his work were more perceptive even amid the near hysteria that greeted the book's appearance. Still, one must admit that he yielded to the temptation to be extravagant, at crucial moments, in presenting scenes of sentiment. Though he often used the word "gently" with ironic intent he used it far too often as he also overworked the even more lush "tenderly." And if sentimentality may be defined as the deliberate distortion of the probable in the in-

terest of what is strikingly picturesque, then it is true that Steinbeck is sometimes sentimental, twisting his characters into dubious postures of nobility. The last scene of *The Grapes of Wrath*
provides an example. In it a girl who has just lost her child at
birth gives her breast, charged as it is with milk, to a man who
has collapsed of starvation. Humanity, one understands, owes
something to humanity which it must cross any gap to pay. But
the symbolic act fails of its own excessive strain. It is patently a
theatrical gesture used to bring down the curtain on an arti-
ficially composed tableau.

But, considering Steinbeck's temperament and the abundance
of his imagination, it is remarkable that such excesses were few.
His style contributed warm benefits of sympathy and spontaneity
to each important book. Reappraising his work one is reminded
that style is the man and that this was a remarkably whole and
wholesome man.

A special dimension is evident in Steinbeck's work when it is
compared with that of most of the writers of his time. He was not
content to be merely an observer of mores and recorder of the
movements of the moment. His books were all products of a
speculative intelligence. The writing of fiction was for him a
means of trying, for his own benefit and that of his readers, to
identify the place of man in his world. His conception of that
world included not merely the interests of economics and sociology but those of science and the realm of the spirit as well. Into
the bloodstream of his work he released a steady flow of ideas to
enrich its vigor.

His interest in science developed, during his middle years,
into a semiprofessional preoccupation when he became part
owner of a laboratory of marine biology. The scientific studies
he engaged in, which were guided by a highly trained friend, Ed
Ricketts, reinforced his belief in the oneness of all life — organic
and inorganic, animal, vegetable, and aquatic. The book *Sea of
Cortez*, written in collaboration with Ricketts, is in part a statement of that belief. It is also an account of a voyage up and down

the Gulf of California to take specimens for a collection which, it was hoped, would constitute in itself a history of the marine life of the region.

What the investigators felt that they found in each tide pool they visited was "a world under a rock," a tiny microcosm of the universe. They comment: ". . . it is a strange thing that most of the feeling we call religious . . . is really the understanding and the attempt to say that man is . . . related inextricably to all reality, known and unknowable. This . . . profound feeling . . . made a Jesus, a St. Augustine, a St. Francis, a Roger Bacon, a Charles Darwin, and an Einstein. Each . . . reaffirmed . . . the knowledge that all things are one thing and that one thing is all things — plankton, a shimmering phosphorescence on the sea and the spinning planets and an expanding universe, all bound together by the elastic string of time."

Such passages have baffled some of Steinbeck's readers, leading them to the conclusion that his personal philosophy amounted to nothing but animalism, the denial that man has a spiritual nature. It is curious that his testimony should have been so misread. In his Nobel address he made two significant declarations: first, that he lived, as a writer, to "celebrate man's proven capacity for greatness of heart and spirit, courage, compassion and love"; second, that "a writer who does not believe in the perfectability of man" cannot claim to have a true vocation. These might be dismissed as the afterthoughts of an elderly convert, apologizing for the heresies of his youth, if Steinbeck had not anticipated such affirmations many years before in *Sea of Cortez*. There he made it clear that a sense of man's oneness with the universe should not drug the mind into passivity. Man is not merely the creature of an unknowable pattern of existence. He has made himself unique among animals by accepting responsibility for the good of others. Only he has this "drive outside of himself," that is, toward altruism. It is the "tragic miracle of consciousness" that has re-created him. "Potentially man is all things" and his impulses urge him often to be greedy and cruel. But he is also "capable of great love." His problem is to learn to accept his cosmic identity, by which Steinbeck means: to become aware of himself as an integral part of the whole design of existence. Tom Joad said it for him more succinctly in *The Grapes of Wrath*: "Well, maybe . . . a fella ain't got a soul of his own, but on'y a piece of a big one."

The theme of oneness is developed in *Sea of Cortez* with illustrations drawn from scientific observation. In an illuminating passage he describes the phenomenon of interdependence among aquatic creatures: "The schools swam, marshaled and patrolled. They turned as a unit and dived as a unit. . . . We cannot conceive of this intricacy until we are able to think of the school as an animal itself, reacting with all its cells to stimuli which perhaps might not influence one fish at all. And this larger animal, the school, seems to have a nature and drive and ends of its own . . . a school intelligence." His sense of unity stirred once more, Steinbeck pushes the speculation on: "And perhaps *this* unit of survival [the school of fishes] may key into the larger animal which is the life of all the sea, and this into the larger of the world."

This is the same concept which animated Steinbeck's imaginative re-creation in *The Red Pony* of the movement which he calls westering. As the old man who has been the "leader of the people" remembers: "It wasn't Indians that were important, nor adventures, nor even getting out here. It was a whole bunch of people made into one big crawling beast . . . Every man wanted something for himself, but the big beast that was all of them wanted only westering. . . . We carried life out here and set it down the way those ants carry eggs. . . . The westering was as big as God, and the slow steps that made the movement piled up and piled up until the continent was crossed." So, as he might have said, the movement of westering keyed into the life of the continent and that into the life of the world.

It was the readiness to search behind the facts of life for a philosophical resolution of their complexity that gave depth and a rich texture to Steinbeck's picture of the life of his time. He had the rare ability to blend speculation into his fiction, making it an integral part of a narrative plan. Only a few of his contemporaries attempted to establish so broad a rapport with the minds of readers. Of such writers Thomas Mann offers the century's most brilliant example. As Joseph Wood Krutch once pointed out, Steinbeck's name must be linked with that of his European counterpart in any discussion of the novelist as thinker. Mann explored his magic mountain and Steinbeck his shimmering sea of contemplation but in doing so neither sacrificed the authority of his voice as storyteller.

Alexander Cowie has suggested, thinking of Steinbeck: "Perhaps this is the final responsibility of the novelist: he must be true to his time and yet save himself for Time."

Steinbeck was certainly true to his time in his eagerness to be identified with scientific enterprise and his willingness to take the guiding principles of science as his own. He might be called a moral ecologist, obsessively concerned with man's spiritual struggle to adjust himself to his environment. It is significant that this storyteller, conscious of a mission, undertook to popularize theories about the salvation of man's total environment long before public attention focused on the discipline of ecology.

He also nourished within himself the attitudes toward social reform that were growing slowly in the national consciousness of his time. His protests, his rejections as well as his affirmative convictions about the hope for regeneration, were exactly those that have been taken up by leaders of opinion in a later day enabling them, as teachers, theorists, and legislators, to change our minds in the direction of greater sensibility concerning human rights. Always the artist, never a practicing reformer, Steinbeck dramatized situations in American life and espoused beliefs about the need of room for growth in a way that helped to awaken the conscience of his fellow Americans.

Steinbeck was in addition a kind of working Freudian in the broad sense that he used the novel to remind readers that the myths of the past contain the wisdom of the race, that they tell us more about ourselves than sources of factual information can convey. Many, perhaps most, of the novelists of the 1930s and 1940s were deeply imbued with the same idea. But Steinbeck, consciously and conscientiously exploring the suggestions of Freud (and of Frazer whose work he may have known even better), covered a far broader field than did his fellow writers. His was an ambitious and inclusive effort to relate contemporary evidence about "the human condition" to that of the great witnesses of the past. His work suggests again and again that the story of humankind is a steadily continuing one, full of passions that seem as familiar in a setting of two thousand years ago as they do in our own time. It is a sense of the past made present that gives Steinbeck's best books their universality of tone. Old perils the like of which still surround us, old aspirations renewed as commitments by our restatement of them — these are the elements that contribute the essence of drama to his stories and give them distinction.

Steinbeck said that the one commandment of life is "to be and survive." His work may be said to fulfill that commandment.

JAMES T. FARRELL

I would say that any genuine artist seeks to give the fullest possible expression to his own psychological life-cycle, and that he seeks to give the best organized form that he can to his own way of seeing the world." James T. Farrell wrote these words in 1948. In a letter to H. L. Mencken two years earlier he had suggested his way of seeing the world and the course his life had taken: "I was, after all, a young man of plebeian origins trying to write. The background from which I came was not one which fostered and affirmed the values of sophisticated literary culture. It was one of spiritual poverty. Through books, I gained something of a vision of possibilities in life . . . As I went on, this . . . new world of envisioned and acquired values . . . stood in striking contrast to the past . . ." He knew that one of his major problems as a writer was to draw upon the "social universe" of his various pasts with truth, and still to make them "consistent with a conception of expanded values, a fuller life, a broader range of perspectives."

This problem was implicit in his first two tales of any substance, "Slob" (1929) and "Studs" (1930). The first shows a young man struggling with his drunken aunt. In the second a young man goes to a wake and listens to the crude talk of the dead

245

man's friends. The young man of each tale is deeply disturbed at human degradation, even to the point of revulsion. But his feelings betray deep involvement with those concerned, and we observe that the author is full of his subject. "Slob" is a germ of Farrell's autobiographical Danny O'Neill pentalogy — Farrell prefers to call it the O'Neill-O'Flaherty series — and the other story is the well-known origin of the Studs Lonigan trilogy. When he wrote these tales, the "plebeian" writer had found books and "expanded values" at the University of Chicago near his home.

James Thomas Farrell was born February 27, 1904, in Chicago, where he lived until April 1931, except for eight months in New York City during the late 1920s. He was the second oldest of Mary and James Francis Farrell's six children who lived to maturity. Mary Farrell was a native of Chicago. Her parents, John and Julia Brown Daly, had come to America during the Civil War from a background of poverty in County Westmeath, Ireland. John Daly became a teamster in Chicago, and on his meager earnings he and Julia reared five children. James Francis ("Big Jim") Farrell also became a Chicago teamster after he left his parents' home in Kentucky. His father was James Farrell of Tipperary, who had been an overseer of slaves in Louisiana before he became a Confederate foot soldier in — Farrell believes — the Second Louisiana Infantry Battalion, known as the Louisiana Tigers. After the war the ex-soldier settled in Kentucky and married.

Farrell's father was a strong and enterprising man — he once tried to start his own saloon in Chicago — but his wages as a teamster were not adequate to support his growing family. When Farrell was three, he was taken to live permanently with his grandparents, the Dalys, who were then comfortably supported by an unmarried son and daughter. This removal was the most important event of Farrell's youth. Eight years later, eager for companionship and filled with dreams, he moved with his grandmother, his Uncle Tom, and his Aunt Ella into the middle-class neighborhood, immediately west of Washington

Park, that was made famous in *Studs Lonigan*. Altogether he attended three of Chicago's parochial schools — once he called his schooling a "mis-education," but later, in 1963, he praised it for having instilled moral values in him. During his high school years (1919–23) he worked summers and after school in the Wagon Call Department of the Amalgamated Express Company and continued there full time after graduation.

Faced with a dreary future of office routine, he enrolled as a prelaw student in De Paul University night school in September 1924. He entered the University of Chicago in June 1925, and in four years, paying his own way, he completed eight quarters. During 1929 and 1930 while working on his *Studs Lonigan* manuscript, he published fiction in *Blues, Tambour,* and *This Quarter* and articles in *Plain Talk* and the *New Freeman*. After eloping with Dorothy Butler in April 1931, he lived for a year in Paris, where he received substantial encouragement from Ezra Pound and Samuel Putnam, editor of the *New Review*. While he was there, James Henle of the Vanguard Press accepted *Young Lonigan*, an act marking the beginning of an important editorial association and friendship. Since 1932 Farrell has made New York City his home, although from 1933 to 1936 he lived for long periods at the Yaddo writers' colony, and for many years he has traveled widely in this country and abroad as a lecturer — his 1956 visit to Israel is related in *It Has Come to Pass* (1958). He has supported himself and his family — he has two sons, Kevin and John — mainly by his writing, at which he works each day wherever he is. In addition he has actively engaged in the public literary and political life of his times, most dramatically, perhaps, in his early and clear-sighted opposition to the Communist literary line during the 1930s. His differences then with Granville Hicks, Michael Gold, Joseph Freeman, Malcolm Cowley, and others led to *A Note on Literary Criticism* (1936) and to his later attacks on the Communist-dominated League of American Writers. On behalf of the artist he has fought against commercialism, censorship, political dictation, and dogmatic theory — such as the Marxian doctrine of art as a weapon for proletarian revolution. Economically his course has not been easy, and personal troubles have compounded his problems. In 1935 he and Dorothy Farrell separated. His later marriage to Hortense Alden also ended in divorce and was followed in 1955 by his remarriage to Dorothy Farrell, from whom he is again separated.

At the University of Chicago Farrell began an intellectual development as unpredictably intense as Melville's unfolding eighty years before. Earlier his reading had been casual and undistinguished, although it included *Huckleberry Finn, Tom Sawyer, Silas Marner, Sartor Resartus, Lord Jim, You Know Me, Al,* portions of Dreiser's *Hey Rub-a-Dub-Dub*, and some Shakespeare. In college he concentrated his studies in the social sciences, but in 1927 he decided to be a writer of fiction, come what might. By 1930 he had formed lasting attitudes and, like Melville, had swum through libraries. William James, Dewey, Mead, Nietzsche, Stirner, Russell, Veblen, Freud, Pater, Ibsen, Chekhov, Mencken, Dreiser, Anderson, Lewis, Hemingway, and Joyce are some who were important to him. The ardent Catholic became a naturalist and pragmatist who affirmed the power of reason to improve society, but his greatest strength lay in a new and liberating sense of ego. He liked fiction, he wrote, having "the pressure of reality," the authority of personal experience he found in Anderson's *Tar*. Also by 1930 he had a bulky stack of manuscript tales and was well into *Studs Lonigan*. As early as 1928, in fact, he had begun to develop a life-plan for writing twenty-five volumes of fiction about the character later named Danny O'Neill and others. These books were to be loosely integrated — as he later wrote, "panels of one work." They would picture life in "connected social areas," first and basically in Chicago and then elsewhere.

In 1957 Farrell published his twenty-fifth book of fiction twenty-five years after his first. Behind him were the Studs Lonigan trilogy, the Danny O'Neill pentalogy, the Bernard Carr trilogy, three other novels, a novelette, ten collections of tales, and a play (with Hortense Alden Farrell), as well as six books of essays and criticism. The fiction re-creates "connected social areas" through its range of characterization and its use of cultural details. Its geographical poles are Chicago and New York City, but other parts of America and Europe come in for attention. A surprising number of memorable characters move about in their homes and neighborhoods, in leisure and working hours. They represent four generations and their actions span half a century. They come from a wide variety of social, economic, professional, national, and ethnic groups. Revealing a steadfast purpose and unrelenting endeavor, Farrell has explored, with a complexity not generally recognized, a representative segment of America, and in doing this he has established his personal style and his mode of realism. Since 1957 he has added other "panels." *Invisible Swords* (1971) is his twenty-second and most recent novel. *Judith and Other Stories* (1973) is his fourteenth collection of tales and novellas and his forty-eighth book. His present hope, time permitting, is to expand his lifework to include approximately sixty books of fiction. Toward that goal he is making steady progress as he continues to bring out portions of his massive new series, *A Universe of Time.*

Farrell's reputation rose rapidly in the early 1930s, those depression years when proletarian fiction was the vogue. But before the end of the decade his reputation with reviewers began to suffer. He soon saw that the current of critical opinion was running against realism — his own brand, in particular, offended many left-wing reviewers, Catholics, and academic critics. To be sure, he has had sympathetic interpreters, notably Joseph Warren Beach and Blanche Gelfant, and he has contemporary admirers, those whom Leslie Fiedler has called "a few surly defenders." Paperback editions of his books have sold into the millions and still sell when available. Many of his major works have been widely translated. He is sometimes called America's greatest living realist or naturalist, just as years before he was sometimes called proletarian. But often praise is tempered with strong reservations, sometimes very strong indeed. Farrell is still breasting the current.

A typical view writes him off as a pessimistic determinist, negative and unwholesome. The Christian critic Nathan A. Scott, Jr., believes Farrell has nothing to say because he lacks mythical and religious imagination. Others think of him as locked up in his boyhood or as simply an expert on adolescent behavior. Still others find that his style is inadequate. They see his writing as repetitious and without form or grace. Another group dismisses him as a notebook writer, a photographic realist who literally reports facts or case histories. Those who hold this view believe he specializes unimaginatively and at random in the external. In effect they say of his work, with Mark Schorer, that "really, the thing is dead." His fiction rarely receives close critical attention; yet no recent American writer has been so variously — and confidently — impaled since the 1930s when William Faulkner was pigeonholed as a pornographer, or a regionalist, or a naturalist, or an uneducated primitive whose formless writing was needlessly complicated and lacking in affirmation.

It is important to see the wholeness of Farrell's fiction. His writing is truly a single body of work because it expresses his "psychological life-cycle" through the development of a unified subject. His novels and stories, following one after the other, are like a group of islands in the sea. Each is separate yet all rise out of one land mass below the ocean's surface, and when seen from above they form an impressive pattern. His poetry as well, and *A Universe of Time* — his work in progress since 1958 — continue to reflect the unified imagination that lies behind his three completed cycles of novels on Studs Lonigan, Danny O'Neill, and Bernard Carr together with the individual novels and the tales related to them.

The scope of Farrell's fiction and its chain-linked social areas are distinctive features, but a quality more in the grain is its inner continuity of feeling, the shifting yet related clusters of emotions experienced by the characters. The sensitive young man of "Slob" and "Studs" is a simple example. Danny O'Neill in the early story "Helen, I Love You" is a better example. There we see the twelve-year-old boy, new in the neighborhood like Tom Sawyer, hoping that pretty red-haired Helen Scanlan will be his girl. But he makes no headway with her because he is bashful. Lonesome and fearful, he indulges in lush fantasies as he walks at dusk in Washington Park wishing Helen were with him. In this tale of a boy's adoration for a girl, there is a cluster of emotions — the devotion, the romantic yearning, the fear of criticism, the pain and guilt of having lost the girl through timidity, the longing to be understood — comparable to those that stir Studs Lonigan when he thinks of his lost Lucy. In *The Face of Time* seven-year-old Danny O'Neill feels much the same way about his Aunt Louise. With shifting emphases the pattern reappears several times in Danny's later life, helping to define his growth. Rooted in similar feelings are Bernard Carr's fantasies of his childhood sweetheart, a symbol of perfection that works creatively in his imagination.

The early story "Boyhood" yields a related set of emotions that has a long history in Farrell's fiction. Danny is thirteen and wants to be one of the gang, but they think he is a "goof." He recoils into himself. Although he is a little ashamed at being a misfit, he vows to fight the injustice and "show them." He will be a great man. With different coloration these feelings bubble up later in Danny, Studs, and Bernard. Other clusters of emotions, like the one centering in nostalgia for the past, similarly recur.

The continuity of Farrell's writing also is seen in the patterns of action flowing from the insistent emotions. Consider three sequences, one each from the completed major cycles about Danny O'Neill, Studs Lonigan, and Bernard Carr. In the first — actually the second to be written — Danny O'Neill is taken from his hard-pressed family at the age of three to live with his grandparents, the O'Flahertys. They share a comfortable apartment in Chicago with their son Al and two unmarried daughters. Because Danny's father, Jim O'Neill, is hurt by this loss of a son to his wife's relatives, he brings Danny home two weeks later. The boy will not eat and he screams day and night. Afraid his son will die in convulsions, Jim carries him back to Mrs. O'Flaherty at 2 A.M. At her apartment door Danny opens his arms and says, "Mother, put me to bed!" He will often be unhappy and fearful in her home, but he will live with her until in his middle twenties, he leaves for New York to write.

Toward the close of *Judgment Day* Studs Lonigan is out of work and desperately ill. Painfully he drags himself through Chicago streets to his unhappy parental home, his only refuge. As he enters the apartment he collapses at his mother's feet and says "Mom, I'm sick. Put me to bed." A few days later, not yet thirty he dies.

At twenty-nine Bernard Carr is a high-principled writer from Chicago living in New York. In the last chapter of *Yet Other Waters* he and his pregnant wife, Elizabeth, have returned to Chicago to visit her parents, whom Bernard once scorned but now respects. We see them in Jackson Park, an old haunt of his, watching Philip, their two-year-old son, play in the grass. Bernard, happily married, is determined that Philip's boyhood shall not be "lost and betrayed" like his own. In the closing scene Philip sleeps peacefully in his father's arms as the parents return to the grandparents' apartment to put him securely to bed.

These sequences are variations on the theme of family loyalty and estrangement, and they focus on the son's place in the family. Turbulent emotions and actions of critical importance mark the personal relationships. Often the characters are unhappy, and even during happy moments they are likely to sense the sadness time will bring. Beginnings, setbacks, new starts, and endings are examined as though to answer the question "Who am I and where am I headed?" Moral indignation and confident rationalism enter strongly into Farrell's sensibility, especially early in his career. But a deeper strain in his fiction, although not as broodingly apparent as in Dreiser's, is humility: an acceptance, tinged with melancholy, of the mysterious and inevitable transfigurations of time.

This tendency in Farrell's fiction often is expressed in suggestive short passages. There is Studs's plaintive recognition not long before his death that "he had never thought . . . his life would turn out this way," or Bernard's thoughts in *The Road Between*: "Chicago! He had once been a boy there, a frightened and ordinary boy, and somehow that boy had grown into this Bernard Carr, an American writer . . . How had it happened? How had he found his road and won the confidence he now felt? The seeds of this change were not here in New York. They had been planted back there . . ." In his fiction Farrell seeks detailed answers to the question "How had it happened?" and also "What happened?" He tries to identify the seeds that flower as qualities of mind and heart. As he fills out his characters' lives, he explores growth, self-discovery, creativity — and their frustration. These are his themes.

The business of Farrell's fiction, then, is to trace the "human destinies" — a favorite phrase — of many characters. Hundreds of his people, to be sure, appear only once or twice and have no proper history. But scores of others do, and these thread their way through separate tales and novels. They include minor characters like Milt Cogswell and Father Doneggan, more important ones like Red Kelly and Ed Lanson who appear time after time, and major ones like Jim O'Neill and Peg O'Flaherty. They prosper or decline, or simply live from day to day busy with their thoughts or with other persons. In the Chicago fiction, for example, their interweaving lives cohere around family, grammar school, boy gang, church, social circle, high school, fraternity, sports team, office or other place of work, poolroom, saloon, bohemian colony, university, political group. These related centers of activity, shown intimately or obliquely, merge to form a colorful neighborhood just as the characters form a spectrum of human possibilities. And as the neighborhood flows into the larger city, so the characters' actions are not contained within neatly plotted sequences. They overflow formal boundaries with the wash of time. The effect is to suggest the novelty and inconclusiveness of life, particularly the surging complexity of city life.

Towering out of this setting is the major dramatic action of Farrell's work to date: the organic story uniting the lives of Studs, Danny, and Bernard, three crucial characters intimately related to each other in the author's imagination. That story affirms love and the creative power of mind and will. It traces the rise of a type of twentieth-century American male — urban, Irish Catholic, aspiring — from a condition of slavish ignorance and appalling human waste (Studs) through a growing aware- ness and independence (Danny) to a state of useful self- fulfillment (Bernard). The story is one of emergence in which Studs represents the life Danny rejects, and Bernard the life he chooses. It presupposes free will not as an endowment but, in Farrell's words, as "an achievement . . . gained . . . through knowledge and the acquisition of control, both over nature and over self." In Farrell's novel *Boarding House Blues* (1961), Danny writes: "A life is blown by wind called destiny, and that wind is controlled by the mind as much as by circum- stances." Elsewhere Farrell calls Danny a "bridge character." Yet the crossover Danny makes from Studs's world to Bernard's has the decisive effect of a breakthrough. In each world habits of mind and circumstances are important, but Danny learns that the key to freedom is the creative use of knowledge — the all- important difference. Bernard, who begins where Danny leaves off, gives additional moral content to the newly won freedom. In his personal and professional life Bernard moves toward the integrity appropriate to each.

In 1941 Farrell wrote to Van Wyck Brooks: "In a sense the theme of my fiction is the American way of life." For one thing, he meant that his books counteracted American myths of easy success. In particular he was thinking of those immigrants "from a poor, bitter and oppressed little island" who fail to find their "land of heart's desire" in America. Their sons and grandsons often grow up in a rootless urban culture, and like Studs they may destroy themselves. Farrell wrote to his publisher, Henle, in 1942 that his books show the ways in which America deprived its youth during his formative years; surely many of his characters are badly twisted — some virtually pinioned — by their experi- ence. In its extreme form the human cost of American growth as seen in Farrell's writing includes education for death.

Education for life also is part of his vision, for some characters build successful futures from past deprivations. "The American way of life" in Farrell's writing presupposes the "social making" of *all* the characters — as his friend Meyer Schapiro phrased it in a letter to Farrell. Just as surely Farrell's vision includes individuals making their culture. The poolroom and the brothel are partronized by Slug Mason and his kind. Others, like Jim O'Neill, Al O'Flaherty, or Paddy Lonigan, all idealists in their way, help build workaday America. Then there are those, including the important Danny and Bernard, who overcome — and creatively use — deficiencies in their pasts to become professional men or artists. Whether Farrell's major characters work with their hands or their minds, and whether they fail or succeed, most of them aspire to rise because they have known privation.

Farrell's subject is the unity of personal and national American growth within the "social universe" of his experience. Following that experience closely, his fiction records an urban America — Irish Catholic at the core — growing up; his large cast of characters merges into part of a nation sluggishly groping upward to the light. Plebeian vigor leads toward cultural sophistication, and cultural clichés stimulate intellectual revolt. A crude self-defeating individualism gives ground to mutual trust and accomplishment. The author rarely neglects for long the darkness of Studs's world: man cherishes his delusions and hostile divisions. Farrell once called that strain in his consciousness "an appalling terror, like a grinning and menacing mask." But the promise is also there. Danny O'Neill and Bernard Carr, especially, represent the creative will and secular reason that give Farrell's work its over-all Zarathustrian and Promethean pattern. They turn the feelings of the young man of "Slob" and "Studs" to account.

Studs Lonigan: A Trilogy (1935) is composed of *Young Lonigan* (1932), *The Young Manhood of Studs Lonigan* (1934), and *Judgment Day* (1935). Usually called Farrell's best work, it is a powerful realistic portrayal of the failure of understanding and potential growth in its hero. Studs is the elder son in a well-to-do Irish

Catholic family that lives in a respectable neighborhood on Chicago's South Side. Essentially he is an aspiring person who responds too readily to what is malignant in his culture. Chiefly through Studs the trilogy dramatizes man's capacity for self-destruction. Its double condemnation of Studs and his culture is rooted partly in the emotions of Farrell's early faith, for it projects Farrell's Catholic imagination through the mode of secular realism.

The action spans fifteen years, one-half of Studs's life, from June 1916 to his death in August 1931. It goes from World War I to early Depression days; Studs declines from a strong young fighter to an impoverished weakling. The structure of his life is built up in massive, architectural fashion. The first book covers five months in 1916, and the last, six months in 1931. In the first, Studs chooses a way of life: he scorns learning, breaks with Lucy whom he adores, joins the tough Prairie Avenue gang, becomes "a man" at fifteen with Iris. *Judgment Day* shows the outcome of his choice: he is an insignificant laborer; loses his work, money, and health; gets his girl, Catherine, pregnant but does not really love her; at twenty-nine dies a miserable death. In *Young Lonigan* life seemingly opens up for him. In *Judgment Day* it relentlessly closes in.

The ironically titled middle volume spans twelve and one-half years, from April 1917 to January 1929. Studs tries to join the army, drops out of school, works as a house painter for his father, and graduates from young punk to accredited poolroom barbarian. When Negro families begin filtering into the neighborhood, the Lonigans move to better surroundings, but Studs cannot move away from his impoverished values. Instead, he pursues them with a certain single-mindedness. The physically strong chauvinistic idealist changes to the helpless, bloodied figure, to whom "most things are just plain crap," draped around the fireplug at Fifty-Eighth Street and Prairie Avenue. The middle volume, then, gives the stages of Studs's corruption, not neglecting his dense "social universe." The trilogy is fashioned to support Farrell's moralistic view of Studs's life as a darkening progress toward death.

Farrell avoided making Studs a slum-dweller because he wanted to explore the interaction of character and culture in his own middle-class neighborhood. He had come to think of human personality as both social product and social cause. Studs and his friends constantly absorb — and then fairly exude — the values of their milieu. Notice Studs in a moment of guilt: after having inwardly belittled Catherine, "he suddenly asked himself who the hell he was, wanting so damn much, and thinking she wasn't enough for him." But the momentary self-recognition fizzles out in renewed social cliché as he wishes "he were a six-foot handsome bastard, built like a full-back . . ." With equal constancy the story returns to the personal origins of social disorganization, dramatized in episodes showing uncontrolled drinking, rapes and beatings, and racial strife.

Studs's character lies at the heart of the work. As a boy Studs is hopeful, imaginative, aware of his feelings, sensitive to criticism — but outwardly already "hard." He is a leader with a romantic and adventurous flair, and he wants his life to count for something. Morally he is often at odds with himself; his conscience is active. Nor does he lack will. His painful hacking at his humanity is a major point of the action. He wills to be tough because he understands how tricky and unreliable his tender feelings can be, and because he knows, on the other hand, that toughness can be controlled and can get results. The young Studs sometimes reminds us of Huck Finn, who also once tried to make himself feel good by doing the conventional and inhuman thing. But if Studs begins as a truncated Huck, he ends as his opposite. Each boy seeks human intimacy, but Studs learns to value his own miserable isolation. He finds self-assurance in rigidity. So he knows he is "the real stuff" by the very act of denying his best impulses. Huck affirms his best impulses in action but without full understanding, and humbly he thinks he acts from the devil. Studs repeatedly wills his own victimization; ironically his environment "takes" on him all too well because he needs to make his life count. Studs is a rather average person who betrays his potentiality for good and descends to disaster. As a spiritually crippled man in *Judgment Day* he condemns himself, although falteringly and darkly, for the self-destruction he has worked.

Farrell wanted to re-create a sense of what life meant to Studs by unfolding the story in Studs's "own words, his own actions, his own patterns of thought and feeling." In this way he hoped to create the vivid illusion of life going on, the very process itself, apparently free from the author's manipulation. This famous and traditional "objective" method is Farrell's convention to get perspective upon personally meaningful material and is not, as some seem to believe, an impossible effort to reveal objective reality as it is, untinged by subjectivity. In practice, Farrell went beyond his description of his method. The writing ranges from the interior monologue, baring Studs's reveries and dreams, to a neutral recording of dialogue, setting, and action — sometimes with Studs not present. Perhaps most typically the external world is shown colored by Studs's awareness, a merging of the inner and outer in varying proportions that helps to determine pace of action, sense of time, and manner of character portrayal.

Standing with "the older guys" in front of the poolroom, Studs at fifteen watches the neighborhood people go by: ". . . they had the same sleepy look his old man always had when he went for a walk. . . . Those dopey-looking guys must envy the gang here, young and free like they were. Old Izzy Hersch, the consumptive, went by. He looked yellow and almost like a ghost; he ran the delicatessen-bakery down next to Morty Ascher's tailor shop near the corner of Calumet, but nobody bought anything from him because he had the con, and anyway you were liable to get cockroaches or mice in anything you bought. Izzy looked like he was going to have a funeral in his honor any one of these days. Studs felt that Izzy must envy these guys. They were young and strong, and they were the real stuff; and it wouldn't be long before he'd be one of them and then he'd be the real stuff."

The author also reveals the external world through the minds of other characters, notably Studs's father and some of Studs's friends. These additional perspectives and the stream of action involving many persons create a strong sense of cultural process. Studs is thereby firmly related to the past and to his contemporaries. He is precisely located in a well-defined historical current.

This method leaves room for ideal and mature elements in Studs's culture. Not all of his friends sink into crime like Weary Reilley or into destitution like Davey Cohen. Many succeed in their business or profession. Other persons like Christy, John Connolly, Danny O'Neill, Mr. Legare, Helen Shires, Catherine Banahan, and Lucy are humane and relatively enlightened. Studs often is in touch with the excellence that might have given him the "something more" he sought. Nor are the issues and institutions of the larger world excluded. Near Lake Michigan Studs overhears two students discuss a Communist demonstration against Japanese imperialism. In this brief episode the reminder of the nearby university and of active world forces underscores his ignorant isolation, while the surging lake in the background suggests the ever accessible vitality of nature. Farrell's method by no means leaves an impression of Studs as merely a helpless victim. His destiny therefore becomes all the more terrible. Because we feel through Studs and still see him in context, we experience both the personal tragedy and the full social implications of the flow of his life toward the trivial and shameful.

Farrell handles that flow with skill. The chronological episodes form a series of penetrations into Studs's experience during sixty-five days selected from fifteen years. Studs's egotistic sense of time — first cocky, later nostalgic, and subject to a haunting fear of death — contrasts vividly with our understanding of what is happening. From the first we feel time's shaping passage as well as its repetitive heaviness, a deathlike stagnancy reflected in Studs's boredom. As the action proceeds, we see Studs's past in shifting ironic lights, while simultaneously we feel time moving invincibly toward Studs's future death.

Farrell's images and symbols are drawn from the empirical world and are used incisively to reveal Studs's changing condition. The city and nature provide patterns of imagery related to rigidity and fluidity, light and dark. Social actions like drinking or dancing and entire scenes reverberate with meaning, both forward and backward in time, through the trilogy. On the surface Father Gilhooley's graduation talk, for example, is a rather heavy-handed satire of Catholic religion and education. Yet the fatuous Father is a true prophet; he foretells the judgment day. His talk works in *Studs Lonigan* something like Father Mapple's sermon in *Moby Dick*. On a deep ironic level his dire Catholic admonitions send out vibrations echoing in Studs's moral imagination and also in Farrell's.

Although flaws in *Studs Lonigan* are easy to find, the objective method is a great success. Studs comes fully alive, and lesser characters also stay with us. In the main Farrell faithfully gave us Studs's world as Studs knew it. At the same time he charged it with the meaningful tensions of his personal feelings. He identified partly with Studs, yet the acceptance falls within a larger pattern of rejection. Farrell also re-created Studs's world from the perspectives he gained through his hard-won study and his growing success. His knowledge of Dewey's thought, and Mead's, was a major constructive force in the trilogy; and in *Judgment Day*, written considerably later than the first two volumes, his growing interest in Marxism had its impact. The method also is well suited to Farrell's view of time and experience. The episodic panorama of Studs and his friends constantly bobbing up in an earthly hell that ends in the blackness of death is itself a fitting expression of an imagination both Catholic and naturalistic.

Farrell's insight that "Studs is a consumer who doesn't know how to consume" applies to Studs as he drinks in platitudes or bootleg gin, a living example of the misuse of leisure in a modern city. But the trilogy strikes deeper, for it accurately pictures those basic evils charged against industrial society by the southern Agrarians, who spoke out at the very time Farrell was publishing his work. Their premises and solutions were poles apart from his, yet every evil they attacked is dramatically alive in *Studs Lonigan*. John Crowe Ransom called industrialism the contemporary form of pioneering, "a principle of boundless aggression against nature." Studs, brought up in a great industrial center, waged a personal war against his nature so that he might realize his dream of the tough he-man. Farrell once called Studs "the aftermath in dream of the frontier days."

The trilogy exposes a middle-class morality that arises more ominously from human urges than it does in Sinclair Lewis's Zenith. In his business Paddy Lonigan practices the aggressive individualism that Studs acts out in fantasy or reality as Lonewolf Lonigan, or a hard guy who beats up Jews and Negroes. As David Owen has shown, Studs strips the clothing of respectability from the illiberal ideal of rugged individualism and so clashes with respectability while remaining a son of the culture. The trilogy also extends the range of social conflict found in Upton Sinclair or Theodore Dreiser. Possibly it affects us most as an intimate picture of personal disintegration, of adult corruption fully at work in a representative boy who in turn convincingly becomes father to the man. For here is much of the terror and agony of our modern cities. We feel the ugly power of man's irrational drive toward the brutal and destructive. The failure of family, school, and church seems to lie in the impotence of love and reason themselves. Yet we know that this black picture is the oblique expression of Farrell's idealism.

Farrell's next major work is the Danny O'Neill pentalogy: *A World I Never Made* (1936), *No Star Is Lost* (1938), *Father and Son* (1940), *My Days of Anger* (1943), and *The Face of Time* (1953). The action covers more than eighteen years in Danny's life. It goes from 1909, when he is an insecure child of five, to 1927 when he resolutely leaves home and his college studies to become a writer in New York City. As a college student, Danny had appeared briefly in *The Young Manhood of Studs Lonigan*. There he condemns the ignorance and inhumanity of the city life around him. He considers his former beliefs to be lies and delusions, "so many maggots on the mouldering conception of God dead within his mind." Through his writing he intends to win recognition and to help build a better world. The pentalogy shows the growth of the child into the young man who has found the means to satisfy the deepest needs of his nature.

This series is central in Farrell's imagination and work. As an exploration of Danny's growth, it is the author's most direct adventure in self-understanding. For Danny's development is patterned upon Farrell's, and Danny's feelings approximate the "way it was" with Farrell during his formative years. The series therefore illuminates Farrell's other work and his life. It is rich in memorable characterizations based upon members of his family. Moreover, taken as a unit the five novels are central in the over-all design of his fiction. The rebel Danny emerges out of a long foreground not unlike Studs's in some respects. He wins his freedom and comes to the threshold of accomplishment. Having discarded supernaturalism, he wants to infuse humanitarian values into the existence that became "plain crap" to Studs. In these books the imagination that shaped Studs's earthly hell turns to the origins of Danny's dream of "a newer, cleaner world."

Those origins go back to Danny's traumatic removal at three from his own family to the O'Flahertys' home. This experience sets the pattern of his future relations to others. For example, it helps to explain the shame he feels toward his mother, and his later strained relationship with his father. As the son in two families, a kind of double outsider, he is a subject of contention. He feels bewildered and insecure. He knows he is different from other boys whose family life is normal, and naturally he seeks an identity. He searches for understanding and a wholesome directness in his personal relations. When these satisfactions are denied him, his reaction is likely to be sharp. Whatever its form, it is intended to assert his importance and independence, to help him leave the past behind and to move on to the new friend, the new neighborhood, or the new belief.

True to this basic pattern, Danny gradually takes on substance and color: Farrell is as interested in showing processes of growth as the end result. In *The Face of Time* Danny is a dependent, impressionable child overshadowed by adults already set in their ways. Sensitive to others' feelings toward him, confused in his loyalties, reaching out for affection, he is like a chip on a torrent of adult emotions. Already the later Danny who wants to be a free man is dimly visible in the small boy, who is effectively contrasted to his dying grandfather, Tom O'Flaherty. As a seven-year-old in *A World I Never Made*, Danny is still an anxious and sheltered little boy, but his experience broadens rapidly. His increasing interest in baseball is a good example of Farrell's use of common materials to suggest the dynamics of his growth. Broad outlines of his character begin to emerge: his family loyalty, a sense of honor, quick guilt feelings, a childish judiciousness, a capacity for faith. These qualities, together with the blunderings and weaknesses of an unsure child, make a balanced picture. Danny is rarely, if ever, sentimentalized.

As a preadolescent in *No Star Is Lost*, Danny lives more in a public world than before. The insecurities arising from family troubles grow more intense, and he reaches out eagerly for acceptance by his classmates. He begins to confront the hierarchy of authority he must eventually reject — the chain of command running from God through parents and relatives, priests and nuns, policemen, other grownups, and older boys. In *Father and Son*, as Danny enters high school, his troubles grow. His efforts to fit the stereotypes of his surroundings build inner pressures that eventually will erupt in the revolt he cannot yet conceive. For he is still the unsuccessful conformist. Yet his very "goofiness" is evidence of an unchanneled creative drive. As the fourth novel ends, Danny still lacks critical awareness, but the ties to his environment are wearing thin and he is beginning to understand the meaning of his father's life and death.

When Danny gets to college in *My Days of Anger*, the old gods tumble rapidly as the tensions of many years find release through knowledge. He develops a naturalistic philosophy with shifting overtones of despair, stoical endurance, confidence, and angry indignation, but he is really not very different from the little boy to whom affection and fair treatment meant the most. Danny's life naturally lacks the gravitational inevitability we feel in Studs's. Yet his reclamation is entirely plausible, for the series elaborately shows the complex interaction of his character and his environment. In the particulars of his daily living we can feel the origin of his sincere aspirations and his emotional needs that eventually lead to the University of Chicago and to New York City. As Danny confronts the nebulous future — the world he wants to make — Farrell ends his series with a sure touch. In the call room of the Express Company we again feel the power of delusion, the sense of people terribly caught in the mechanisms of our civilization, the opposite of what Danny wants. Yet there, too, is the vigorous authority of an established way of life that puts Danny's highfalutin and untested aspirations in a realistic perspective.

Of all Farrell's work, these novels are richest in major characters. Jim O'Neill is the proud, self-reliant workingman, a person of moral force and Danny's true spiritual father. His wife, Lizz, is an aggressive, salty woman, central in the pentalogy as wife, mother, daughter, sister, neighbor. Her father, old Tom O'Flaherty, is fundamentally a gentle, understanding man still not at ease in America after many years. Mary, Tom's wife, is one of Farrell's finest characters, a shrewd, resourceful woman who never loses her zestful will to live and to control. Mary's other children are also exceptional creations, especially the rigid and lonely Al, and the self-tormented Peg who keeps the family in turmoil. These characters, patterned after members of Farrell's family, are created out of the mature author's love and understanding. The pentalogy in effect is an act of piety toward his own people, an effort to recapture their feelings, to show how their lives went in the city they helped to build. To be an honest tribute, the picture had to include in all relentlessness their violence and weakness as well as their affection and will to live.

The adult O'Neills and O'Flahertys intimately affect Danny

and form a relatively stable human backdrop to his story. We measure his growth against it as he changes from a dependent child among towering adults to the young man whose educated perception reduces them to true scale. Yet they are far more than adjuncts to Danny's growth, for they are seen and created as autonomous characters. Much of the pentalogy traces their lives and faithfully explores their personal feelings. Moreover they add a special blend of comedy and pathos. For example, Al's childlike illusion that the true wise guy achieves cultural status through decorum contrasts effectively with Jim's hardheaded realism. Lizz sprinkles holy water or has a mass said to shape the future to her desire. We are amused but sympathetic, for her action reflects a naive concept of the power of spirit, and her faith measures the immensity of her need. Particularly through Lizz and Mrs. O'Flaherty, Farrell develops a broad and rich humor, a quality of his writing that often goes unrecognized.

Compared to Danny, whose urgent needs drive him *through* experience, the members of his family show little radical development, except, perhaps, Jim O'Neill. For instance, Al remains loyal to his ideals of business success and self-improvement through a study of Lord Chesterfield's letters and the dictionary. The repetition of such effects, emphasizing the cultural naiveté of the family, heightens our sense of what Danny must overcome before he finds his way. The repeated family quarrels over him or over Peg's affairs, for example, and the adults' occasional harshness toward Danny burn the pattern of shame and fear into him, thereby making his ultimate revolt more certain. Also, while reiteration of Al's pretensions to culture, his brother Ned's New Thought, Peg's vain resolutions to reform, and Mary's verbal onslaughts says a great deal about the deprivation in their lives, it conveys as well their stubborn vitality. Farrell's repetition of these traits simultaneously shows the O'Neills' and O'Flahertys' strong will to live and the cultural stunting that affects them as it does Studs and his friends. As first- or second-generation immigrants struggling in a competitive world, they transmit a heritage that is terribly inadequate, but it has the validity of a bludgeoning weapon forged of necessity in the heat of battle.

Again, as in *Studs Lonigan*, the development of individual character is used to reveal historical process in human life. In love and strife Danny's family act out social forces, seen as individual habits or predispositions. They quarrel but they stick together and help each other. Their loyalty shows the common need of first- and second-generation Americans for support from family and cultural tradition. Their belligerence derives from their violent past. The scheming, the shouting, the blows, the talk of splitting skulls with skillets is deeply ingrained and shows them, in effect, meeting their problems with the habits and language developed from their Irish past. Their actions also reveal the clash of cultural patterns between the generations and between economic classes. Farrell's method spotlights his characters under institutional pressures, typically from the Church and the job. We feel the power of money and dogma in their lives. These books show what it means to have been a big-city Irish American Catholic, of modest income, during the first three decades of this century — one reason Farrell is a significant Catholic novelist — and they display the broad human meaning of early twentieth-century capitalism, from its drudgery and harsh competition to its genuine opportunities.

The Danny O'Neill series keeps to the episodic and objective method of *Studs Lonigan*, for it presents life as felt by the characters during selected segments of time. Studs's limited awareness dominates in the trilogy, but in the later work the family members establish many viewpoints. The resulting autonomy of these convincing people strengthens Danny's characterization, for he grows through involvement with other persons. Farrell's procedure in the pentalogy suits the theme of individual growth, just as the method in *Studs Lonigan* dramatizes the substance of lonely spiritual impoverishment.

Farrell again uses the Chicago setting with a sure and revealing touch. But for various reasons neighborhood plays a less crucial role than it did in the trilogy. Instead we feel the confining apartment or job more strongly. Even so, the pentalogy yields a broader spectrum of life than *Studs Lonigan*, which is dominated by the dramatic curve of one meager destiny. It includes more characters, traces more careers, presents several persons with explosive emotional lives, ranges more widely in action, and follows up Danny's drive toward a spacious world. For these reasons the city is more broadly present in the pentalogy but less immediately and fatally than in the trilogy, which makes such effective use of urban imagery. In keeping with its theme of emergence, the Danny O'Neill cycle, unlike *Studs Lonigan*, leaves a sense of an open society despite the limitations of individual characters.

The 2500 pages of the loosely jointed Danny O'Neill books show little formal plotting, although causal relationships are everywhere and narrative strands, like the story of Peg and Lorry Robinson, hold some suspense. The episodes are most easily seen as a panorama, a vast succession of scenes leading to many climaxes and to a fitting conclusion for Danny. It would indeed be difficult to justify formally all the episodes; yet when the five books are examined as a unit they reveal a unique structure with its own logic. This structure is appropriate to Danny's position as a son in two families, to the slowly rising curve of his personal development, to the three-generation process which transforms immigrant stock from laborer to intellectual American, and to the large rhythms of life flowing through the books: birth and death, growth and decay, regeneration and sterility. The result is not as intensely dramatic as *Studs Lonigan* but it is more inclusive, for here Farrell significantly extends his story of the making of Americans. He broadens the implicit indictment of reigning values and urban conditions, and in Danny he presents the emerging artist — his awakening identity and sources of courage.

Farrell rounded out his basic story with the Bernard Carr trilogy: *Bernard Clare* (1946) — after a libel suit brought by a man of that name, *Clare* was changed to *Carr* in the second novel —

The Road Between (1949), and *Yet Other Waters* (1952). The over-all
movement in the three major series is this: Studs goes under,
Danny discovers his true calling and escapes from Chicago, and
after considerable floundering Bernard succeeds as a writer in
New York City. The action occurs between 1927 and 1936, over-
lapping Studs's later years and in effect taking up the thread
where Danny dropped it. The work fulfilled Farrell's long-
standing ambition to write of New York literary life and radical
political groups.

The trilogy brings together several matters of importance to
Farrell. He wanted to indicate what happened, spiritually and
artistically, to a generation of New York writers and intellectuals
who were either Communists or fellow travelers. (In this respect
The Road Between and *Yet Other Waters* approximate *romans à clef*.)
He felt that their relatively sophisticated story also would enrich
his picture of contrasting values and milieus in America.
Moreover, he intended his hero to mirror the economic and
spiritual struggles he had known. From a working-class family,
Bernard illustrates Chekhov's statement used as the epigraph to
Bernard Clare: "What writers belonging to the upper class have
received from nature for nothing, plebeians acquire at the cost
of their youth." As Farrell wrote to Henle in 1944, Bernard
wrestles with "the problem of sincerity" and seeks his identity.
Eventually he defines himself vis-à-vis his boyhood past, the
economic order, his lovers and wife, and especially the American
Communist party, which tries to use him for its political ends. In
this work Farrell returned to familiar themes, and like James,
Dreiser, Anderson, and others before him, he took up the artist's
relation to society — a special case of his general interest in the
social making of Americans. Bernard's life, somewhat like
Farrell's, becomes a search for integrity, the struggle to be himself through serious writing.

Farrell used the Communist theme to underscore the continuity of his three major cycles. Ironically, the party brings Bernard to himself. In effect he learns that Communists are moral
cousins to Studs: absolutists whose idealism — or fanatic faith —

sanctions their efforts to be strong and tough and the real stuff in politics and art; or, less kindly, hooligans with a philosophy. But they pay the price of a shattered integrity and a withered inner life. Whereas they behave like Studs on a higher level, Bernard becomes more and more like a mature version of Danny. Three crowd scenes show his progression. In 1927 on the night Sacco and Vanzetti were executed the rebellious Bernard, although no Communist, is strong for social justice and as capable of "solidarity" with Communist-manipulated demonstrators as Studs is with his gang. In 1932 with some reservations he marches in the Communist May Day parade. Finally in 1936 he watches the May Day marchers from the curb, aloof, seeing them as both dupes and deceivers, Stalin's "local boys," corrupters of the Revolution. He thinks: "He was alone here, as he had been in Chicago in his boyhood." But his is the isolation of integrity and not that arising from aggressive hostility toward others as in Studs, or from rejection by others as in Danny. Like Danny he is a stranger in a world he never made and has a tough endurance Studs never really had, but he has outgrown Danny's frustration and rage. Instead of feeling Danny's early insecurity — *A Legacy of Fear* was Farrell's first choice of title for *The Face of Time* — he knows he can "walk the streets with confidence." Like Farrell, he becomes more aware of the evil flowing straight out of men's hearts and minds, as distinct from the evil of social injustice. In *Judgment Day* the Communist parade held out hope for the deceived, the "prisoners of starvation" like the Lonigans, but in *Yet Other Waters* the Communist marchers are themselves prisoners of the deceit they practice.

As in the Danny O'Neill series, the central story is the hero's growth. At twenty-one Bernard is an immature, confused romantic who spends half of 1927 in New York City trying to write. His view of life as a drab affair and a race with Time in which Death is the ultimate winner masks his angry determination to expose life's shame and injustice through his writing. He publishes nothing, but he grows in self-understanding and compassion. His identification with the executed Sacco and Vanzetti and his affair with Eva, a young married woman, enable him to define his aims with greater certainty. His menial jobs teach him the plight of misfits in a society all out for money and progress. He begins to see his chosen craft and the flaws in his writing more clearly. As *Bernard Clare* ends, he is still relatively immature, a parochial Nietzschean who can be disagreeably egotistical; but at the core of his personality is a strong will to fight tenaciously for what he wants — and he knows that he is a "collection of somebodies wanting to be a synthesis of somebodies" through his art.

The Road Between opens in 1932 with Bernard, newly married to his Chicago sweetheart, Elizabeth Whelan, receiving recognition for his first novel. He still feels a Zarathustrian defiance and loneliness, yet his art permits him to harness much of his inner torment. Emerging from the 1920s into the 1930s, he is well along on the road between his conventional Chicago past — reflected in chapters about his and Elizabeth's families — and his radically different New York life. His growing understanding of each world is the measure of his development. With increasing flexibility he comes to understand his crude father's sexual and cultural frustrations and his own similarity to his pious Catholic mother, who seeks immortality not through art but through religion. He sees that, to the faithful, the Church he has rejected clothes life with meaning and dignity — as he tries to do in his writing — and he begins to see significant differences between Communist theory and practice. The road between that he travels thus leads from mind to heart. Eventually the journey will enable him to heal a split in his consciousness between the rational and the emotional. His earlier condemnation of his past and his acceptance of Marxism were steps toward freedom, but his heart now feels the tug of loyalty to family and to native traditions as part of the truth he will affirm in his writing. *The Road Between* ends in 1933: Bernard publishes his second novel, he wins a Loewenthal Fellowship, and Elizabeth's baby is born dead.

Yet Other Waters traces Bernard's life for a year and a half beginning in the spring of 1935; and as before, interspersed Chicago scenes take us back to his origins. Now fairly well off, the Carrs have a son, Philip, and Bernard has written a third novel. He pickets in a strike directed by the party, and he speaks at the 1935 American Writers Congress where he sees Communist intrigue from the inside. He successfully resists inducements to make his fiction and his criticism follow the party line, explaining that he seeks "to rediscover and put down . . . some of my own continuity." Before long he publicly denounces the party for its disruptive tactics and its deceit. As the trilogy ends, Bernard's mother dies and Elizabeth is expecting their second child.

The third volume makes clear that the trilogy, like much of Farrell's work, sets up an opposition between forces of life and death in modern America and shows the growth of life out of death. Bernard believes that death is life's framework and end, the extinction of awareness, and that whatever diminishes awareness, whether because of rigid attitudes or cultural sterility, is a form of death-in-life. It may be said, then, that absolutisms like the Church and the party, although meeting deep human needs, are blinders to help fearful men cope with the fact of death. Bernard regards his writing as an opposite method of outwitting death: a splurge of consciousness, a sustained effort to intensify awareness and understanding. He learns that to write with truth he must constantly return to the flux of experience — to *his* feelings and thoughts — and must distrust all systems claiming perfection and finality; "for other and yet other waters are ever flowing on." This Heraclitean, pragmatic theme is restated through a parallel set of symbols, the women in Bernard's life. The vision of Elsie that haunts his imagination is a boyhood ideal of perfection like the Church, and Alice is his seductive Communist mistress who would like him to knuckle under. Elizabeth, one of Farrell's best women characters, is intuitive, warm, sensible, and loyal to Bernard and to the needs of her family — a good example of feminine "realism" in contrast to masculine "idealism." Bernard's renewed affection for her is a return to a love which, like a heightened consciousness, is a creative breach of death's power and one that gives added point to Bernard's — and Danny's — earlier angers and hates. Bernard grows through his ability to perceive and reject the disembodied ideal, the seductive Absolute, in his emotional life and in his thinking. His final wisdom is to seek the attainable ideal in the ever-changing present reality and not to locate it in a fantasy of the past or future, as Studs does, or in a Utopia of this world or a heaven of the next. It is the wisdom, strangely echoing Hawthorne, of Saint-Just's phrase, "Happiness is a new idea." For Bernard, this saying sums up a way of life embracing a democratic social philosophy, a pragmatic trust in experience, a naturalistic metaphysics, and an ethics of self-fulfillment in one's personal and occupational lives.

Judged as fiction, the trilogy is weaker than the two earlier series — unfortunately so, for its climactic position calls for strength. At the heart of the difficulty lies Farrell's uncertain conception of Bernard's character and fate. The original intention to have Bernard return to Mother Church or Stalinism — as some of the characters in Bernard's fiction do — did not square with Farrell's compelling need to have Bernard become triumphantly self-sustaining. The cloudiness in Bernard's character cannot be entirely accounted for by the effort to highlight the problem of identity or to avoid the "gianticism" of "Wolfeism," as Farrell explained to F. O. Matthiessen in 1946.

Nor do the Bernard Carr books flow from the visceral knowledge of environment and manners evident in Farrell's Chicago novels. Bernard does not really know his world; he is homeless in a way Studs and Danny never are. Although this quality is not inappropriate to a seeker, Farrell's method, as Blanche Gelfant has shown, fails to convey the density of Bernard's inner life — that very flux he learned to trust. Moreover, for a fertile writer, he is shown too seldom in creative interplay with ideas, and too often, perhaps, in merely hostile relationship to his environment. Farrell justified his plebeian hero's character to James Henle in 1946: he had tried to place Bernard "on the same plane as the other characters," and he did not want to have "culture . . . conceal reality in the books." Yet we miss a compelling sense in Bernard that human culture, in its broader sense, *is* his reality, his very livelihood as a writer. The autonomous "social universe," the seething background Farrell wished to catch, is clouded over by Bernard's narrow self-absorption. To be sure, the Chicago scenes, some of the Chicago characters — notably Mr. Whelan and Mrs. Carr — and a number of objective New York sequences show much of Farrell's earlier power. Some of the Communists, especially Jake, Sam, and Sophie, come alive at intervals, but by and large the New York writers and radicals are ghostly figures who inadequately project social realities of magnitude. Although Bernard succeeds in his significant quest, the world he moves in lacks the solidity and meaningful implication of that other rejected world in *Studs Lonigan*, and Bernard himself insufficiently represents the positive ideal made real.

Nevertheless, with a brilliance of conception, the trilogy rounds out the organic story begun in *Young Lonigan*, for Bernard's hard-won wisdom and freedom are ultimately a triumph over spiritual rigidity, seen in rudimentary form in Studs. In its concern with the artist's entanglement with modern society, the work is unusually ambitious and partly successful. Unquestionably it extends and enriches Farrell's picture of America.

Farrell's other novels and his short stories interlace with his three major series through characters, settings, and themes. They help to round out his fictional world.

In Paris during the fall of 1931, he wrote *Gas-House McGinty* (1933), a novel whose composition influenced the last two volumes of *Studs Lonigan*. The new work was the first book of a projected trilogy on the Amalgamated Express Company in Chicago. Originally called "The Madhouse" and intended as "a Romance of Commerce and Service," it focuses on the hectic Wagon Call Department presided over by Chief Dispatcher Ambrose J. McGinty during the summer of 1920. The slight narrative centers on the frustrated McGinty and his demotion to route inspector, paralleling the "fall" of the old song, but in a real sense the office itself is the protagonist (the anonymous, blaring telephone conversations of the clerks and the incessant sadistic banter create a nightmarish collective personality), and Farrell constructed his work accordingly. He explained to Henle, probably in July 1931, that his new work would be "something in which the characters are massed" to give a "composite picture . . . a sense of them squirming inside this large institution." Scenes of McGinty at home or on the street, inter-chapters about the outside route men, and echoes of current events in the men's talk and in McGinty's thoughts add perspective; but the crowded, claustrophobic office remains the central stage. Farrell accurately wrote to Henle in September 1931 that his characters "bring everything down to the Call Department, and, so to speak, dump it."

Awake or dreaming, McGinty is a small triumph of characterization, and his co-workers, including Jim and Danny O'Neill, are created deftly and surely. Dialogue used for narration is overworked (Farrell cut the Vanguard text for the Avon reprint edition), yet the men's frantic talk, functioning as release from devitalizing routine, makes its point and shows Farrell at his best in handling a robust vernacular. Despite the evident influence of Joyce's *Ulysses* in particular, the novel remains fresh and meaningful. It vividly dramatizes the shaping — and scarring — of character through occupation and thus complements the stories of Studs and Danny, which constantly return to the effect of leisure activity and family relationships upon personal growth. It vigorously re-creates the human significance of the commercial purgatory Danny fled.

This Man and This Woman (1951), a successful minor novel, returns to the milieu of the Express Company almost incidentally in relating the domestic catastrophe of the aging Walt and Peg Callahan. Farrell's theme is "biological tragedy," earlier developed in the stories of Jim O'Neill, Tom O'Flaherty, and Bernard's parents. It is the erosion of human life through physical and psychological causes, and is seen here particularly in Peg's aberration. The action is limited to a few days during the 1940s and builds upon Peg's growing paranoia that suffocates her former buoyant spirit. The novel's strength lies in the convincing and sympathetic portrayal of her change into the very thing she thinks she sees in the likable Walt. Appropriately minimizing the social background, the story explores seemingly unbridgeable differences between the sexes with an intensity suitable to Peg's obsessional character.

Ellen Rogers (1941) also is a story of blighted love in Chicago, this time an affair in 1925 between Edmond Lanson and Ellen, just out of high school. Begun as a novelette, the work developed into a full-length chronicle whose mounting climax, as Mencken wrote to Farrell in September 1941, was managed with impressive effect. Because Farrell believed he had established the middle-class social context of his characters in earlier books, he played down the background and concentrated on his lovers' personal relationships. The story thus lacks the massive impact of *Studs Lonigan*, and the origins of Ed Lanson's destructive egotism are left in obscurity; its specific quality is suggested by Thomas Mann's judgment that it "is one of the best love-stories I know, of unusual truthfulness and simplicity."

Mann believed that Ellen's agony and humiliation following her abandonment by Ed were brilliantly portrayed. She is, indeed, Farrell's far lesser Anna Karenina, the female in the grip of passion. Once she is in love, her calculating worldliness and her self-sufficiency fall away. Depths of devotion, suffering, and fury open up, and her superficial life takes on meaning. Although Ellen is the source of emotional strength in this novel, her destroyer, Ed Lanson, interests us more as an individual and as a symbolic figure of the 1920s. Farrell imagined him as a mixture of a middle-class Sanine, a shallow Raskolnikov, and an eighteenth-century rogue transplanted to the 1920s; in short, a vulgarized product of "the Ben Hecht, Bodenheim, Cabell, Nietzsche influence." Ed is a character of calculated ambiguity. He is not merely morally starved or conventional, but a man who directs his charm, his courage, and his intelligence toward wicked ends. A rebel in the cause of romantic, selfish egotism, he is more dangerous than Studs because he is aware — an accomplished technician in evil. Like Studs, he is a foil to Danny (significantly *Ellen Rogers* came just before *My Days of Anger*), for he grows toward irresponsibility and ill will. He takes a road more deathlike than Studs's; he is incapable of true love even in dream. *Ellen Rogers* is remarkable as a love story and as a study of the deceitful heart that awakens love for the pleasure of strangling it.

Ed Lanson and Danny O'Neill are key figures in *Boarding House Blues* (1961), Farrell's fifteenth published novel. The action of this uneven but haunting work takes place in 1929 while Danny is back in Chicago trying to get his career started by writing "about the 58th Street boys in the old neighborhood." The surface story is the tawdry conflict between Ed and Bridget O'Dair, a nymphomaniac grandmother, over a disintegrating rooming house for bohemians on Chicago's near North Side. But the deeper concern is with Danny's new-found maturity that is set against a background of triviality and moral irresponsibility symbolized by the house. The theme is man's use of his brief lifetime — Farrell's old concern with the mysterious alternatives and rhythms of human life. As the moralist Danny writes in his notebook: "The question is which 'to be' before we are 'not to be.' There are no Hamlets today who are of Hamlet's quality."

Farrell's approximately two hundred and forty published short stories, most of them collected in fourteen volumes — and many others in manuscript as well — provide ample evidence, if more is needed, of his expressed intention to shake reality like a sack until it is empty. A few of them, to use Robert Morss Lovett's phrase, literally are chips off the blocks of his novels: preliminary experiments, deletions, or parts of abandoned works. The great majority were written as independent pieces, yet many of these mesh with the novels and among themselves. All the stories remain faithful to his version of reality while reflecting his continuing experience. Thus they reinforce our impression of his writing as a loosely organized, expanding work-in-progress. Danny O'Neill or his near equivalent turns up in over fifty stories, often at a new time and place like Italy in the mid-1950s. Familiars like Red Kelly and Willie Collins carry on through several tales. The stories tighten the personal relationships among Farrell's vast body of characters, yet leave his "social universe" open and permit quick probings of unexplored regions. They add significantly to Farrell's picture of youth and age, family life and marriage, the Church and clergy, education up through the university, unions and the laboring man, the politics of the ward heeler and the radical, bohemian and literary circles, organized urban violence and organized sports, and the everyday life of city people from the down-and-outer to the chain-store magnate. Working outwards from numerous Chicago communities — not confined to what is loosely called Farrell's "South Side" — the stories eventually reach to New York, Paris, and Europe at large. Their relentless pursuit of a fallible humanity is tempered by rare understanding, whether the quarry is a sheik "looking 'em over" on a Chicago beach in the twenties or a contemporary writer sardonically aware of his self-deception.

The stories range from mere scraps of experience to *Tommy Gallagher's Crusade* (1939), a novelette about a Studs-like character of the 1930s who gives his floundering life direction through fascism. Farrell has written that an experience may call for translation into anecdote, sketch, tale, novelette, or novel. Regardless of the genre, what matters most in the re-created experience is "the sense of life" arising with "internal conviction" when character is not sacrificed to ideology or to frozen form. To this end Farrell has most often, but not invariably, used the "plotless short story," the artifice of an intentionally primitive method. Not surprisingly his tales have been profoundly affected by Chekhov's short fiction, which also emphasizes character over plot and portrays the ordinary experience of common people. In Chekhov's prodigal output Farrell found strong support for his view of short stories as "doors of understanding and awareness opening outward into an entire world." About the time he read the Russian realist Farrell learned from Anderson ("Mary O'Reilley"), Hemingway ("A Casual Incident"), Dreiser ("The Open Road"), and probably Lardner. Severely controlling a preference for descriptive and metaphorical language to be seen in his earliest fiction, he rapidly developed his manner of "letting life speak" by presenting characters through their own consciousness, or their own language:

"Jesus, we sure get paper on the floor here, don't we?" Jim said, seeing the paper stacked and piled under the dining-room table as he came into the room, wearing his work clothes.

"Well, Jim, I always think this. When the children are playing, I think to myself that if they got their health, it's good, and the paper they throw on the floor don't hurt the floor, not this floor full of slivers. You couldn't hurt a floor in this dump," Lizz said, standing in the door.

"The floor's sometimes so covered with papers that we can't even see it," Jim said.

"Our Lord was born in a stable. It isn't what the outside looks like. It's what the inside looks like. If your soul is clean, that counts more than if your house is. Many there are in the world with clean houses and dirty souls. And this morning, the souls in this house are clean. This morning, everyone who's old enough to in my house received the Body and Blood of our Blessed Lord," Lizz said, her voice rising in pride as she drew to the end of her declamation.

"Well, it isn't necessary to have a dirty house in order to have a clean soul," Jim said. [From *No Star Is Lost*.]

This style has its limitations, as critics have freely shown. Yet it permits effective and colorful contrasts of idiom and it achieves dramatic immediacy, for character is directly exposed through the interplay of dialogue and through the free association of interior monologues. At its best the style *is* the character-in-action.

Experimenting in his new manner during the prolific years between 1928 and 1932, Farrell quickly came to his lyrical vein of boyhood loves and sorrows in early stories like "Autumn Afternoon" and "Helen, I Love You," and to his fiercely ironic style in stories like "The Scarecrow" and "Two Sisters." He progressively opened up the broader world of his Chicago youth in such tales as "A Jazz Age Clerk," "Spring Evening," and, somewhat later, "Comedy Cop" and "The Fastest Runner on Sixty-First Street." "They Ain't the Men They Used to Be," "The Girls at the Sphinx," and "An American Student in Paris" are examples of superior stories, completed later, that take us outside Chicago. During the past two decades as Farrell has gone farther afield in his settings, he also has increasingly experimented with different styles in his tales. He has tried the monologue, the stream-of-consciousness, and other variants of the first-person point of view. In many of the late tales he has moved away from the vocally dramatic method of dialogue and from other methods that yield a direct impression of particularized experience, relying instead upon a generalized narrative manner somewhat like the summary of a rather detached chronicler of human events.

Farrell's stories can be heavy-handed and verbose ("Honey, We'll Be Brave"), tendentious ("Reverend Father Gilhooley"), synthetic ("Just Boys"), more skilled in portraying belching and banalities ("Thanksgiving Spirit") than nuances of feeling or thought ("The Philosopher"). Perhaps they are most moving when he gives the illusion of dramatic objectivity to simple, compact action known from the inside. Then, most likely, truth to individual character becomes social revelation, and we feel the story as a self-sufficient unit. At the same time we seem to be confronted not by a discrete and packaged experience but by an ongoing actuality momentarily spotlighted in the stream of time. We might say with Danny O'Neill in *Boarding House Blues*: "It is not a story at all. It is an account of . . . that which has happened, has come to pass and has passed to become part of the welter of all that has happened." Although Farrell has succeeded best in his novels, which impressively embody his concern with time and human emergence, his tales are an integral part of his work, and a surprising number of them are individually memorable.

With few exceptions, Farrell's other imaginative writing also has been in the form of prose fiction. In 1940 he and Hortense

Alden wrote the three-act drama "The Mowbray Family" (in-cluded in *When Boyhood Dreams Come True* [1946]), a mediocre domestic comedy of "penthouse Bolshevism" in New York City. A selection of Farrell's poems appeared in 1965 as *The Collected Poems of James T. Farrell*. Almost half of the forty-four poems in the volume date from Farrell's sustained creative period of the late 1920s and early 1930s, and the remainder were written after 1960 while Farrell was launching, during his "second career," as he called it, his new multicycled series of novels entitled *A Universe of Time*. In general the earlier poems, expressing a wide range of Farrell's youthful emotional turmoil, are more success-ful than the later.

Whatever the deficiencies of Farrell's poetry, many of his verses hold up exceptionally well. Moreover, his poetry intimately exposes the sensibility that has created important fiction in our time. In it may be seen the author's zealous dedication to his work, his romantic temperament, and his susceptibility to beauty and love — sources of the equally evident hatred of all that is vulgar and defiling in his "ugly and hideous corner" of the world. Here too is expressed his broad understanding of hu-manity and the enduring will and the hardy optimism which has sustained him in the face of his naturalistic philosophy.

Farrell considers *A Universe of Time*, his current cycle of novels, tales, and poems, to be the culmination of his life work. Based upon a reassessment of his experience, it aims to present "a relativistic panorama of our times." At present, Farrell believes the entire project should run to about thirty volumes, to be organized into four divisions: I. When Time Was Young (1924–31). II. Paris Was Another Time (1931–32). III. When Time Was Running Red (1932–37). IV. A Universe of Time (1937 to the present). Occasionally the action of the series will dip backwards in time to the mid-nineteenth century, thus creating a countermovement to the over-all forward progression.

Much of the action of *A Universe of Time* will relate to Eddie Ryan (roughly Danny O'Neill's equivalent), whom Farrell thinks of as the integrating image of the total work. Yet, as the author has remarked, "The world is bigger than Eddie. Through a pattern of associations, many characters are introduced, and many paths are traced. From book to book, the past shall grow, and change, and grow and swell." Farrell intends *A Universe of Time* to interlock with his earlier work but to yield a more comprehensive view of experience than do any of his other series. Presumably, if Farrell realizes his purpose, the interpretation of modern life emerging from the new cycle will reinforce the large patterns of meaning implicit in the interrelated series on Studs Lonigan, Danny O'Neill, and Bernard Carr. For the author has maintained that the basic themes of his current cycle will be "man's creativity and his courageous acceptance of impermanence."

From 1963 through 1971, in addition to various related tales and poems, Farrell had published seven volumes in *A Universe of Time*: *The Silence of History* (1963), *What Time Collects* (1964), *When Time Was Born* (1966), *Lonely for the Future* (1966), *A Brand New Life* (1968), *Judith* (1969), and *Invisible Swords* (1971). These works do not compose a continuous narrative, and in most instances the positions they ultimately will assume in the vast cycle are open to conjecture.

Farrell has asserted about *The Silence of History*, however, that it was planned to "carry and predicate" the entire series. Its essential action, covering a year in the mid-1920s, explores Eddie Ryan's spiritual growth which climaxes in his fateful decision to give up the job that financed his university education. Eddie tends to see his problem as one pitting artistic destiny against business success. His decision in favor of the former demands personal sacrifice and risk, but he sees it as "an assertion, an irrevocable step toward freedom" — his way of saying "No" to the sacred values of an acquisitive society that he increasingly mistrusts. Eddie knows that through education he can gain a valuable training and also establish a relationship to a wider and nobler reality than any his impoverished past has offered. Nevertheless, his decision to drop out is an existential affirmation of uniqueness that he hopes will nullify, in his life, the anonymity that befalls most men — the silence of history. The novel, therefore, is a study of the individual growth of an incipient artist at a crucial stage in his development. To point up the theme, Farrell makes extensive excursions into the past history and the psychology of numerous other characters — ranging from professors to commercial flunkies — whose directions in life are at variance with the course Eddie takes.

Lonely for the Future continues the exploration of Eddie Ryan's past. The action opens in Chicago in March 1927, some eight months after Eddie's decision to give up his job. It closes in mid-July as Eddie and his friend George Raymond (the equivalent of Ed Lanson) hitchhike to New York. Eddie, George, and their close friend Alec McGonigle become implicated in the affairs of the Bohemian Forum, a night spot near Eddie's South Side Chicago home. This discotheque of the prohibition 1920s is the setting in which each of the three friends comes to understand better the values he wishes to live by. Alec will return to law school and eventually to the conventional commonplaces of Chicago politics and law. George, the pseudo-Nietzschean, travels farther down the self-destructive road of the "superman beyond good and evil." Eddie, already a naturalist, finds that in practice he cannot approve of George's callous use of other people. Furthermore, Eddie's awareness that men are caught in a trap of time and nothingness intensifies his need to find order and meaning through art, while life may last.

Major themes of *The Silence of History* and *Lonely for the Future* permeate *When Time Was Born*, a prose poem of several thousand words. This brief work is Farrell's celebration of the creation and creativity, of "the undying wonder of the world," the incessant surge of existence toward more complex states of awareness and being as the self interacts with others and with the world as experienced. Farrell's use of the Adam and Eve theme presents man's creativity as springing from his weakness and his need for another person. Love in all its forms is linked to the growth of personal awareness — the strengthening of "the inner wind of consciousness" — and to the beat and pace of time itself.

What Time Collects is an important, ambitious addition to Farrell's canon. In this novel the present time is approximately 1924 to 1925, but long stretches of the action look to the past, as far back as the 1870s, to explore the antecedents of Anne and Zeke Daniels of Valley City (Indianapolis). None of the characters of *The Silence of History* or *Lonely for the Future* enter this novel — the connections will come in later books — but *What Time Collects* parallels Eddie Ryan's story in its concern with a "decision to make some kind of leap into life" in pursuit of self-liberation. Anne Duncan Daniels, a girl in her early twenties, focuses this theme. What time collects in Anne is precisely the strength to break out of her degrading marriage to Zeke Daniels and to reject her past. She belongs with seekers like Danny O'Neill and Eddie Ryan, who develop the self-knowledge and the courage that permit them to act decisively in response to individual needs. What time has collected for Zeke is a spiritually crippled self, the end result of "the whole loveless heritage" of the Daniels family over several generations. Zeke is a victim as well as a monster of crudity and aggression. Like Studs, he symbolizes a spiritual malady in his society. He is an excrescence of the solid, middle-class Protestants of Valley City, who are smug, materialistic, and puritanical to the core. *What Time Collects* projects Farrell's exceptional understanding of the many characters in three generations of the Duncan and Daniels families. It effectively adds a new panel to Farrell's picture of America.

In *A Brand New Life* Anne Duncan Daniels, newly divorced from Zeke, is living in Chicago seeking "the real Anne" through love, first with Roger Raymond and then with his brother George, two friends of Eddie Ryan. Thus she moves close to the periphery of Eddie's life, although Eddie enters the book only indirectly through the conversation of Anne's lovers. They recognize Eddie's strength of purpose, his compassion, and his obsession with time and impermanence — qualities commenting on the frantic and passion-bound interests of Anne and her lovers. But the story is Anne's, her search to overcome loneliness. Her tragedy is that neither of her lovers really wants her or anyone else to breach the spiritual walls behind which he feels secure; and, by herself, Anne is inadequate to the task. At the moment when she believes she has found genuine oneness with George, he already has discarded her in his thoughts. Presumably, in later novels, Anne's search for a satisfying, truly mutual love will continue.

Judith, an excellent short novel, brings Eddie Ryan to the center of the stage as narrator and chief actor. The tale is his first-person retrospective account of his on-and-off affair with Judith, an internationally known concert pianist of New York City, during the years 1951 to 1954. Eddie, now in his early fifties, is an established professional writer. He and Judith are both hard-driving, successful artists in mid-career. Eddie recognizes that "we had both hemmed ourselves within our separate loneliness," inevitable for the artist, and that each craved a liberating love. But the ever-present obstacle to a stable relationship that will satisfy the craving is the inescapable contradiction, felt by each, between the demands of art and the demands of love. The emotional seesaw tossing them up and down is effectively comic. But ultimately each of these artists must go his own way. As Farrell has written in a private letter, the theme of *Judith* appears to be "Artists and Egos go on." Much of the excellence of this novella lies in the ability of Eddie as narrator, for he is factual, accurate, honest, and sensitive. Through Eddie, Farrell has provided a terse, swiftly moving first-person narrative of remembered experience, including generous passages of dialogue that provide still another level of dramatic immediacy. Presumably *Judith* fits into the final division of Farrell's plan for *A Universe of Time*.

Invisible Swords, Farrell's latest novel, makes a strong cumulative impact. With *Judith* it belongs in the fourth part of *A Universe of Time*. It is the story of a child's congenital retardation and its effect upon the parents, Bill Martin, a New York City editor, and his wife Ethel; and as such it reflects the experience of Farrell and Hortense Alden with their child John. In addition, the important character Tod Johnson, a writer somewhat similar in his honesty to Eddie Ryan of *Judith*, reflects important aspects of Farrell the mature novelist. The story, set in New York City from 1946 to 1949, simultaneously relates the growth of the Martins' harrowing realization of what the hopeless retardation of their beautiful child Billy means, the consequent damaging strain upon their marriage, and the connection between the overpowering despair of such "biological tragedy" as Billy's idiocy to the creation of art that earnestly explores the meaning of the most searing events. The lingering death from cancer of Tod Johnson's wife, an ordeal he honestly faces in his novel *Caroline's Destiny*, parallels the experience of the Martins with Billy. But Bill Martin, Johnson's editor, blocks the publication of the novel because its honesty forces him to face up to personal realities he cannot handle. In the concluding pages of *Invisible Swords*, Bill Martin's evasiveness and Tod Johnson's tormented grappling with his experience effectively suggest two ways of meeting the horror that lurks behind the beauty of little Billy.

At present *A Universe of Time* is too incomplete to judge as a cohesive work. Evidently as it grows, it will continue to be compatible in themes and patterns of experience with Farrell's earlier work; but also it may develop new techniques suitable to its own purpose, and it may give fresh emphases to Farrell's interpretation of the past. For the novelist has long believed that the emergence of novelty in the present means that "new pasts are always rising behind us." Whatever may be the potential of *A Universe of Time*, its published portions do not as yet make the strong and unified impact of either *Studs Lonigan* or the O'Neill-O'Flaherty series.

"'You live badly, my friends. It is shameful to live like that.'" Maxim Gorki's words express the sad indictment of humanity he found implied in Chekhov's fiction. They suggest the reproach in Farrell's writing, although the American's attitude is more yeasty with indignation. Like Chekhov in his way, Farrell makes us aware of life as it might be by showing life as he often found it: riddled with contempt for mind and fear of affection. But his

critical realism recognizes man's idealism as well as his shabbi-
ness, and its constant assumption is man's capacity for reason
and dignity. His humanism is friendly to reformist social
thought and to modern pragmatism. His fiction says to us that
the only real ends are earthly consequences and that in human
society consequences are men and women, affected for better or
worse by their culture. Also it says that elemental emotions impel
men and women toward self-fulfillment or self-deception. At the
heart of his fiction is an ethics of self-development more basic
than his rationalism and displayed in his rise from "plebeian"
origins and in his stubborn independence of mind. This ethics is
a kind of Emersonian individualism without the supernatural
aura. It asserts the possibility of radical self-improvement
through the right and the will to grow. As he has written: "Man
is my concern. Freedom is my concern. . . . the dream that
each and all have the opportunity to rise to the full stature of
their potential humanity." Farrell is a philosophic naturalist who
simultaneously sees life in the context of death and affirms with
utter seriousness the values of the Enlightenment. A cantanker-
ous Irishman with a zest for living, he never sees life as "absurd."
Nor does he reject modern civilization as an irreclaimable wasteland. Nostalgia in a Farrell character is not a sign of abhorrence
for the bases of modern society. Instead it is a technique of
character revelation, a sign of one man's failure to live the good
life.

The same values are alive in his historical and critical writing: *A
Note on Literary Criticism* (1936), *The League of Frightened Philistines*
(1945), *Literature and Morality* (1947), *Reflections at Fifty* (1954), and
even the sly mouthings of Jonathan Titulescu Fogarty in *The
Name Is Fogarty: Private Papers on Public Matters*. These values
may be seen in his political development through various stages
of anti-Stalinist socialism to the liberal internationalism of
Stevenson and Kennedy. His social criticism, often joyously
pugnacious but sometimes shrill, employs touchstones of human
freedom and of growth toward excellence. It identifies shoddy
cultural products of the profit system ("The Fate of Writing in

America") and of political orthodoxy ("The Literary Popular Front before the War"). It condemns what he believes is intellectually regressive ("The Faith of Lewis Mumford") or morally insensitive ("Moral Censorship and the Ten Commandments"). Because it attacks sources of cultural stagnancy and personal frustration, his social criticism is blood brother to his fiction and demonstrates anew the unity of his work.

So does his thinking about literature. Books freed him (Bernard links *library* and *liberty*) and helped him to grow. The unforgettable lesson was that literature intensifies awareness, expands what George H. Mead called "the sense of the other," so narrowly developed in Studs. By assuring the cultural continuity that crowns life with meaning, literature "humanizes the world." It brings men back to the essence of all "destinies": "the struggles, aspirations, joys, and sorrows of human beings." The writer works at "shaping . . . life itself into literary form" in order to convey his vision through "the structure of events, the quality of the characterization, the complex impact of the work itself." The critic's role is to illuminate the work. He should explore its internal relationships and patterns, then relate these to social processes. Farrell's criticism of Joyce, Tolstoi, and others takes this approach, in keeping with his idea of the two uses of literature, aesthetic and functional, elaborated in *A Note on Literary Criticism*.

Farrell's initial advantage as a writer was his thorough possession of an urban, Irish Catholic world. As a child in two families he sought acceptance and identity, and as a talented boy in culturally illiterate surroundings he groped to find himself. His need charged his youthful experience with unforgettable tensions and burned it into his consciousness. His fiction, an extension of his search for himself, brings his Chicago experience into focus. It creates the larger self — his famous "South Side" in its spatial, temporal, cultural, and emotional dimensions — by opening out to include family, society, and cultural process extending over half a century. It explores this past with great objective validity, employing a method and style appropriate to his view of life and drawing upon a constructive imagination both

informed and savage. The writing remains intensely personal —
and this is a deep strength — if only because its subject, the
education of Americans, is rooted in his early predicament and
in his accomplishment, just as many of his characters are imagined versions of the possibilities and actualities of his experience.

This personal and ultimately self-centered quality of his art
helps to explain its limitations. His shaking the sack of reality —
his intimate reality — until it is empty shows his unqualified
desire to master what is genuinely his own and to get it all down,
and critics have responded according to their disposition: he is
truthful, honest, thorough, stubborn, or repetitious. Surely this
quality sometimes hampers control and selectivity, and it may
make for writing that lacks sufficient aesthetic distance in spite
of the objective method. Moreover his imagination is most vi-
tally engaged with his pre-University of Chicago life, that experience of the nerve-ends and the emotions that absorbed him
for years before he found the essential intellectual tools to shape
it into clarity. So he best creates the wounded and confused boy,
the aspiring or rebellious young man, the adult grotesque, in
short, those very human personalities in his fiction who are
defined by deep involvement with their family and their severely
limited culture. Yet the dynamics of his social philosophy and
the grand design of his fiction call for an equally convincing
picture of men and women who have emerged into larger
worlds — social, intellectual, and psychological. As Robert
Gorham Davis has cogently argued (in the *New York Times Book
Review* for November 2, 1947), his fiction does not do complete
justice to what is rich and creative in human consciousness,
Farrell's included.

This is to say that Farrell has not realized the full potential in
his vision. But his vision is large and single, and step by step he
has created a single world of ample proportions. His cycles of
novels with his other fiction approximate a sequence, a rarity in
our literature. At its best, the American past he creates is deeply
authentic, like Cather's Nebraska or Faulkner's South. It is espe-

cially meaningful to us because, through its rich details of urban manners, it shows the heavy cost exacted of people and institutions by the modern city. His characters' lives expose social process; time slowly brings change, and the making of personality and the formation of society merge. His Lonigans, O'Flahertys, and O'Neills are deeply immersed in their time and place — interesting contrasts to Hemingway's disengaged Americans — and his work is exceptional in our fiction for the number of its living characters. The contrast between their often blind groping for a better future and the grimness of their present, flowing inevitably out of their past, is a subject with tragic power.

SELECTED BIBLIOGRAPHIES

SELECTED
BIBLIOGRAPHIES

STEPHEN CRANE

Works

NOVELS

Maggie: A Girl of the Streets (A Story of New York), "by Johnston Smith" (pseud.). N.p. [1893]. Revised edition, *Maggie: A Girl of the Streets*. New York: Appleton, 1896. There have been three recent reprints of note: one edited by Joseph Katz (Gainesville, Fla.: Scholars' Facsimiles and Reprints, 1966); another by Maurice Bassan (*Stephen Crane's Maggie, Text and Context*, Belmont, Calif.: Wadsworth Publication, 1966); and the third by Donald Pizer (San Francisco: Chandler, 1968).
The Red Badge of Courage. New York: Appleton, 1895.
George's Mother. New York and London: Edward Arnold, 1896.
The Third Violet. New York: Appleton, 1897.
Active Service. New York: Frederick A. Stokes, 1899.
The O'Ruddy. New York: Frederick A. Stokes, 1903.
The Complete Novels of Stephen Crane, edited by Thomas A. Gullason. New York: Doubleday, 1967.

SHORT STORIES AND SKETCHES

The Little Regiment and Other Episodes of the American Civil War. New York: Appleton, 1896.
The Open Boat and Other Tales of Adventure. New York: Doubleday and McClure, 1898. (The English edition, *The Open Boat and Other Stories*, published by W. Heinemann in 1898, contains more stories.)
The Monster and Other Stories. New York: Harper, 1899. (Contains only "The Monster," "The Blue Hotel," and "His New Mittens.")
Whilomville Stories. New York and London: Harper, 1900.
Wounds in the Rain. New York: Frederick A. Stokes, 1900.

293

Great Battles of the World. Philadelphia: Lippincott, 1901.

The Monster. London: Harper, 1901. (Contains "The Monster," "The Blue Hotel," "His New Mittens," "Twelve O'Clock," "Moonlight on the Snow," "Manacled," and "An Illusion in Red and White.")

Last Words. London: Digby, Long, 1902.

Men, Women and Boats, edited with an introduction by Vincent Starrett. New York: Boni and Liveright, 1917. (Contains seventeen stories and sketches.)

A Battle in Greece. Mount Vernon, N.Y.: Peter Pauper Press, 1936. (Contains a reprint of the battle sketch which appeared in the *New York Journal* of June 13, 1897.)

The Sullivan County Sketches, edited by Melvin Schoberlin. Syracuse, N.Y.: Syracuse University Press, 1949.

The Complete Short Stories and Sketches of Stephen Crane, edited by Thomas A. Gullason. New York: Doubleday, 1963.

The New York City Sketches of Stephen Crane and Related Pieces, edited by R. W. Stallman and E. R. Hagemann. New York: New York University Press, 1966.

Stephen Crane: Sullivan County Tales and Sketches, edited by R. W. Stallman. Ames: Iowa State University Press, 1968.

WAR DISPATCHES

The War Dispatches of Stephen Crane, edited by R. W. Stallman and E. R. Hagemann. New York: New York University Press, 1964.

POETRY AND PLAYS

The Black Riders and Other Lines. Boston: Copeland and Day, 1895.

A Souvenir and a Medley. East Aurora, N.Y.: Roycroft Printing Shop, 1896. (Contains seven poems, as well as a sketch entitled "A Great Mistake" and a fifteen-line piece printed in capitals, "A Prologue," which reads like stage directions.)

War Is Kind. New York: Frederick A. Stokes, 1899.

The Collected Poems of Stephen Crane, edited by Wilson Follett. New York: Knopf, 1930.

The Poems of Stephen Crane, a critical edition by Joseph Katz. New York: Cooper Square Publishers, 1966.

At Clancy's Wake, in *Last Words.* London: Digby, Long, 1902.

The Blood of the Martyr. Mount Vernon, N.Y.: Peter Pauper Press, [1940]. (A play originally printed in the Sunday magazine of the *New York Press* on April 3, 1898.)

Drama in Cuba, in *The War Dispatches of Stephen Crane,* edited by R. W. Stallman and E. R. Hagemann. New York: New York University Press, 1964.

COLLECTED EDITIONS

The Work of Stephen Crane, edited by Wilson Follett. 12 vols. New York: Knopf, 1925–27. Reprinted in 6 vols., New York: Russell and Russell, 1963.

Stephen Crane: An Omnibus, edited by R. W. Stallman. New York: Knopf, 1952.

Stephen Crane: Uncollected Writings, edited with an introduction by Olov W. Fryckstedt. Uppsala: Almqvist and Wiksell, 1963.

The Works of Stephen Crane, edited by Fredson Bowers. 10 vols. Charlottesville: University Press of Virginia, 1969–. Vol. I, *Bowery Tales,* 1969. Vol. IV, *The O'Ruddy,* 1971. Vol. V, *Tales of Adventure,* 1970. Vol. VI, *Tales of War,* 1970. Vol.

VII, *Tales of Whilomville*, 1969. Vol. VIII, *Tales, Sketches, and Reports*, 1973. Vol. IX, *Reports of War*, 1971. Others in preparation.

LETTERS AND NOTEBOOK

Stephen Crane: Letters, edited by R. W. Stallman and Lillian Gilkes. New York: New York University Press, 1960.
The Notebook of Stephen Crane, edited by Donald J. Greiner and Ellen B. Greiner. Charlottesville: University Press of Virginia, 1969.

Bibliographies

Since 1963 Syracuse University has issued an annual Crane bibliography in *Thoth*.

Gross, Theodore L., and Stanley Wertheim. *Hawthorne, Melville, Stephen Crane: A Critical Bibliography*. New York: Free Press, 1971.
Stallman, R. W. *Stephen Crane*. New York: Braziller, 1968.
  sity Press, 1972.
Williams, Ames W., and Vincent Starrett. *Stephen Crane: A Bibliography*. Glendale, Calif.: John Valentine, 1948.

Biographies

Beer, Thomas. *Stephen Crane*. New York: Knopf, 1923.
Berryman, John. *Stephen Crane*. New York: Sloane, 1950. Reprinted in 1962 as a Meridian paperback with an additional preface.
Gilkes, Lillian. *Cora Crane*. Bloomington: Indiana University Press, 1960. (Although centered on Cora, this contains much information on the life of the couple in England.)
Raymond, Thomas L. *Stephen Crane*. Newark, N.J.: Carteret Book Club, 1923.
Stallman, R. W. *Stephen Crane*. New York: Braziller, 1968.

Critical Studies

Bassan, Maurice. "Crane, Townsend, and Realism of a Good Kind," *Proceedings of the New Jersey Historical Society*, 82:128–35 (April 1964).
Berryman, John. "The Red Badge of Courage," in *The American Novel*, edited by Wallace Stegner. New York: Basic Books, 1965.
Berthoff, Warner. *The Ferment of Realism: American Literature 1884–1919*. New York: Free Press, 1965.
Cady, Edwin H. *Stephen Crane*. New York: Twayne, 1962.
Cazemajou, Jean. *Stephen Crane, écrivain journaliste*. Paris: Didier, 1969.
Colvert, James B. "The Origins of Stephen Crane's Literary Creed," *University of Texas Studies in English*, 34:179–88 (1955).
Ellison, Ralph. Introduction to *The Red Badge of Courage*. New York: Dell, 1960. Reprinted in *Shadow and Act*. New York: Random House, 1964.
Furst, Lilian R., and Peter R. Skrine. *Naturalism*. London: Methuen, 1971.
Geismar, Maxwell. *Rebels and Ancestors*. Boston: Houghton Mifflin, 1953.
Gibson, Donald B. *The Fiction of Stephen Crane*. Carbondale: Southern Illinois University Press, 1968.
Gordan, John D. "*The Ghost* at Brede Place," *Bulletin of the New York Public Library*, 56:591–96 (December 1952).

Greenfield, Stanley B. "The Unmistakable Stephen Crane," *PMLA*, 73:562–72 (December 1958).

Gullason, Thomas. "Stephen Crane's Private War on Yellow Journalism," *Huntington Library Quarterly*, 22:200–8 (May 1959).

———, ed. *Stephen Crane's Career: Perspectives and Evaluations*. New York: New York University Press, 1972.

Hoffman, D. G. *The Poetry of Stephen Crane*. New York: Columbia University Press, 1957.

———. "Stephen Crane's Last Novel," *Bulletin of the New York Public Library*, 64:337–43 (June 1960).

Holton, Milne. *Cylinder of Vision*. Baton Rouge: Louisiana State University Press, 1972.

Katz, Joseph. "'The Blue Battalions' and the Uses of Experience," *Studia Neophilogica*, 38:107–16 (1966).

———, ed. *Stephen Crane in Transition*. De Kalb: Northern Illinois University Press, 1972.

———, ed. *Stephen Crane Newsletter*, Fall 1966 to date.

Kazin, Alfred. "American Fin de Siècle," in *On Native Grounds*. New York: Reynal and Hitchcock, 1942.

La France, Marston. *A Reading of Stephen Crane*. Oxford: Clarendon Press, 1971.

Lytle, Andrew. "'The Open Boat': A Pagan Tale," in *The Hero with the Private Parts*. Baton Rouge: Louisiana State University Press, 1966.

Martin, Jay. *Harvests of Change: American Literature, 1865–1914*. Englewood Cliffs, N.J.: Prentice-Hall, 1967.

Modern Fiction Studies, 5:199–291 (Autumn 1959). (Essays on Crane by Thomas A. Gullason, Robert F. Gleckner, Peter Buitenhuis, James B. Colvert, R. W. Stallman, Hugh Maclean, Eric Solomon, James T. Cox; also contains a good selective bibliography.)

Nelson, Harland S. "Stephen Crane's Achievement as a Poet," *University of Texas Studies in Literature and Language*, 4:564–82 (Winter 1963).

Pizer, Donald. *Realism and Naturalism in Nineteenth-Century American Literature*. Carbondale: Southern Illinois University Press, 1966.

Ross, Lillian. *Picture*. London: Penguin Books, 1962. Reprinted from the *New Yorker*, May–June 1952. (An account of the filming of *The Red Badge of Courage* for MGM under the direction of John Huston.)

Schneider, Robert W. *Five Novelists of the Progressive Era*. New York: Columbia University Press, 1965.

Solomon, Eric. *Stephen Crane: From Parody to Realism*. Cambridge, Mass.: Harvard University Press, 1966.

Vasilievskaya, O. B. *The Work of Stephen Crane*. Moscow: Nayka Editions, 1967. (A critical study in Russian.)

Walcutt, Charles Child. *American Literary Naturalism, a Divided Stream*. Minneapolis: University of Minnesota Press, 1956.

Weisenberger, Bernard. "The Red Badge of Courage," in *Twelve Original Essays on Great American Novels*, edited by Charles Shapiro. Detroit: Wayne State University Press, 1958.

Weiss, Daniel. "The Red Badge of Courage," *Psychoanalytic Review*, 52:32–52 (Summer 1965), 52:130–54 (Fall 1965).

Westbrook, Max. "Stephen Crane's Poetry: Perspective and Arrogance," *Bucknell Review*, 11:23–34 (December 1963).

Ziff, Larzer. *The American 1890s*. New York: Viking, 1966.

FRANK NORRIS
Works

Yvernelle. Philadelphia: Lippincott, 1892.
Moran of the Lady Letty. New York: Doubleday and McClure, 1898.
McTeague. New York: Doubleday and McClure, 1899.
Blix. New York: Doubleday and McClure, 1899.
A Man's Woman. New York: Doubleday and McClure, 1900. (Serialized in 1899.)
The Octopus. New York: Doubleday, Page, 1901.
The Pit. New York: Doubleday, Page, 1903.
The Responsibilities of the Novelist and Other Literary Essays. New York: Doubleday, Page, 1903.
Vandover and the Brute. Garden City, N.Y.: Doubleday, Page, 1914.
Complete Edition of Frank Norris. Garden City, N.Y.: Doubleday, Doran, 1928. (Contains the works listed above, and in addition reprints Norris's short stories, Vol. IV, and journalistic writings, Vol. X.)
The Letters of Frank Norris, edited by Franklin D. Walker. San Francisco: Book Club of California, 1956.
The Literary Criticism of Frank Norris, edited by Donald Pizer. Austin: University of Texas Press, 1964. (Collects, with illuminating commentary, all Norris's important criticism.)

Bibliography

Lohf, Kenneth A., and Eugene P. Sheehy, compilers. *Frank Norris: A Bibliography*. Los Gatos, Calif.: Talisman Press, 1959.

Critical and Biographical Studies

Åhnebrink, Lars. *The Beginnings of Naturalism in American Fiction*. Cambridge, Mass.: Harvard University Press, 1950.
Biencourt, Marius. *Une influence du naturalisme français en Amérique: Frank Norris*. Paris: Giard, 1933.
Cargill, Oscar. *Intellectual America: Ideas on the March*. New York: Macmillan, 1941. Pp. 89–107.
Chase, Richard. *The American Novel and Its Tradition*. Garden City, N.Y.: Doubleday, 1957. Pp. 185–204.
Collins, Carvel. Introduction to *McTeague*. New York: Holt, Rinehart and Winston reprint, 1950.
Cooperman, Stanley. "Frank Norris and the Werewolf of Guilt," *Modern Language Quarterly*, 20:252–58 (September 1959).
Folsom, James K. "Social Darwinism or Social Protest? The 'Philosophy' of *The Octopus*," *Modern Fiction Studies*, 8:393–400 (Winter 1962–63).
Geismar, Maxwell. *Rebels and Ancestors*. Boston: Houghton Mifflin, 1953. Pp. 3–66.
Hart, James D., ed. *A Novelist in the Making: Frank Norris*. Cambridge, Mass.: Harvard University Press, 1970.
Hicks, Granville. *The Great Tradition*. New York: Macmillan, 1933. Pp. 168–75.
Howells, William Dean. "Frank Norris," *North American Review*, 175:769–78 (December 1902).
Kazin, Alfred. *On Native Grounds*. New York: Reynal and Hitchcock, 1942. Pp. 97–102.

Lynn, Kenneth S. Introduction to *The Octopus*. Boston: Houghton Mifflin (Riverside Editions reprint), 1958.

Marchand, Ernest. *Frank Norris: A Study*. Stanford, Calif.: Stanford University Press, 1942.

Millgate, Michael. *American Social Fiction: James to Cozzens*. New York: Barnes and Noble, 1964. Pp. 38–53.

Pizer, Donald. *The Novels of Frank Norris*. Bloomington: Indiana University Press, 1966.

Taylor, Walter F. *The Economic Novel in America*. Chapel Hill: University of North Carolina Press, 1942. Pp. 282–306.

Walcutt, Charles Child. *American Literary Naturalism, a Divided Stream*. Minneapolis: University of Minnesota Press, 1956. Pp. 114–56.

Walker, Franklin D. *Frank Norris: A Biography*. Garden City, N.Y.: Doubleday, Doran, 1932.

THEODORE DREISER

Works

Sister Carrie. New York: Doubleday, Page, 1900.

Jennie Gerhardt. New York: Harper, 1911.

The Financier. New York: Harper, 1912.

A Traveler at Forty. New York: Century, 1913.

The Titan. New York: John Lane, 1914.

The "Genius." New York: John Lane, 1915.

Plays of the Natural and Supernatural. New York: John Lane, 1916.

A Hoosier Holiday. New York: John Lane, 1916.

Free and Other Stories. New York: Boni and Liveright, 1918.

The Hand of the Potter. New York: Boni and Liveright, 1918.

Twelve Men. New York: Boni and Liveright, 1919.

Hey Rub-a-Dub-Dub. New York: Boni and Liveright, 1920.

A Book about Myself. New York: Boni and Liveright, 1922. Republished as *Newspaper Days*. New York: Horace Liveright, 1931.

The Color of a Great City. New York: Boni and Liveright, 1923.

An American Tragedy. 2 vols. New York: Horace Liveright, 1925.

Moods Cadenced and Declaimed. New York: Boni and Liveright, 1926.

Chains: Lesser Novels and Stories. New York: Boni and Liveright, 1927.

Dreiser Looks at Russia. New York: Horace Liveright, 1928.

A Gallery of Women. New York: Horace Liveright, 1929.

Dawn. New York: Horace Liveright, 1931.

Tragic America. New York: Horace Liveright, 1931.

America Is Worth Saving. New York: Modern Age Books, 1941.

The Bulwark. Garden City, N.Y.: Doubleday, 1946.

The Stoic. Garden City, N.Y.: Doubleday, 1947.

Critical and Biographical Studies

Beach, Joseph Warren. *The Twentieth-Century Novel: Studies in Technique*. New York: Appleton-Century-Crofts, 1932. Pp. 321–31.

Campbell, Louise, ed. *Letters to Louise*. Philadelphia: University of Pennsylvania Press, 1959.

Cargill, Oscar. *Intellectual America: Ideas on the March*. New York: Macmillan, 1941. Pp. 107–28.

Elias, Robert H. *Theodore Dreiser: Apostle of Nature*. New York: Knopf, 1949. Emended edition, Ithaca, N.Y.: Cornell University Press, 1970.

————, ed. *Letters of Theodore Dreiser*. 3 vols. Philadelphia: University of Pennsylvania Press, 1959.

Geismar, Maxwell. *Rebels and Ancestors*. Boston: Houghton Mifflin, 1953. Pp. 287–379.

Hicks, Granville. *The Great Tradition*. New York: Macmillan, 1933. Pp. 226–37.

Kazin, Alfred. *On Native Grounds*. New York: Reynal and Hitchcock, 1942. Pp. 78–91.

———— and Charles Shapiro. *The Stature of Theodore Dreiser*. Bloomington: Indiana University Press, 1965.

Lehan, Richard. *Theodore Dreiser, His World and His Novels*. Carbondale: Southern Illinois University Press, 1969.

Matthiessen, F. O. *Theodore Dreiser*. New York: Sloane, 1951.

Moers, Ellen. *Two Dreisers*. New York: Viking, 1969.

Shapiro, Charles. *Theodore Dreiser: Our Bitter Patriot*. Carbondale: Southern Illinois University Press, 1962.

Swanberg, W. A. *Dreiser*. New York: Scribner's, 1965.

Spiller, Robert E., *et al. Literary History of the United States*. Revised edition, New York: Macmillan, 1953. Pp. 1197–1208.

Warren, Robert Penn. *Homage to Theodore Dreiser, August 27, 1871–December 28, 1945, on the Centennial of His Birth*. New York: Random House, 1971.

Walcutt, Charles Child. *American Literary Naturalism, a Divided Stream*. Minneapolis: University of Minnesota Press, 1956. Pp. 180–221.

JACK LONDON

Works

NOVELS AND COLLECTIONS OF SHORT STORIES

The Son of the Wolf, Tales of the Far North. Boston: Houghton, Mifflin, 1900.

The God of His Fathers and Other Stories. New York: McClure, Phillips, 1901.

A Daughter of the Snows. Philadelphia: Lippincott, 1902.

Children of the Frost. New York: Macmillan, 1902.

The Call of the Wild. New York: Macmillan, 1903.

The Faith of Men and Other Stories. New York: Macmillan, 1904.

The Sea-Wolf. New York: Macmillan, 1904.

The Game. New York: Macmillan, 1905.

Moon-Face and Other Stories. New York: Macmillan, 1906.

White Fang. New York: Macmillan, 1906.

Before Adam. New York: Macmillan, 1906.

Love of Life and Other Stories. New York: Macmillan, 1906.

The Iron Heel. New York: Macmillan, 1907.

Martin Eden. New York: Macmillan, 1909.

Lost Face. New York: Macmillan, 1910.

Burning Daylight. New York: Macmillan, 1910.

When God Laughs and Other Stories. New York: Macmillan, 1911.

Adventure. New York: Macmillan, 1911.

South Sea Tales. New York: Macmillan, 1911.

The House of Pride and Other Tales of Hawaii. New York: Macmillan, 1912.
Smoke Bellew Tales. New York: Century, 1912.
A Son of the Sun. New York: Doubleday, Page, 1912.
The Night-Born. New York: Century, 1913.
The Abysmal Brute. New York: Century, 1913.
The Valley of the Moon. New York: Macmillan, 1913.
The Strength of the Strong. New York: Macmillan, 1914.
The Mutiny of the Elsinore. New York: Macmillan, 1914.
The Scarlet Plague. New York: Macmillan, 1915.
The Star Rover. New York: Macmillan, 1915.
The Little Lady of the Big House. New York: Macmillan, 1916.
The Turtles of Tasman. New York: Macmillan, 1916.
The Human Drift. New York: Macmillan, 1917.
The Red One. New York: Macmillan, 1918.
On the Makaloa Mat. New York: Macmillan, 1919.
Hearts of Three. New York: Macmillan, 1920.
Dutch Courage and Other Stories. New York: Macmillan, 1922.
The Assassination Bureau, Ltd. (completed by Robert L. Fish). New York: McGraw-Hill, 1963.

PLAYS

Scorn of Women. New York: Macmillan, 1906.
Theft. New York: Macmillan, 1910.
The Acorn-Planter. New York: Macmillan, 1916.

ESSAYS, TRACTS, TRAVEL, AUTOBIOGRAPHY, LETTERS

The Kempton-Wace Letters (with Anna Strunsky). New York: Macmillan, 1903.
The People of the Abyss. New York: Macmillan, 1903.
War of the Classes. New York: Macmillan, 1905.
The Road. New York: Macmillan, 1907.
Revolution and Other Essays. New York: Macmillan, 1910.
The Cruise of the Snark. New York: Macmillan, 1911.
John Barleycorn. New York: Century, 1913.
Letters from Jack London, edited by King Hendricks and Irving Shepard. New York: Odyssey Press, 1965.

JUVENILES

The Cruise of the Dazzler. New York: Century, 1902.
Tales of the Fish Patrol. New York: Macmillan, 1905.
Jerry of the Islands. New York: Macmillan, 1917.
Michael, Brother of Jerry. New York: Macmillan, 1917.

SELECTED EDITION

The Bodley Head Jack London, edited by Arthur Calder-Marshall. 3 vols. London: Bodley Head, 1963–64.

Bibliography

There is no adequate bibliography for London. "A Jack London Bibliography" appears in Charmian London, *The Book of Jack London* (New York: Macmillan,

1921), II, 397–414. Bibliographical information may also be found in Joseph Gaer's *Jack London* (Monograph No. 1 of California Literary Research Project, 1934) and J. Haydock's "Jack London: A Bibliography of Criticism," *Bulletin of Bibliography*, 23:42–46 (May–August 1960).

Critical and Biographical Studies

Feied, Frederick. *No Pie in the Sky: The Hobo as American Cultural Hero in the Works of Jack London, John Dos Passos and Jack Kerouac.* New York: Citadel, 1964.

Foner, Philip S. *Jack London: American Rebel.* New York: Citadel, 1947, 1964.

Geismar, Maxwell. *Rebels and Ancestors.* Boston: Houghton Mifflin, 1953. Pp. 139–216.

Herrick, Robert. *The Memoirs of an American Citizen.* New York: Macmillan, 1905.

James, George W. "A Study of Jack London in His Prime," *Overland Monthly*, 69:361–99 (May 1917).

Johnson, Martin. *Through the South Seas with Jack London.* New York: Dodd, Mead, 1913.

Lane, R. W. "Life and Jack London," a serial in *Sunset* extending from October 1917 to May 1918.

London, Charmian. *The Book of Jack London.* 2 vols. New York: Century, 1921.

———. *The Log of the Snark.* New York: Macmillan, 1915.

———. *Our Hawaii.* New York: Macmillan, 1917; revised edition, 1922.

London, Joan. *Jack London: an Unconventional Biography.* New York: Doubleday, 1939.

McDevitt, William. *Jack London as Poet.* San Francisco: Recorder-Sunset Press, 1947.

Mencken, H. L. *Prejudices: First Series.* New York: Knopf, 1921. Pp. 236–39.

Mumford, Lewis. *The Golden Day: A Study in American Literature and Culture.* New York: Boni and Liveright, 1926. Pp. 247–50.

Noel, Joseph. *Footloose in Arcadia: A Personal Record of Jack London, George Sterling, Ambrose Bierce.* New York: Carrick, 1940.

O'Connor, Richard. *High Jinks on the Klondike.* Indianapolis: Bobbs, Merrill, 1954.

———. *Jack London: A Biography.* Boston: Little, Brown, 1964.

Pattee, Fred L. *Side-Lights on American Literature.* New York: Century, 1922. Pp. 98–160.

Payne, Edward B. *The Soul of Jack London.* London: Rider, 1926.

Schorer, Mark. *Sinclair Lewis: An American Life.* New York: McGraw-Hill, 1961. Pp. 164–66 and *passim*.

Stone, Irving. *Sailor on Horseback.* Boston: Houghton Mifflin, 1938. Reissued as *Jack London, Sailor on Horseback: A Biographical Novel.* New York: Doubleday, 1947.

Walcutt, Charles Child. *American Literary Naturalism, a Divided Stream.* Minneapolis: University of Minnesota Press, 1956. Pp. 87–113.

Williams, Blanche C. *Our Short Story Writers.* New York: Moffat, Yard, 1920. Pp. 256–57.

SHERWOOD ANDERSON
Works

NOVELS AND COLLECTIONS OF SHORT STORIES

Windy McPherson's Son. New York: John Lane, 1916. Revised edition, New York: B. W. Huebsch, 1922.

Marching Men. New York: John Lane, 1917.
Winesburg, Ohio: A Group of Tales of Ohio Small Town Life. New York: B. W. Huebsch, 1919.
Poor White. New York: B. W. Huebsch, 1920.
The Triumph of the Egg: A Book of Impressions from American Life in Tales and Poems. New York: B. W. Huebsch, 1921.
Horses and Men: Tales, Long and Short, from Our American Life. New York: B. W. Huebsch, 1923.
Many Marriages. New York: B. W. Huebsch, 1923.
Dark Laughter. New York: Boni and Liveright, 1925.
Beyond Desire. New York: Liveright, 1932.
Death in the Woods and Other Stories. New York: Liveright, 1933.
Kit Brandon: A Portrait. New York: Scribner's, 1936.

POETRY AND PLAYS

Mid-American Chants. New York: John Lane, 1918.
A New Testament. New York: Boni and Liveright, 1927.
Plays: Winesburg and Others. New York: Scribner's, 1937.

AUTOBIOGRAPHY AND OTHER PROSE

A Story Teller's Story: The Tale of an American Writer's Journey through His Own Imaginative World and through the World of Facts . . . New York: B. W. Huebsch, 1924.
The Modern Writer. San Francisco: Lantern Press, 1925.
Sherwood Anderson's Notebook. New York: Boni and Liveright, 1926.
Tar: A Midwest Childhood. New York: Boni and Liveright, 1926.
Hello Towns! New York: Liveright, 1929.
The American County Fair. New York: Random House, 1930.
Perhaps Women. New York: Liveright, 1931.
No Swank. Philadelphia: Centaur Press, 1934.
Puzzled America. New York: Scribner's, 1935.
A Writer's Conception of Realism. Olivet, Mich.: Olivet College, 1939.
Home Town. New York: Alliance, 1940.
Sherwood Anderson's Memoirs. New York: Harcourt, Brace, 1942.

EDITIONS AND COLLECTIONS

Sherwood Anderson's Memoirs. New York: Harcourt, Brace, 1942.
The Sherwood Anderson Reader, edited by Paul Rosenfeld. Boston: Houghton Mifflin, 1947.
The Portable Sherwood Anderson, edited by Horace Gregory. New York: Viking, 1949.
Letters of Sherwood Anderson, edited by Howard Mumford Jones and Walter B. Rideout. Boston: Little, Brown, 1953.
Winesburg, Ohio, edited by Malcolm Cowley. New York: Viking, 1960.
Sherwood Anderson: Short Stories, edited by Maxwell Geismar. New York: Hill and Wang, 1962.
6 Mid-American Chants by Sherwood Anderson [/] *Midwest Photographs by Art Sinsabaugh*, with a note by Edward Dahlberg and a poem by Frederick Eckman. Highlands, N.C.: Nantahala Foundation, 1964.
Return to Winesburg: Selections from Four Years of Writing for a Country Newspaper,

edited by Ray Lewis White. Chapel Hill: University of North Carolina Press, 1967.

A Story Teller's Story: A Critical Text, edited by Ray Lewis White. Cleveland: Press of Case Western Reserve University, 1968.

Sherwood Anderson's Memoirs: A Critical Edition, edited by Ray Lewis White. Chapel Hill: University of North Carolina Press, 1969.

Tar: A Midwest Childhood, a Critical Text, edited by Ray Lewis White. Cleveland: Press of Case Western Reserve University, 1969.

The Buck Fever Papers, edited by Welford D. Taylor. Charlottesville: University Press of Virginia, 1971.

Marching Men: A Critical Text, edited by Ray Lewis White. Cleveland: Press of Case Western Reserve University, 1972.

Sherwood Anderson/Gertrude Stein: Correspondence and Personal Essays, edited by Ray Lewis White. Chapel Hill: University of North Carolina Press, 1973.

Bibliographies and Checklists

Gozzi, Raymond D. "A Bibliography of Sherwood Anderson's Contributions to Periodicals, 1914–1946," *Newberry Library Bulletin*, Second Series, No. 2 (December 1948), pp. 71–82.

Rideout, Walter B. "Sherwood Anderson," in *Sixteen Modern American Authors*, edited by Jackson R. Bryer. Durham, N.C.: Duke University Press, 1974.

Sheehy, Eugene P., and Kenneth A. Lohf. *Sherwood Anderson: A Bibliography*. Los Gatos, Calif.: Talisman, 1960.

White, Ray Lewis. *The Merrill Checklist of Sherwood Anderson*. Columbus, Ohio: Merrill, 1969.

———. "A Checklist of Sherwood Anderson Studies, 1959–1969," *Newberry Library Bulletin*, 6:288–302 (1971).

Critical and Biographical Studies

Anderson, David D. *Sherwood Anderson: An Introduction and Interpretation*. New York: Holt, Rinehart and Winston, 1967.

Asselineau, Roger, ed. *Configuration critique de Sherwood Anderson*, in *La revue des lettres moderne*, Nos. 78–80 (1963).

Burbank, Rex. *Sherwood Anderson*. New York: Twayne, 1964.

Chase, Cleveland B. *Sherwood Anderson*. New York: McBride, 1927.

Fagin, Nathan Bryllion. *The Phenomenon of Sherwood Anderson: A Study in American Life and Letters*. Baltimore: Rossi-Bryn, 1927.

Howe, Irving. *Sherwood Anderson*. New York: Sloane, 1951.

Newberry Library Bulletin, Second Series, No. 2 (December 1948). "Sherwood Anderson Memorial Number."

Newberry Library Bulletin, Vol. 6, July 1971. "Special Sherwood Anderson Number."

Schevill, James. *Sherwood Anderson: His Life and Work*. Denver: University of Denver Press, 1951.

Shenandoah, Vol. 13, Spring 1962. "Sherwood Anderson Number."

Story, Vol. 19, September–October 1941. "Homage to Sherwood Anderson" number.

Sutton, William A. *The Road to Winesburg: A Mosaic of the Imaginative Life of Sherwood Anderson*. Metuchen, N.J.: Scarecrow, 1972.

White, Ray Lewis, ed. *The Achievement of Sherwood Anderson: Essays in Criticism*. Chapel Hill: University of North Carolina Press, 1966.

Works

JOHN STEINBECK

NOVELS

Cup of Gold. New York: Covici-Friede, 1929.
To a God Unknown. London: Heinemann, 1932.
Tortilla Flat. New York: Covici-Friede, 1935.
In Dubious Battle. New York: Covici-Friede, 1936.
The Red Pony. New York: Covici-Friede, 1937.
The Grapes of Wrath. New York: Viking, 1939.
Of Mice and Men. New York: Viking, 1940.
The Moon Is Down. New York: Viking, 1942.
Cannery Row. New York: Viking, 1945.
The Wayward Bus. New York: Viking, 1947.
The Pearl. New York: Viking, 1947.
East of Eden. New York: Viking, 1952.
Sweet Thursday. New York: Viking, 1954.
The Winter of Our Discontent. New York: Viking, 1961.

COLLECTIONS OF SHORT STORIES

The Pastures of Heaven. New York: Covici-Friede, 1932.
The Long Valley. New York: Viking, 1938.

PLAYS

Of Mice and Men (dramatic version with George Kaufman). New York: Viking, 1940.
The Moon Is Down (dramatic version). New York: Viking, 1942.
Burning Bright. New York: Viking, 1950. (A play in story form.)

NONFICTION

The Forgotten Village. New York: Viking, 1941.
Bombs Away. New York: Viking, 1942.
A Russian Journal. New York: Viking, 1948.
Sea of Cortez (in collaboration with Edward F. Ricketts). New York: Viking, 1951.
The Log from the Sea of Cortez. New York: Viking, 1951.
The Short Reign of Pippin IV. New York: Viking, 1957.
Once There Was a War. New York: Viking, 1958.
Travels with Charley. New York: Viking, 1962.
America and Americans. New York: Viking, 1966.
Journal of a Novel: The East of Eden Letters. New York: Viking, 1969.

Critical Studies

Allen, Walter. *Tradition and Dream*. London: John Dent and Son, Phoenix House, 1961.
Astro, Richard. *John Steinbeck and Edward F. Ricketts: The Shaping of a Novelist*. Minneapolis: University of Minnesota Press, 1973.
Beach, Joseph Warren. *American Fiction, 1920–1940*. New York: Macmillan, 1941.
Cowie, Alexander. *The Rise of the American Novel*. New York: American Book, 1948.

Fontenrose, Joseph Eddy. *John Steinbeck: An Introduction and Interpretation*. New York: Barnes and Noble, 1963.

French, Warren. *The Social Novel at the End of an Era*. Carbondale: Southern Illinois University Press, 1966.

Geismar, Maxwell. *Writers in Crisis*. Boston: Houghton Mifflin, 1942.

Hoffman, Frederick. *The Modern Novel in America*. Chicago: Regnery, 1951.

Kazin, Alfred. *On Native Grounds*. New York: Reynal and Hitchcock, 1942.

Lewis, R. W. B. *The Picaresque Saint*. Philadelphia: Lippincott, 1959.

Lisca, Peter. *The Wide World of John Steinbeck*. New Brunswick, N.J.: Rutgers University Press, 1958.

Moore, H. T. *The Novels of John Steinbeck: A First Critical Study*. Chicago: Normandie House, 1939.

Tedlock, E. W., ed. *Steinbeck and His Critics: A Record of Twenty-five Years*. Albuquerque: University of New Mexico Press, 1957.

Watt, Frank William. *John Steinbeck*. New York: Grove Press, 1962.

Wilson, Edmund. *The Boys in the Back Room: Notes on California Novelists*. San Francisco: Colt Press, 1941.

Articles

Aaron, D. "The Radical Humanism of John Steinbeck: *The Grapes of Wrath* Thirty Years Later," *Saturday Review*, 51:26–27 (September 28, 1968).

Brown, C. "The Callus behind the Fiction," *New Republic*, 161:26–32 (December 20 and 27, 1969).

Hyman, Stanley Edgar. "Some Notes on John Steinbeck," *Antioch Review*, 2:185–200 (June 1942).

Shuman, R. B. "Initiation Rites in Steinbeck's *The Red Pony*," *English Journal*, 59:1252–55 (December 1970).

Shaw, P. "Steinbeck: The Shape of a Career," *Saturday Review*, 52:10–14 (February 8, 1969).

JAMES T. FARRELL

Works

NOVELS

Young Lonigan: A Boyhood in Chicago Streets. New York: Vanguard, 1932.

Gas-House McGinty. New York: Vanguard, 1933.

The Young Manhood of Studs Lonigan. New York: Vanguard, 1934.

Judgment Day. New York: Vanguard, 1935.

Studs Lonigan: A Trilogy. New York: Vanguard, 1935. (Includes *Young Lonigan*, *The Young Manhood of Studs Lonigan*, *Judgment Day*.)

A World I Never Made. New York: Vanguard, 1936.

No Star Is Lost. New York: Vanguard, 1938.

Father and Son. New York: Vanguard, 1940.

Ellen Rogers. New York: Vanguard, 1941.

My Days of Anger. New York: Vanguard, 1943.

Bernard Clare. New York: Vanguard, 1946.

The Road Between. New York: Vanguard, 1949.

This Man and This Woman. New York: Vanguard, 1951.

Yet Other Waters. New York: Vanguard, 1952.

The Face of Time. New York: Vanguard, 1953.

Boarding House Blues. New York: Paperback Library, 1961.
The Silence of History. New York: Doubleday, 1963.
What Time Collects. New York: Doubleday, 1964.
Lonely for the Future. New York: Doubleday, 1966.
New Year's Eve/1929. New York: Horizon, 1967.
A Brand New Life. New York: Doubleday, 1968.
Invisible Swords. New York: Doubleday, 1971.

SHORT STORIES AND NOVELLAS

Calico Shoes and Other Stories. New York: Vanguard, 1934.
Guillotine Party and Other Stories. New York: Vanguard, 1935.
Can All This Grandeur Perish? and Other Stories. New York: Vanguard, 1937.
The Short Stories of James T. Farrell. New York: Vanguard, 1937. (Includes the
   three volumes above.)
Tommy Gallagher's Crusade. New York: Vanguard, 1939. (Reprinted in *To Whom It
   May Concern and Other Stories,* 1944.)
$1,000 a Week and Other Stories. New York: Vanguard, 1942.
To Whom It May Concern and Other Stories. New York: Vanguard, 1944.
When Boyhood Dreams Come True. New York: Vanguard, 1946.
The Life Adventurous and Other Stories. New York: Vanguard, 1947.
A Misunderstanding. New York: House of Books, 1949. (A limited edition of 300
   copies; reprinted in *An American Dream Girl,* 1950.)
An American Dream Girl. New York: Vanguard, 1950.
French Girls Are Vicious and Other Stories. New York: Vanguard, 1955.
An Omnibus of Short Stories. New York: Vanguard, 1957. (Reprints *$1,000 a Week
   and Other Stories, To Whom It May Concern and Other Stories, The Life Adventurous
   and Other Stories.*)
A Dangerous Woman and Other Stories. New York: New American Library, Signet
   edition, 1957. (Followed by Vanguard photolithograph edition.)
Side Street and Other Stories. New York: Paperback Library, 1961.
Sound of a City. New York: Paperback Library, 1962.
Childhood Is Not Forever. New York: Doubleday, 1969.
Judith. Athens, Ohio: Duane Schneider Press, 1969. (Reprinted in *Judith and Other
   Stories,* 1973.)
Judith and Other Stories. New York: Doubleday, 1973.

POETRY AND PROSE POEM

The Collected Poems of James T. Farrell. New York: Fleet Publishing Corporation,
   1965.
When Time Was Born. New York: Horizon, 1966.

OTHER PROSE

A Note on Literary Criticism. New York: Vanguard, 1936.
The League of Frightened Philistines and Other Papers. New York: Vanguard, 1945.
Literature and Morality. New York: Vanguard, 1947.
The Name Is Fogarty: Private Papers on Public Matters, "by Jonathan Titulescu
   Fogarty, Esq." (pseud.). New York: Vanguard, 1950.
Reflections at Fifty and Other Essays. New York: Vanguard, 1954.
My Baseball Diary. New York: A. S. Barnes, 1957.
It Has Come to Pass. New York: Theodor Herzl Press, 1958.

Dialogue on John Dewey, edited by Corliss Lamont. New York: Horizon, 1959.
(Farrell was one of eleven persons who contributed to this transcription of an
evening of reminiscences and personal impressions of Dewey.)

Bibliographies

Branch, Edgar M. *A Bibliography of James T. Farrell's Writings, 1921–1957.*
Philadelphia: University of Pennsylvania Press, 1959.
———. "A Supplement to the Bibliography of James T. Farrell's Writings," *American Book Collector*, 11:42–48 (June 1961).
———. "Bibliography of James T. Farrell: A Supplement," *American Book Collector*, 17:9–19 (May 1967).
———. "Bibliography of James T. Farrell: A Supplement, 1967–August, 1970,"
American Book Collector, 21:13–18 (March–April 1971).

Books, Articles, and Chapters of Critical Studies

Aldridge, John W. "The Education of James T. Farrell," in *In Search of Heresy:
American Literature in an Age of Conformity*. New York: McGraw-Hill, 1956.
Beach, Joseph Warren. "James T. Farrell: Tragedy of the Poolroom Loafer" and
"James T. Farrell: The Plight of the Children," in *American Fiction, 1920–1940.*
New York: Macmillan, 1941.
Branch, Edgar M. "American Writer in the Twenties: James T. Farrell and the
University of Chicago," *American Book Collector*, 11:25–32 (June 1961).
———. "Freedom and Determinism in James T. Farrell's Fiction," in *Essays on
Determinism in American Literature*, Kent Studies in English, Number 1, edited
by Sydney J. Krause. Kent, Ohio: Kent State University Press, 1964.
———. *James T. Farrell*. New York: Twayne, 1971.
———. "James T. Farrell's Studs Lonigan," *American Book Collector*, 11:9–19 (June
1961).
———. "The 1930's in James T. Farrell's Fiction," *American Book Collector*, 21:9–12
(March–April 1971).
Curley, Thomas F. "Catholic Novels and American Culture," *Commentary*,
36:34–42 (July 1963).
Dyer, Henry Hopper. "James T. Farrell's Studs Lonigan and Danny O'Neill
Novels." Unpublished dissertation, University of Pennsylvania, 1965.
Fried, Lewis F. "The Naturalism of James Farrell: A Study of His Major Novels."
Unpublished dissertation, University of Massachusetts, 1969.
Frohock, Wilbur M. "James T. Farrell: The Precise Content," in *The Novel of
Violence in America*, second edition. Dallas: Southern Methodist University
Press, 1958.
Gelfant, Blanche H. "James T. Farrell: The Ecological Novel," in *The American
City Novel*. Norman: University of Oklahoma Press, 1954.
Glicksberg, Charles I. "The Criticism of James T. Farrell," *Southwest Review*,
35:189–96 (Summer 1950).
Grattan, C. Hartley. "James T. Farrell: Moralist," *Harper's*, 209:93–94, 96, 98
(October 1954).
Gregory, Horace. "James T. Farrell: Beyond the Provinces of Art," *New World
Writing: Fifth Mentor Selection*. New York: New American Library, 1954.
Hatfield, Ruth. "The Intellectual Honesty of James T. Farrell," *College English*,
3:337–46 (January 1942).
Howe, Irving. "James T. Farrell — The Critic Calcified," *Partisan Review*, 14:
545–46, 548, 550, 552 (September–October 1947).

Kazin, Alfred. *On Native Grounds: An Interpretation of Modern American Prose Literature.* New York: Reynal and Hitchcock, 1942. Pp. 380–85.

Lovett, Robert Morss. "James T. Farrell," *English Journal*, 26:347–54 (May 1937). (Reprinted as the Introduction to *The Short Stories of James T. Farrell*.)

Lynch, William James. "The Theory and Practice of the Literary Criticism of James T. Farrell." Unpublished dissertation, University of Pennsylvania, 1966.

Mitchell, Richard. "*Studs Lonigan:* Research in Morality," *Centennial Review*, 6:202–14 (Spring 1962).

O'Malley, Frank. "James T. Farrell: Two Twilight Images," in *Fifty Years of the American Novel: A Christian Appraisal*, edited by Harold C. Gardiner. New York: Scribner's, 1951.

Owen, David H. "A Pattern of Pseudo-Naturalism: Lynd, Mead, and Farrell." Unpublished dissertation, University of Iowa, 1950.

Reiter, Irene Morris. "A Study of James T. Farrell's Short Stories and Their Relation to His Longer Fiction." Unpublished dissertation, University of Pennsylvania, 1964.

Walcutt, Charles Child. "James T. Farrell: Aspects of Telling the Whole Truth," in *American Literary Naturalism, a Divided Stream*. Minneapolis: University of Minnesota Press, 1956.

ABOUT THE AUTHORS

ABOUT THE
AUTHORS

JEAN CAZEMAJOU is a professor of English at the University of Bordeaux (France). He is the author of a book-length study of Stephen Crane and co-author of a book on the mass media in the United States, both in French.

W. M. FROHOCK is a professor of French at Harvard University. Among his books are *André Malraux and the Tragic Imagination, Rimbaud's Poetic Practice, The Novel of Violence in America,* and *Style and Temper: Studies in French Fiction.*

CHARLES CHILD WALCUTT is the author of numerous books including *American Literary Naturalism, a Divided Stream,* and *Man's Changing Mask: Modes and Methods of Characterization in Fiction.* He teaches at Queens College and the City University of New York.

BROM WEBER, professor of English at the University of California, Davis, has edited *An Anthology of American Humor* and *The Letters of Hart Crane.*

JAMES GRAY, literary critic, novelist, and historian, is a former professor of English at the University of Minnesota and former literary editor of the *Chicago Daily News* and of the *St. Paul Pioneer Press–Dispatch.*

EDGAR M. BRANCH is research professor of English at Miami University, Oxford, Ohio. He is the author of *The Literary Apprenticeship of Mark Twain* and *Clemens of the "Call,"* and has written articles for numerous journals.

311

INDEX

INDEX